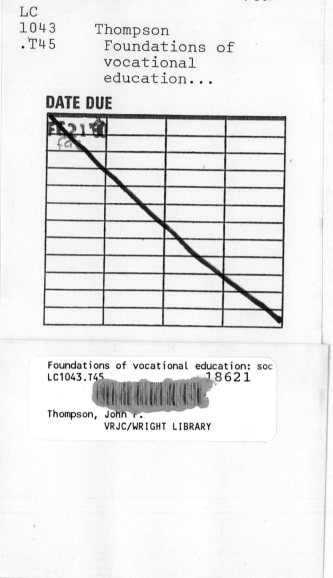

FOUNDATIONS
OF
VOCATIONAL
EDUCATION

PRENTICE-HALL, INC.
ENGLEWOOD CLIFFS, NEW JERSEY

JOHN F. THOMPSON
UNIVERSITY OF WISCONSIN, MADISON

FOUNDATIONS
OF
VOCATIONAL
EDUCATION

SOCIAL AND PHILOSOPHICAL CONCEPTS

Library of Congress Cataloging in Publication Data

THOMPSON, JOHN F.
    Foundations of vocational education

    Includes bibliographical references.
    1. Vocational education. I. Title
LC1043.T45   370   72–5193
ISBN   0–13–330068–4

Chart on page 187 based upon material from pp. 63–64,
p. 66 from *The Conditions of Learning*, Second Edition, by
Robert M. Gagne. Copyright © 1965, 1970 by Holt, Rinehart
and Winston, Inc. Used by permission of Holt, Rinehart and
Winston, Inc.

PRENTICE-HALL INTERNATIONAL, INC., London
PRENTICE-HALL OF AUSTRALIA, PTY. LTD., Sydney
PRENTICE-HALL OF CANADA, LTD., Toronto
PRENTICE-HALL OF INDIA PRIVATE LIMITED, New Delhi
PRENTICE-HALL OF JAPAN, INC., Tokyo

CONTENTS

I DEVELOPMENT 1

1. SOCIAL FOUNDATIONS OF VOCATIONAL EDUCATION 3.   Introduction 3.
The Nature of Education 7.   The Nature of Educational Decisions 12.
The Social Setting for Vocational Education 14.   Vocational Education,
Economic and Manpower Policy 17.   Vocational Education and a Con-
cept of the Learner 21.   A Social Contribution to Be Made by Vocational
Education 23.

2. A HISTORICAL REVIEW OF SELECTED FACTORS THAT INFLUENCED VOCA-
TIONAL EDUCATION 27.   Introduction 27.   The Change from an Agrarian
Society 28.   An Economic View of the Worth of Man 29.   Pluralism of
Institutions 30.   Wars 31.   National Study Panels 34.   Employer Associ-

ations and Labor Organizations 43. The Development of Technology 47. Change in Occupational Structure 53. Other Factors 55.

3. VOCATIONAL EDUCATION AND NATIONAL LEGISLATION 57. Early Legislative Acts 57. Separation of Church and State 60. The Move Toward Nationalism 64. The Move West 65. The Land Grant College Movement 68. The Smith-Hughes Act of 1917 69. The GI Bill of Rights 76. The Vocational Education Act of 1963 77. The Vocational Education Amendments of 1968 79. Impact of Federal Legislation 83.

II INTERPRETING THE DEVELOPMENT 87

4. ASSUMPTIONS OF VOCATIONAL EDUCATION 89. A Philosophical Problem 89. Democratic Assumptions 90. World of Work Assumptions 93.

5. DEFINITIONS FOR VOCATIONAL EDUCATION 105. The Accident Theory 105. Legal Definitions 107. Definitions by Good and Harris 111. Observations 112. Additional Definitions 113. Summary 115.

6. A MODEL OF CONVENTIONAL VOCATIONAL EDUCATION 118. Relating Vocational and General Education 118. Critical Orientation Points 120. Another Consideration 128. Summary 128.

III THE PRESENT PROGRAMS 131

7. THE CONTEMPORARY PROGRAM 133. Introduction 133. Agricultural Education 134. Business and Office Education 136. Distributive Education 138. Health Occupations 139. Home Economics Education 140. Technical Education 142. Trade and Industrial Occupations 142. Occupational Experience Programs 143. Youth Organizations 146.

8. CURRICULA FOUNDATIONS 150. Developing Occupational Competency 150. What Constitutes Occupational Competency 152. Approaches to Curriculum 155. Examples of Curricular Approaches in Vocational Education 160. Postscript 173.

IV THE EMERGENT 177

9. THE CHANGING EDUCATIONAL SCENE 179.   Introduction 179.   The Reform Movement 180.   The Emergent School 193.   New Characterizations of the Educational System 196.

10. THE EMERGENT IN VOCATIONAL EDUCATION 203.   Growth and Development Concerns 203.   Vocational Education Defined 213.   Learn What an Occupational Area Is All About 219.   A Unifying Effect 222.   A Contemporary Model for Vocational Education 223.

11. OCCUPATIONAL EDUCATION FOR ALL 231.   A Modern Philosophy 232. The Purpose of Vocational Programs 238.   Summary 249.

INDEX 251.

PREFACE

Several factors conspire to make evident the need for a book presenting the social and philosophical foundations of vocational education. First, there has been no previous systematic analysis and presentation in one source of the social and philosophical foundations of vocational education. Second, most books in vocational education describe existing programs and practices. I want this book to analyze what is being done and attempt to influence change. Hence current developments in vocational education are identified and assessed against a background of traditional practices. Vocational education is at a crucial point in its development and therefore its foundations need to be scrutinized by its every practitioner.

Third, education is changing rapidly, and vocational education has shown little willingness to adjust to these educational changes. Most of the recent changes in vocational education have moved it closer toward a manpower-delivery policy.

Further, society's demands upon the educational enterprise are changing. These changes entail not only the provision of increased opportunities for formal education in all segments of society, but conceptions about the purposes of education in responding to changing patterns of work must be reformulated. Finally, vocational education as a maturing social science can be analyzed and described now in ways not possible in its early, less mature eras.

Current programs in vocational education, relatively long on practice and short on theory, often reflect considerable inertia on the one hand and on the other, an almost frantic search for innovation to alleviate current problems.

This book is committed to the idea that vocational education does make a contribution to our educational progress. Vocational education was added to the schools' curriculum to achieve a particular set of purposes. Those purposes are still held valid by most vocational educators in spite of the fact that we now have a society that differs rather sharply from the society of the early 1900s. This work sets forth the social and philosophical foundations of vocational education as they have developed and identifies the current choices that are available to vocational educators. Every educator needs to understand these foundations and current choices if he is involved in planning programs for, advising students in relation to, or making judgments about vocational education.

Many persons have contributed significantly to my development and thus to the development of this book. T. C. Martin, a retired teacher and school administrator currently living in Beaverdam, Virginia, made it all possible. Two professors at Michigan State University, Dr. H. Paul Sweany and Dr. Raymond M. Clark assisted in many very direct ways as did Dr. V. Ray Cardozier, then at the University of Maryland. I have also had an opportunity to exchange, shape, and refine ideas with a large number of outstanding vocational educators including Dr. Larry Borosage, Dr. Harold Byram, Dr. Beverly Crabtree, Fred Eberle, Dr. Peter Haines, Dr. Russ Hosler, Dick Nelson, Dr. Harland Samson, Dr. Clodus Smith, Dr. Jake Stern, and Dr. Robert Taylor.

Two colleagues are very much a part of this book. Dr. William E. Gleason, at the University of Wisconsin, and Dr. Donald L. Stormer, at Texas A&M University, have assisted me in many ways. Bill and Don, in the half dozen years that I have known them, were often the first recipients of my ideas. They read drafts of some ideas, and, in general, critiqued many of my ideas as they were being developed. Their contributions are deeply appreciated.

Dr. Walter T. Bjoraker created an administrative atmosphere where my writing on this book was encouraged. And thanks also to Miss Gail Zwecki, Mrs. Jill Prochaska, Miss Kathy Stephenson, Mrs. Marjorie Gleason, and Miss Carol Skram who assisted with the typing.

Finally, deep appreciation is extended to Jan, Brenda Jayne, and Kevin Andrew.

JOHN F. THOMPSON

Madison, Wisconsin
March, 1972

INTRODUCTION

The phrase "vocational education" is used throughout this book. A precise definition will not be offered at the outset, for this generic term has been used historically with a variety of meanings. In some instances it refers to very narrow skill training; in others it relates to attitudes and values. More generally, the phrase describes educational programs that assist people as they develop toward occupations and careers. That is its intended use here. A new definition of vocational education will be offered later in this book (Chapter 10) to describe the emerging philosophy in career and vocational education.

The institution of vocational education is understood in relation to three components: people, society, and technology. All institutions, including vocational education, grow discontinuously and are directed and shaped by strong and sometimes strange forces. In general, each stage in the development of vocational education begins with the existence of a social condition. Philosophical inquiry establishes a new view of what is possible for man to become. Out of this disparity between the social condition (what is) and the philosophical condition (what should be) grows a recognition of a need to bring *what is* more in line with *what should be*. At some point in time a technological advance is achieved to close the gap between the social condition and the philosophical position. Adjustment in this manner leads to a new social condition and the cycle is repeated. Overemphasis on one component at a time causes discontinuous growth.

At one point in our history, for example, the worker was not expected to consume the products he made. The worker had limited means of accumulating capital and the production of goods such as automobiles was for rich people. As larger blocks of workers were paid wages the notion emerged that the worker had a right to enjoy the benefits of his labors: to spend his money and to enjoy the same benefits of society that all other men enjoyed. It just was not fair for him to be denied the right to his own automobile. Changing the idea from worker to worker-consumer also increased the demand for the products. Through the efforts of such persons as Henry Ford, technology was used to close the gap between the worker's social condition and his changed philosophical condition.

All of the components of vocational education are changing. American society during the early stages of our technological revolution was described as being shaped like a squat pyramid. Such a description indicated that most of the jobs were at the base of the pyramid. For these jobs little education and little experience was demanded. It also indicated that specialization was not a particularly important concept. Currently, the shape of American industrial society is being described as a tall urn.[1] Such a description indicates that the greatest demand for occupational specialization occurs in the slightly bulging middle. In order to obtain jobs, potential workers need to possess higher educational achievements and more experience. The structure also implies that vertical specialization is an important concept, which in turn opens up the possibility for differentiated entry points in occupational areas. Patterns of work that enable a worker to start at the lowest level and work to the top occur infrequently in the present "urn-shaped" society. Managers are hired into the system with a particular set of educational credentials. Persons without these credentials, regardless of their amount of experience, generally find that their current occupational pattern stops short of managerial positions.

Upgrading, vertical specialization, and differentiated entry points can be observed in many current occupational areas. The beauticians' lobby in New Jersey, for example, has succeeded in persuading the state legislature to pass a bill requiring all licensed beauticians to have high school diplomas. In that same state it is being urged that all state patrolmen be graduates of a four-year college course in police science. The job of meter maid who patrols the parking areas of the city noting those who are in violation of parking ordinances has been added to the police force of many cities. Such a position is not the training ground for future regular patrolmen. The meter maid is not likely to advance to other police functions thus providing specialization and differentiated entry points for police work. Another example is the American Nurses Association's announcement in 1967 that the attainment of the bachelor's degree should be a requisite to becoming a registered nurse.

The professional worker in vocational education needs to understand the foundations of vocational education in our modern "urn-shaped" industrial society. He needs to understand how vocational education has come to be what it is and where it is likely to be headed. This book will assist the vocational educator as he gains that understanding. In addition, many others, such as the curriculum worker, the educational sociologist, the educational philosopher, and the educational theorist, will find the book useful as they relate their area of specialization to vocational education.

The book is divided into sections. Part I sets the social and philosophical context of vocational education. Chapter 1 describes the social setting for vocational education, which is seen first of all as a vast and varied enterprise. It has, as do all aspects of education, a normative base; that is, it grows out of social norms. All societies are organized and create institutions to provide stability. The institution of education, including vocational education, must use a fact-to-value continuum in its decision-making processes. The social setting of vocational education is seen within an institutionalized set of relations between education, the labor market, and the community.

A major question confronting decision-makers in the political arena is what occupational roles in our society should be institutionalized and what policy should be stressed to perform that function. The three phases of manpower policy—employment, human resources development, and manpower allocation—are analyzed and described. It is noted, for example, that employment policy—providing employment for those willing and able to work—is currently receiving much emphasis and is judged by politicians to be more in line with the current national interests. Hence funds provided by the U.S. Congress for vocational education are being shifted in that direction.

The final section of this chapter discusses the impact that economic concerns have on decisions made by vocational educators. Vocational education, for example, is sold on the basis that a job exists and if you take this training for it you are likely to earn more money than those who don't take such training.

Chapter 2 describes some of the forces that have shaped and directed vocational education. Such factors are not presented in chronological sequence, but are discussed in relation to the way they have shaped the development of vocational education. Factors such as our change from an agrarian society, an economic view of man, the pluralism of institutions, wars, national study panels, employer associations and labor organizations, and the development of technology are discussed. Technology is exerting a number of influences that direct changes in society and in types of vocational education programs deemed appropriate for our present society. The implications for changed programs include the need for better educated workers, more general education preceding specialized vocational education, more programs to update workers, systematic educational programs for new careers, and new programs in areas other than industry, manufacturing, and agriculture.

Perhaps the most significant development in the history of vocational education is the change in occupational structure that is occurring. The "heavy" industries of manufacturing and trades have been replaced by the "service" industries as the faster growing occupational areas. The United States emerged from the 1940s with more workers producing goods than providing services. Service-producing industries—government, transportation, public utilities, finance, real estate—took the lead in the number of jobs in the mid-1950s. By 1980 the service-producing industries are expected to employ twice as many workers as the goods-producing industries.[2] Women seeking jobs for longer periods of their life and seeking jobs traditionally held by men also influence the occupational structure.

Chapter 3 examines the national legislative development of vocational education. The colonists were basically pleased with the educational systems that they left in Europe, so their early educational actions in this country emulated what they had known. It provided one kind of education for the children of the poor and another for the children of the rich. Education was eventually removed from the absolute control of the church when the doctrine of separate church and state won out as the dominant political view. Schooling for all citizens, under public control and extending to higher education, was to become a distinctively American contribution. Pride in and loyalty toward America developed slowly. Early in the history of the United States persons began to move from East to West and South, and from farm to city. City residents had to be fed and new ones had to be allocated to existing jobs. Persons often moved to new areas without the trained technicians to support their activities. These technological gaps had to be closed and legislation was designed to do just that.

Part II—Chapters 4, 5, and 6—draws upon the social and historical background to set forth the current philosophical foundations of vocational education through a set of assumptions. These assumptions are the basis from which the purposes and objectives of vocational education in our society are derived. In short, assumptions guide behavior. A complete search of the literature of vocational education was undertaken to derive a set of democratic and world of work assumptions that guide vocational education; these form the content of Chapter 4. Each of these assumptions is examined for its validity.

Chapter 5 describes the definitions of vocational education. The original legal definition of vocational education was formulated by the Smith-Hughes Act of 1917. This legal definition has been the core of all other definitions contained in laws passed by the U.S. Congress.

The legal definition dominating vocational education is seen to have led the vocational education system that developed to be monolithic in character and uniform in structure. Many additional examples of new programs or practices outside of the legal structure are discussed, but these are usually formulated without reference to another definition of vocational education.

Thinking about vocational education is a conceptual problem. Most conceptual problems can be viewed in the form of a model that helps to clarify and explain many variables that must be related in a conceptual problem. The development of a model to conceptualize the prevailing ideas and structure within vocational education is the focus of Chapter 6.

The contemporary programs of vocational education, the focus of Part III, reflects a cross section of the occupational world of work as it has been divided for funding and supervisory considerations. Each division of vocational education is charged with the responsibility of bridging the gap between the educational system and its part of the labor market. Chapter 7 is divided into sections on agricultural education, business and office education, distributive education, health occupations, home economics education, technical education, and trade and industrial education.

Every vocational education program is designed to develop a degree of occupational competency through a program or curriculum. Occupational or job analysis is the prime technique used by vocational education to keep its courses in touch with the occupational world. If the future worker, enrolled in a vocational education program, is taught what the current worker is doing, he will possess occupational competency. Job analysis identifies what the current worker does. Additional methods of insuring occupational competency include the integrated approach, clusters, functions of industry, and conceptual approach. Each of these curriculum patterns is discussed in Chapter 8 following a discussion of what constitutes occupational competency in modern American society.

The focus of the book changes in Part IV from describing existing programs to examining emerging philosophies of vocational education. The basic description of vocational education is left, and we begin to see what is possible for vocational education in contemporary society. Chapter 9 examines the changing educational scene. Experimentation is needed if improvements in education are to be made. Continuous reform has led to the belief that if schools and programs are to be significantly better, they must be substantially different. Most of the current educational reform comes from persons outside the educational sector. Implosions, those forces outside the educational environment, are shaping and directing education. These forces include man's accepting a mode of change, mathematical and scientific illiteracy, prosperity, education for all, values, knowledge explosion, leisure, and urbanization. Within the educational sector, forces are also directing and shaping education. These forces, explosions, include new insights into learning, the discovery method of teaching, change in institutional arrangements, methods of curricular change, and the way curriculum content is identified. These forces have given rise to a new emergent school committed to (1) more flexibility, (2) being a middle-class school, (3) letting students seek and discover, (4) exploring new systems of evaluation, (5) industrial and community involvement, and 6) being an agent of new values.

In Chapter 10, titled "The Emergent in Vocational Education," we begin to see my view of vocational education as it could function in our contemporary society. A new social and philosophical basis for vocational education is emerging. Vocational education must be concerned with vocational development, a process of growth and development that enables an individual to find a satisfying work role and to become established in an occupation. This leads to a new definition of vocational education, one that has it concerned first of all with assisting in the growth and development of people. This definition suggests that vocational education is any education that provides experiences, visual stimuli, affective awareness, cognitive information or psychomotor skills, and that enhances the vocational development processes of exploring, establishing, and maintaining oneself in the world of work. This is followed by a contemporary model designed for flexible and continuous vocational education.

This theme of the emergent in vocational education and in contemporary society is continued in Chapter 11, the final chapter of the book. Titled "Occupational Education for All," it suggests that as vocational education adjusts to contemporary society, a new set of assumptions will be developed. One possible set of social, philosophical, and psychological assumptions is offered here. The purpose of vocational education in the future will be quite different than it is at present. Discussion of its purpose in elementary schools, middle schools, secondary schools, and in adult education is offered.

The framework of the book should assist the reader as he comes to grips with his own assumptions and examines his area of work in relation to the assumptions made here. The social and philosophical foundations are indeed just what we have been talking about—assumptions.

NOTES

[1]These characterizations are described by John K. Galbraith, *The New Industrial State* (Boston: Houghton Mifflin Company, 1967), pp. 238–39.

[2]U.S. Department of Labor, *U.S. Manpower in the 1970's: Opportunity and Challenge* (Washington, D.C.: Government Printing Office, 1970), pp. 10, 14.

FOUNDATIONS
OF
VOCATIONAL
EDUCATION

I

DEVELOPMENT

1

SOCIAL FOUNDATIONS
OF VOCATIONAL EDUCATION

INTRODUCTION

Education is an integral and indispensable aspect of the American way of life. It would be difficult, lacking the social heritage of democracy, to understand or explain why there is no single, centrally organized or controlled school system in America. Authority for the administration and support of American public schools has become the responsibility of the states and their local school districts. The phrase "school system" may be accurately used to describe an educational system for a town, a township, a city, a county, a state, or the entire nation. American education is pluralistic in character. That is, educational systems privately controlled or supported exist alongside public schools. Church-related and other private schools are found at all levels in our society. These factors and dozens more are a part of the social foundations of education.

The social foundations of vocational education have a divided authority base, are pluralistic, and are an integral part of the American way of life. Vocational education finds its basic strength in culture, society, and institutions. A study of it finds an institutionalized set of relationships embracing both the educational system and the labor market.

VOCATIONAL EDUCATION IS VAST

Studies of America's educational enterprise reveal that nearly 30 percent of all Americans, young and old, are engaged in education on a full-time basis as students, teachers, administrators, supervisors, or board members. To this figure one could add the lay persons who are members of educational advisory committees. The exact number of persons involved in vocational education is difficult to determine, as many persons, such as secondary school principals, are concerned with all phases of a secondary program and devote only a small portion of their time to each program under their supervision. The same is true for the post–high school institutions where the administrator of a community, technical, or junior college may be responsible for as many nonvocational as vocational programs.

There were slightly in excess of 146,000 teachers of vocational and technical education in 1968. These teachers were at many grade levels and include the post–high school teachers. This figure represents approximately 1 percent of all secondary and postsecondary (including college level) teachers in the United States. Another indication of the vastness of vocational education is its enrollment figures. In 1968 there were slightly more than 7,500,000 pupils enrolled in vocational education courses. Of these, nearly 50 percent were at the secondary level. Provisional statistics from the U.S. Office of Education indicate that the official 1970 total will be over 9,500,000 pupils. Projecting these figures to 1975 shows an enrollment of 14,000,000 pupils in vocational and technical education. These data are displayed in Table 1.

A fourth index of the vastness of vocational education is a consideration of expenditures. The total expenditures for all education in 1968 was reported to be $61.1 billion, of which $39.8 billion was expended at the elementary and secondary levels. The amount of monies projected to be expended by public educational institutions for the school year 1978 is $87.4 billion. Fair estimates of the expenditures (federal, state, and local) for vocational education in 1970 approach $8 billion. These figures represent vocational education offered in public educational institutions and do not include the monies expended for vocational education in industry. Expenditures for vocational education in regular educational institutions are not expected to decrease in the years ahead although there may be sharp shifts in how the federal dollars are allocated.[1]

TABLE 1. Actual and Projected Enrollment in Education and Vocational Education

Year (Fall)	EDUCATION (K–12)[1]		VOCATIONAL EDUCATION[2]			
	Total Public	Total Public Secondary (9–12)	Total	Secondary	Post-secondary	Adult
1964	44,884,000	11,391,000	4,566,390[2]	2,140,756	170,835	2,254,799
1966	47,385,000	12,000,000	6,105,838[2]	3,061,541	438,469	2,546,452
1968[3]	50,761,000	12,721,000	7,533,936[3]	3,842,896[3]	592,970[3]	2,987,070[3]
PROJECTED						
1970			9,600,000[2]	4,525,000	650,000	4,050,000
1975			14,000,000	5,500,000	1,250,000	6,500,000
1974[4]	53,859,000	15,100,000				
1978[4]	55,748,000	15,400,000				

[1]Projection of Educational Statistics to 1975–1976, OE–10030–66 (Washington, D.C.: Government Printing Office), Table I, 1966.
[2]What's Ahead for Vocational Education, PPDB Series No. 1, U.S. Office of Education, Division of Vocational and Technical Education (does not include students with special needs).
[3]Vocational and Technical Education Annual Report Fiscal Year 1968, OE–80008–68, Office of Education, U.S. Department of Health, Education and Welfare (Washington, D.C.: Government Printing Office), 1970.
[4]Projection of Educational Statistics to 1978–1979, OE–10030–69 (Washington, D.C.: Government Printing Office), 1969.

VOCATIONAL EDUCATION IS VARIED

Vocational education is vast in scope and is characterized by a great variety of types of units and areas for instruction. Some of the units are public; others are private. Public units of vocational education usually include vocational education in agriculture, business, distribution, health, home economics, and trades and industries. A brief description of each of these areas of vocational education will be offered later (Chapter 7). Nonpublic vocational education programs refer to those programs operated by private industry to train and update the training of their employees and to private schools that provide specific occupational training. It is very difficult to obtain an exact figure of the vastness of vocational education in industrial institutions due to the way companies are structured and budgeted. Nearly every company of size has a training budget to identify the salaries and materials of those directly involved in the training. This training budget seems to represent approximately a fifth of what a company is likely to spend on upgrading and training its employees. When a worker leaves the job for an hour or a week of training, the cost of his time is generally budgeted to the production, not the training, division of the company.

Private vocational education also includes the many private post–high school institutions that offer specific training. Many business colleges and computer programming schools are examples of nonpublic vocational schools that derive their income primarily from student tuition; they are referred to as proprietary schools. It is estimated that there are 7,000 proprietary schools in the United States serving 1.5 million students.[2]

The thesis that vocational education on a formal organized basis is varied can be substantiated from observation. Make a list of all types of institutions that you know of that offer some phase of vocational education under the direction or control of public agencies. For young people aged 14 through 17 such a list would include comprehensive public secondary schools, private and parochial secondary schools, various trade, industrial, and vocational schools, and penal institutions. Beyond high school those who desire vocational education can experience these programs in a continuing variety of institutions. Trade, industrial and vocational schools, area vocational schools, junior colleges, community colleges, penal institutions, proprietary schools, and four-year colleges all have vocational education programs. Many of these institutions are maintained by a district, a community, a city government, or a state or a federal agency. Monies for these programs may be some combination of local, state, federal, and private sources.

THE NATURE OF EDUCATION

Education is a normative enterprise; that is, it grows out of social values and norms. This makes education a highly complex arena as a wide variety of persons, institutions, and situations influence its directions. Havighurst and Neugarten state that:

> In a changing society there is always some divergence between what society is and what it wants to be, between practices and its ideals. Thus, the educational system, being part of the culture, has two supplementary functions: to be a mirror that reflects the society as it is, and at the same time, to be an agent of social change and a force directed toward implementing the ideals of society.[3]

Some would deny that the school as a public institution should do more than reflect society as it is. Such a position does not square with recent developments in modern American society and becomes hardly more than an interesting, subsidiary academic question.

Schools have moved to the forefront as agents of social change.[4] Decisions of national policy are being implemented through the public school. Changes in the national policy of school desegregation of neighborhood schools, and of school readiness (Head Start) are cases in point. In the national school desegregation policy, drastic shifts in normal operations are being introduced through such things as busing youngsters long distances and assigning students to schools out of their "neighborhood." Interestingly enough, school desegregation is not the only and perhaps not even the main policy point. Schools are being used to implement a policy that seeks to help solve the problems of ghettos, poor housing, slum neighborhoods, and so on.[5] The public schools are now being cast in the role of a principal change agent for implementing public policy. Such policy emerges by political processes of the national government.

The nature of education, then, has an inherent value conflict. Anytime a teacher acts, say Hicks and Blackington, "He will offend someone's idea of what he ought to be and what he ought to be doing...one can choose which groups he will please or displease. Somewhere a stand(ard) must be taken."[6] That is the nature of education: stand taking, thus valuing. Hence schools have the potential of being an architectural force in a society as they set standards and implement ideals.

EDUCATION AND CULTURE

The people of every society are confronted with the problem of teaching its immature members the ways of the culture. A cultural barbarian at birth—in that he has none of the habits, ideas, attitudes, and skills of the culture—the individual as he matures acquires those items that characterize the adult members of society. In advanced societies the acquisition of cultural ways becomes partly a specialized function, and a specialized institution—the school—is created for this purpose.

The handing down of culture from generation to generation is an educative process: The individual as he grows and develops is "socialized" or "educated" into the ways of his particular culture. Culture, as Malinowski defines it, is composed of "inherited artifacts, goods, technical processes, ideas, habits and values."[7] These items are the content of education as it bridges the gaps between father and son, group and individual.

Vocational education is a distinctive product of the democratic culture that surrounds and supports it. Education in its broadest sense, and perhaps in its most conservative sense, is the principal means that society has of maintaining and perpetuating itself. Education may also be a system of culture creation. That is, education can create new goods, technical processes, ideas, habits, and values. A democratic culture in which vocational education finds itself is evolutionary. Thus, vocational education must also be evolutionary. The kinds of technical processes perpetuated and the kinds to be developed evolve and change from one generation to another.

The elements of a culture may be put into three categories.[8] The first category, *universals*, includes all of the things that are generally accepted by the members of the society. Individuals may eat the same foods, use the same language, possess the same religious ideals, wear the same style of clothes, practice the same or similar political ideals, and greet one another in the same way.

The second category contains *specialties*, those elements found among only a portion of the adult population, things that only a part of the people know about or can do. Specialties are divided primarily by occupational area or social position. Each occupational area has a set of knowledge and skills unique to its practitioners. Also, in some societies, the recognizable social elite or the lower social classes have ways of thinking and believing and behaving that are unique to each group. The wife in a very rich family, for example, does not work to earn an income. The behavioral expectation for her is one of work that is directed toward social projects. On the other hand, the poor of the southern and border states scour the countryside in early spring for "poke" and "cress." Pokeweed and fieldcress become their first green food of the season. In a highly industrial society the meaning of specialties tends to be blurred in the public mind and has impact only to those persons immediately engaged in them. Indeed, labor and products are so specialized and complex that not even the laborers themselves fully understand the processes or outcomes of production.[9]

The third category of elements of a culture, *alternatives*, includes those ways of obtaining results that depart from accepted techniques and procedures. Essentially, alternatives are those elements about which the individual can exercise personal choice. For example, one may choose between private or public education, between hybrid or open pollinated corn, between an electric, gas, or a microwave oven. Alternatives usually include the new and innovative of a culture and after gaining in acceptance are likely to be absorbed by either the specialties or the universals.

CULTURE AND SOCIETY

Human beings must have some kind of relationship with other human beings in order to achieve any goals. Thus, human interaction is inevitable. When this interaction occurs regularly and assumes some pattern or system, society becomes that complex of behavior patterns of a group of human beings who relate to one another and who think of themselves as a distinct group.

Society has structure and process as a result of these complex behavior patterns. One result of structure is a division of labor in society. Some persons, such as teachers, perform a set of unique tasks. In some societies the division of labor is assigned by status and role, which is acquired accidentally by birth; that is, the one performing the task may not be the most competent. One boy is expected to be a goldsmith simply because he is the son of a goldsmith. Another presides over the decision-making process simply because his father passed that right to him.

In a democratic society that is pluralistic and industrial, the division of labor is a complex process. Occupational selection is assumed to operate freely: The interests, ability, and potential of the individual are more significant in his occupational choice than are parental status, social group, or projected manpower needs. A formal educational system is needed to insure that society's needs are met within the assumption of occupational free choice. A part of that formal educational system is vocational education. In the pursuit of carrying out a style of life, it is necessary to engage in certain basic activities. For example, a person must obtain the basic necessities of food and shelter. A systematic set of relationships to govern the pursuit of these activities is necessary. These are referred to later in this chapter as the social setting for vocational education. Once a set of relationships emerges, they tend to become fixed so that culture may have some stability.

Education is directly related to the culture it serves; it's never separate or autonomous. How do you describe American culture in such a way that it reflects accurately the system of vocational education that it developed? We can use the following phrases as beginners.

It is *democratic*; it has a social framework where respect for the individual and the welfare of the group are of prime importance. Priorities are set by the group rather than being imposed on it.

It follows the *democratic process*; a social process whereby man may shape things to his higher purpose. Each individual is to participate in this social process. When decisions need to be made for the larger group, officials selected by and responsible to the group make those decisions in the name of the group.

It is *pluralistic*; it exists in more than one form or shape. Individuals belong and report to a variety of organizations, which may have conflicting values and purposes.

It is an *industrial* society, with a diversity of industry and manufacturing.

SOCIETY AND INSTITUTIONS

As a society seeks a greater diversity of goals, stability is achieved by "fixing" or "institutionalizing" its rules and functions and the interaction pattern becomes consistent and predictable in generalized conditions. As these interaction patterns become normal they are called institutions. Eight institutions in society are generally recognized: kinship, occupation, exchange, property, authority, stratification, religion, and education.[10] Each institution has fundamental interrelationships with all the other institutions.

Schools are a relatively new organization within the institution of education. Schools arose in society when other, older agencies could no longer transmit the cultural heritage. American society has always had a complex culture and has had schools for all but a few years of its existence. Vocational education, which helps man create, understand, and use technology, has a diverse set of specialized knowledge and skills. This diversity has always been so great that vocational education has always been contending for a place in American schools. The adult master or the father could not pass on all of the diverse skills needed. Also, the risk of transmitting by incidental means the diverse cultural heritage of the institution of occupation was too great a risk for society to take. Thus, vocational education finds itself based in two social institutions: occupation and education.

The institution of occupation refers to the organization of work or job roles, learned behaviors associated with the processes of occupational choice and implementation. These have been classified in many ways:

White collar, blue collar; professional, nonprofessional; laborer and non-laborer are a few of the classification schemes. When one leaves this nominal scheme there are many other ways of classifying work roles. A broader and more meaningful grouping of work roles into six occupational groups is frequently used: professional and technical, proprietary and managerial, clerical and sales, skilled, semiskilled, and unskilled. No one system of work role classification results in the best description of roles within *all* areas. This has led to some classification schemes by industry, such as manufacturing jobs, hospital jobs, police and security jobs, agricultural jobs, building trade jobs, selling jobs, and distribution jobs. Within each industry, jobs are then classified by level, so that within hospitals there are unskilled, semiskilled, skilled, clerical, managerial and professional jobs.

Within the institution of education, Hartford classifies three groups of educational agencies.[11] One group is those agencies designed to serve one or more major functions in education. Another is those agencies that serve basic societal needs, including some effective educational functions. The third group is numerous commercial and voluntary establishments and organizations that appeal to various interests but serve some incidental educational purposes. Vocational education is effective in all three groups. The first group, of course, includes formal vocational education. It also includes educational television, camps, churches, and any other formal agency that uses vocational education. Occupational choice and exposure to work roles is the major vocational aspect of the second group. The family and peer groups comprise the bulk of these primary groups. The third group is the broadest, and includes such diverse activities as newspapers, advertisements, workers educational groups, improvement activities of professional organizations, and industry-sponsored tours. It is through these activities that technology—its development, use, and work roles—are learned in society.

VOCATIONAL EDUCATION

We can accept the generalized notions that culture is handed down from generation to generation, that society is based on a developing complex of behavior patterns, and that stability is achieved as the individual internalizes what the agents of the culture transmit to him. We cannot identify with a high degree of assurance all the specific institutions and situations that influence the outcomes of vocational education. Nor can we measure the exact influence that a specific institution has had or does have on vocational education.

Subcultures also exist within the broader culture. Vocational education may be regarded as a subculture as it possesses in its behavior patterns some elements that differentiate it from the larger culture. It has a set of complex behaviors that relate it to other formal and informal educational agencies, to the community, to labor organizations, to social structure, to occupational choice, and to career patterns. It also has a culture of technical processes, ideas, habits, and values. Investigations to establish the social foundation of vocational education have been limited, and, as a result of lacking a clear understanding, confusion exists as to the purpose of vocational education: What should it transmit to the next generation? What of the present should it preserve? What should it seek to transform? How can it choose among the diverse ends of education?[12]

THE NATURE OF EDUCATIONAL DECISIONS

The educational decision-making process is complex; it is not simply a matter of gathering facts and using them as the sole basis for decisions. Since education is normative, educational decisions must reflect values. An excellent examination of the ingredients of educational decision-making has been offered by Fischer and Thomas.[13] They indicate that educational decisions are based on: (a) facts, (b) purpose, (c) values, and (d) outlook on life. The first three of these are examined here.

FACTS. Certainly before we begin to work through any problem we must gather relevant data or facts. But they do not solve the problem. They do not provide direction. In essence they are amoral—they possess no inherent morality—or neutral. They may be used quite diversely by equally competent persons.

It may be a fact, for instance, that in a given community three out of four of the unemployed are not high school graduates. They were enrolled in school but dropped out prior to graduation. Some school officials would shrug their shoulders and assert that the dropouts were once given a chance to get an education and chose not to do it. Such an official might now reason that the school has no obligation to help the students obtain skills for employment or to examine its own curriculum for appropriateness. Another school official might assert that the school should have a program to help nongraduates obtain occupational skills and that the curriculum needs some overhauling. There must be something more to educational decision-making than gathering facts!

PURPOSE. Once facts are gathered, educational decision-makers must look for some guidelines to help them use the facts. Purpose is one of the guidelines, for educational purpose is the end sought. Purpose is not to be confused with means. Much of the dialogue concerning vocational education reflects a confusion on these two points. Purpose is that "which directs or guides a particular activity. A purpose held is a fact.

Whether or not it should be held raises a question of value."[14] For a more complete analysis of the "Purpose of Purpose" the reader is referred to Houston, Blackington, and Southworth.[15]

VALUES. Once we have discerned the facts and have a clear concept of our purposes, what then? We raise the question of "ought." What ought to be done? In solving this question, we state those things that we believe to be right, proper, decent, or moral.[16] (Do not be trapped here. This is a psychological or behavioral definition of value. The philosophical axiological dimensions are untouched.) Is there a difference between a conceived and a behavioral value? My conceived (belief) value is that smoking is bad for my health and I ought to quit. But my behavioral (operational) value is to continue smoking as I enjoy the habit.[17] Examples of educational values are voluminous: The schools should insure that all children develop to the fullest extent of their ability. The public schools should (should not) teach religion. Vocational education should (should not) be taught. The schools must (must not) be concerned with the dropouts. Thus, when we make purpose operational we implement and make explicit our values. When one school official says "no" to the dropout and another says "yes," they are making their values explicit.

Perhaps we can make the point by constructing a parallel case in the field of television programming. Each year much controversy is generated about the role of the sponsor and the types of programs that are offered. The first question that we might ask to help bring order to the problem is: Who should decide on the programs that are to be shown on television? The answers would be varied but might include: (a) the general public, (b) the producers, (c) the sponsors, (d) experts, (e) opinion polls, (f) directors, or (g) the Federal Communications Commission.

We follow that question with: What should their decision be? Here the replies would include: (a) what the public wants, (b) what will hold people's attention, (c) what will sell products, (d) the most popular shows, (e) a balance of news, variety, and quiz shows, (f) what is good, and (g) what the people need.

Finally we ask: What is the primary purpose of television? Our range of responses would include: (a) to inform the public, (b) to entertain, (c) to sell the sponsors' products, and (d) to be educational.

Which of the three questions is the most relevant? It is the question of *purpose.* It is the only question that gets at the ultimate value dimensions of the problem, and an answer to it logically answers the other questions. Values become explicit when purpose is chosen. For if the purpose of television is to sell the sponsors' products, then the sponsor should decide on what programs are shown based on what research says will sell products. The answers to the first two questions are factual in nature and have instrumental value only.

To summarize this discussion: Vocational educators are decision-makers. As such, they need to gather the relevant sociological, psychological, economic, and occupational data about education and vocational education. In order to implement this task and to develop programs, it is necessary to have a clear understanding of what vocational education is to accomplish: its purpose. A purpose held is a fact, but whether or not it should be held is a value decision. Decisions that educators make to implement purposes must reflect a consideration of the ultimate value questions.

THE SOCIAL SETTING FOR VOCATIONAL EDUCATION

FORMAL ALLOCATION OF OCCUPATIONAL ROLES

A study of vocational education in American society finds an institutionalized set of relationships embracing many other significant institutionalized structures, for vocational education is directly related to the educational system and the labor market. But it is even more closely associated with the social structure of the community and the values it produces. Adequate evidence supporting this close relation between the community on the one hand and the schools and the labor market on the other hand has been assembled.[18]

Vocational education is the formalized vehicle in American society that facilitates the allocation of occupational roles. As such, it is an extension of those social mechanisms that differentiate persons within the community and prescribe the types of stations and roles that they are expected to assume. Vocational education is usually the only link between educational institutions and the institutionalized labor market.[19]

If we accept the notion that the social dimension of vocational education is the formal preparation of youth for the world of work, then vocational education is found in all societies that have occupational structures. Occupations, of course, are not found in all societies.[20] In modern American society, which is characterized as urban and highly industrialized, the occupational system is highly structured. So an allocation system and formal preparation of youngsters for the world of work is an important aspect of this society. We have already seen that at one point in our history the occupational allocation system was personal and informal. Today it is an impersonal market system far removed from the modern home and often the neighborhood. The daily activity and contact of today's youth permits only a very limited socialization toward work (with the exception of rural farms and other family-owned businesses).

If vocational education allocated and prepared youth for the world of work in a clear and straightforward manner, always maintaining a balance between individual, community, and societal needs, curricular adjustment in vocational education would be an easier problem for educators. But this is not the case. Vocational education has often been used as a vehicle to keep youngsters in school and too often has been designed for those who were thought to be unable to handle the other offerings of the school.[21]

The structure within the formal allocation system (in this case vocational education) has not helped to make its curriculum more appropriate for its clientele or to the community. Offerings are based on an analysis of present labor markets with some adjustment for future rates of growth. No effective system of "opportunity forecasting" has been developed that will feed change from the occupational system into the formal allocation system. Thus, changes occur in the labor market prior to curricular adjustments in vocational education. Attempts to eliminate this lag are not systematic but occur periodically and sporadically. Vocational education has found itself concentrating to provide instruction for jobs that were already declining in numbers and of decreasing importance to the occupational system. A history of the developments in training key punch operators is a case in point.

That we do not have a system that could forecast long-range manpower needs is discussed by Tebbel.[22] It was generally promoted that while machines would put people out of jobs, they would concurrently create so many new jobs in our technological society that unemployment would not result. Theoretically this was true. Unfortunately, the theory presumed that those displaced would be the ones trained for the jobs that technology created, and that has not happened on any significant scale. The rise in unemployment during the last half of 1967 was attributed primarily to women whose skills were displaced by machines. This displacement continues all the way from the assembly line to white-collar middle management.

The social setting for vocational education, described here so briefly, is a highly institutionalized set of relationships between the school, the community, and the labor market. It is important to recognize that these relationships are at present strained and the assumptions on which they are based need careful scrutiny.

WHAT OCCUPATIONAL ROLES?

We have seen that our advancing society has institutionalized, under fairly orderly conditions, the process of transmitting from one generation to the next knowledge, craftsmanship, and cultural values. Boulding has asserted that the only key to accelerations in the rate of such social evolution is found in new methods of transmitting such knowledge.[23] Within this context there are a number of rationales that purport to identify and describe the institutionalized relationship between man, the educational system, and the labor market. Ray as well as Kaufman and Brown analyzes a significant body of recent research supporting these rationales.[24]

One rationale suggests that vocational education is efficient when it assures an adequate labor supply. This rationale was developed prior to the others. One of the basic principles underlying each national vocational education act was that people would be trained for occupations (supply) for which society had a need (demand). The rationale was developed on the assumption that education was an investment good: Education can increase the economic well-being of society. Consequently it was necessary to develop a comprehensive manpower policy. Kaufman and Brown describe one definition of manpower policy as a combination of employment policy (aimed at providing employment opportunities for those willing and able to work), human resources development policy (designed to increase the skills, knowledge, and capabilities of the labor force), and manpower allocation policy (specifically aimed at matching men and jobs).[25] When vocational education and the labor market are discussed in the literature it appears that the manpower allocation policy tends to dominate.

In order for it to work even in a gross or crude manner, labor economists would need to project the needs of society before vocational educators could adjust their programs if an allocation policy or a broader manpower policy were followed. Kaufman and Brown conclude that it is almost impossible to obtain sufficient detailed and accurate knowledge of the labor market to make useful manpower projections.[26] Furthermore, they state, national projections are of limited use to the vocational educator, who is primarily concerned with a local area, and local areas' statistics are not widely available.

This brings into sharp focus the question of what occupational roles should be transmitted from one generation to another. Beginning with the Smith-Hughes Act of 1917, the federal government indicated that it was interested in people being trained for occupations needed by society and vocational education was created to follow an allocation policy. It was also indicated that the public school had an important role to play in the institutionalized setting of allocating people to jobs. This policy, based on a broad view of the role of occupational education as an allocating mechanism, stood basically undisturbed until 1962.

In the early 1960s, unemployment was high, especially in large geographical pockets; jobs and people were not well matched; vocational

education was criticized for failing to respond to contemporary manpower needs; and there was an emerging concern for persons with special
needs. It was evident that supporters of vocational education did not
have the means to identify contemporary manpower trends and that they
desired to expand their program, particularly at the secondary level. This
led to the passage of the Area Redevelopment Act of 1961, the Manpower
Development and Training Act of 1962, the Vocational Education Act
of 1963, and the Economic Opportunity Act of 1964. The Senate subcommittee on manpower stated that it was important to separate education from training for specific skills or occupations.[27] In essence, at a
time when proponents of vocational education were pushing for more
federal monies to support broad programs, the supporters of manpower
(employment policy) programs also put forth their firm conviction that
preparation for employment was not an appropriate objective of the
public school. The narrow employment policy concept prevailed and took
precedence over the allocation policy in deciding how federal monies
were to be spent.

One is cautioned not to overgeneralize from the above discussion. The
narrow employment policy concept prevails only to the extent that
federal monies are involved in vocational education, not to the broad
spectrum of vocational education.

There are those who maintain, and who are supported by a significant
body of research, that vocational education has the responsibility of
passing from one generation to the next the broadest possible knowledge
about occupations, a knowledge that includes much more than skills.
This rationale is based on the very clear chain of reasoning that occupations are a source of personal identity. Man, as he works, is attempting
to implement a meaningful existence for himself. As he chooses an occupation he is implementing a self-concept. This belief suggests that
rather than vocational education being limited to narrow skills after
high school graduation, it is important subject matter for the senior high
school student, the junior high school student, and even for the elementary student. Frank, supported by this rationale, proposed that a new
vocationally oriented educational path begin at the junior high level
for those who have not benefited from the traditional curriculum and its
enrichment for the academically oriented, high-achieving students.[28]

VOCATIONAL EDUCATION, ECONOMIC
AND MANPOWER POLICY

When really pushed on the point, few vocational educators believe that
economic concern—the allocating policy of matching men and jobs—

is the primary base of vocational education. They would more likely opt for a concern for the individual. But an examination of their operational beliefs finds economic concerns in first priority. Youth, for example, are "sold" vocational education on the basis that a high school graduate can earn more than one with an eighth grade education. An eighth grade dropout can expect to earn slightly over $100,000 in his lifetime, a high school graduate nearly $200,000, and a college graduate even more.

The Panel of Consultants on Vocational Education states the case for the economic effects of vocational education in a most succinct manner: "Indeed, this correlation [between years of schooling attained and life-time earnings] is so apparent that it stimulates parents and children to forego enjoyment of goods and services in order to invest in education. Intuitively or rationally, they thus recognized that education is an investment in higher future earning power of the individual."[29] The following relationships between the individual and education have been documented: (a) For males at all age levels, annual income increases as years of schooling increase. (b) Total lifetime income increases as educational attainment increases. (c) The favorable relationship between income and educational attainment has persisted through the years, even though the amount of formal schooling attained by the population has increased. (d) When lifetime income is discontinued or equated to return on current investment, the contribution of additional education is positive and significant.[30]

It is also readily apparent that education and vocational education are directly related to the annual total output of goods and services produced by a specific labor force. As the skills of the labor force are enhanced through education, output is expanded even if technology, capital, and labor remain at fixed levels. Between 1929 and 1956 only one-half to three-fourths of the national output can be attributed to increased utilization of capital and labor. The other one-fourth to one-half has been attributed to education.[31]

Hence it is apparent that the needs of the economic system are very important to the individual and to society. It is a generally held view that vocational education is to serve the economic system and, thus, the labor market. This view is expressed in nearly every piece of literature that discusses economics and vocational education. For example, the 1968 General Report of the Advisory Council on Vocational Education, when discussing Social and Manpower Environments of Vocational Education, states, "All of these changes in the manpower environment have many implications for vocational education in its traditional economic role of facilitating the adjustment of the skills of the workers to the changing demands of the labor market."[32]

Vocational education entered the public schools as a result of national legislation that was passed to create a pool of trained manpower for industry, including agriculture. The nation was concerned about a number of problems: population growth in cities, increasing industries, and an unsettled world condition. It was important that those persons leaving the rural areas for the cities be able to work at the jobs existing in these urban settings. When it occurred in 1917, legislation promoting national policy was not new in education. It happened in the closing of the technological gaps that were evident in the westward movement (see Chapter 2). It occurred in the early 1800s after American markets were closed to foreign manufactured goods and a way had to be found to produce American goods with American labor, capital, and raw materials.

Vocational education was an instrument of national manpower policy in the late 1960s, also, and it is projected to continue so into the 1970s. During the 1960s a large volume of literature emerged on this topic. One of the latest was a concise policy written for the 1968 advisory committee on vocational education.

The Vocational Education Act of 1963 is significant both for its expansion of Federal Investment and its redirection of vocational education efforts. However, this expansion and redirection were not isolated incidents but parts of a major expansion and redirection of Federal Manpower policy. The objectives of the Vocational Education Act of 1963 are better understood in the context of the total manpower policy environment in which they were formulated and in relation to other manpower programs designed to achieve the same or related objectives. Therefore, this section defines manpower policy and identifies its overall objectives, provides historical perspectives for the present stage of manpower policy, describes and appraises the Manpower Development and Training Act, the Job Corps, the Work Experience and Training Program, some manpower aspects of the community action program and the vocational rehabilitation program, all of which share common origins and objectives with VEA 1963. It also discusses the complex administrative problems which have accompanied the proliferation of programs.

Manpower policy is concerned with the development and use of human labor as an economic resource and as a source of individual and family income. The relative priorities given these two aspects of manpower policy depend upon the economic and political circumstances. Current manpower policy tends to consider efficient allocation of resources important but secondary to the welfare of the workers themselves.

A clearer definition of manpower policy is made difficult by its overlap with employment and education policies, among others. But, precise lines of demarcation are important only when jurisdictional issues are at stake. It is more useful to define manpower policy in terms of its goals and the tools with which it pursues those goals, grateful that those same goals are pursued simultaneously with other policy tools. The goals of manpower policy are:

1. Employment opportunities for all who want them in jobs which balance

free occupational choice and adequate income with society's relative preferences for alternative goods and services.

2. Education and training capable of fully developing each individual's pro-
jective potential.

3. The matching of men and jobs with a minimum of lost income and production.

To distinguish it from other policy tools, at least for the purposes of this paper,
employment policy involves the use of the Federal Government's fiscal and
monetary powers to affect the general levels of employment, while education
policy is concerned with general education as opposed to training in specific
skills. Manpower policy embraces the demand side of the economic equation
in the creation of jobs for specific individuals, groups, and locations. It covers the
supply side in the development of skills. It bridges the two in the matching
process. In its concern for the welfare of the workers it inevitably becomes involved in income distribution and wage issues. Manpower policies involve
individuals, employers, labor organizations, and state and local governments,
but the most significant developments of the past five years have been those
occurring within the Federal Government.[33]

The second paragraph of the above quotation is of particular importance. "Manpower policy is concerned with the development and use
of human labor as an economic resource and as a source of individual
and family income." If this statement was true in 1968, it was always true
during the history of vocational education. There is, however, an additional phase that is gradually being added to manpower policy. Ray
describes this addition as a philosophy stressing "the Development of
Human Resources."[34] This new dimension of manpower policy places
less emphasis on matching the best man with an existing job but emphasizes providing a suitable job for each man or equipping the man
to fill a suitable job. The emphasis, then, is less on manpower as an
economic resource but more on employment as a source of income and
status for workers.

Manpower policy, even with this slight shift in emphasis, still places
man on one side of an economic equation and jobs on the other. As an
instrument of national policy, present manpower policy does not have a
human development base. Such a base is necessary. A human development base regards man as a developing creature, one who can change
and respond, and one whose total entity must be considered when
dealing with him.

When man works his total entity is involved, not just his ability to
perform selected physical skills. To isolate skill development from man's
totality is to run the risk of having a worker with limited survival skills.
This point is made vividly by Meade, who stresses that to survive in
our fast-changing society, man needs five basic skills: the ability to reason,
the ability to readjust oneself on one's own terms to cultural flux, the

ability to control and spend one's time with intelligence and purpose, the ability to achieve and sustain rewarding relationships with others, and the ability to persevere and extend one's uniqueness while participating harmoniously in the society.[35]

VOCATIONAL EDUCATION AND A CONCEPT OF THE LEARNER

A concept of the learner is an important dimension of the social foundation of vocational education, for it determines how we prepare, structure, and execute programs of vocational education. This concept finds most of its support in the field of psychology. Some of it, however, can be legitimately included in our discussion here because a part of the concept of the learner deals with man as a philosophical and social being.

One concept held by some educators is that man finds formal learning a distasteful process and by his basic nature will resist it. Under such an assumption the teacher is not to trust students, not to elicit ideas from them, and is justified in the use of threats. Such a teacher would use firm control in class. A sign over the door might remind the students to "Speak only when you are spoken to by the teacher." The teacher's task would be to expose the students to the accumulated knowledge of the past. Thus exposed, those students who are "educable" would grow to like learning, while the others would drift into occupations that do not require a high degree of literacy.

Other traditionalists view man as being born with a blank mind and expect the school to write upon his wax tablet those things that he should learn. Still others view man as being born with potential that formal education sharpens and draws out. Some feel that man is born in sin, is deprived, and is inherently bad, and that formal education is to show him how to achieve salvation.

Vocational educators tend to reject such assumptions of man as learner. Man is assumed to be, by nature, a curious person. He enjoys learning, is curious about it, and has a desire for it. A teacher's task in this case is to take advantage of this curiosity and interest and use them for educative activities. This view of the learner sees man as the product of organic, biological evolution. Man, on the phylogenetic scale, differs from other organisms in degree but not in kind. He is continuous with nature but has evolved unique abilities, including a powerful mental ability. A child has social, moral, intellectual, and physical potentials. The extent to which these potentials are developed depends upon the number and quality of experiences he has. These may be planned directly by the child or by the school and other social institutions.

The teacher has a humane attitude toward the learner who is appreciated for his own sake. The teacher guides the learner in developing self-control and a sense of responsibility appropriate to his age. Watching and waiting, helping and guiding become activities of the teacher who realizes that the learner evolves through recognized stages of growth and development. Varying needs and interests of the learner are considerations for the teacher.

Vocational educators generalize that each student is an individual; each is motivated and driven by a different set of mechanisms. To say that each student is an individual is really a tautological statement and is used to such an extent it is also nearly a cliché. It does, though, represent a notion that each student is important. Another assumption is that students can make a contribution to their own learning. Teacher-pupil planning and the problem-solving method of teaching are indicative of this assumption. Students can help identify problems, can help plan the solution, and can help test for the appropriateness of solutions. For example, a class in distributive education might not be convinced of the best method of merchandise display. They would probably plan various displays in a supermarket to evaluate their effectiveness.

The student must have purposeful goals to guide his learning activities. Purposeful behavior is more effective than impulsive behavior but it must be the pupil's rather than the teacher's purpose. Another way of saying this is that all students must have a goal toward which they direct their activity if learning is to be meaningful. The student will not be motivated by abstract activities that are inserted to facilitate learning for the sake of learning. W. F. Stewart, known to many as a master vocational teacher, comments,

There is rather general agreement today that the conditions for learning are much more favorable when the learner experiences a feeling of need for the subject matter, and when the mastery of the subject matter results in personal satisfactions. Schools should endeavor to have pupils learn only things and processes which are of use and value in life situations.[36]

Growing out of this assumption is another assumption: The learner must apply, try out, what is being learned if he is to learn it effectively.

Supporting the above is another assumption that the learner needs practice if he is to retain what he learns. Practice refers to performance, not merely repetition of an act, nor is it limited to manipulative use.

A final assumption is that people learn in different ways. These different ways include in a classroom, in a shop, in informal settings, on field trips, and on the job. Vocational instruction is not to be classroom bound. Much of what the student needs to know can be learned only in a concrete situation affected by time, supervision, cooperation, and other real-life factors.

A SOCIAL CONTRIBUTION TO BE MADE
BY VOCATIONAL EDUCATION

Work has taken on a number of meanings at various stages in our history. At one point, economists say, we had a "scarcity" condition. In this situation the function of work—defined in terms of physical effort—was to produce goods. A man's status and salvation was determined by the amount of goods he was able to produce. It was considered evil not to work, and the harder a man worked the more likely he was to be "saved."

Our present condition is one of abundance for the dominant social groups. Machines and machines run by machines can produce and do much "work" in its traditional sense. Nearly two-thirds of our work force today, compared to one-fourth in 1900, are in the white-collar and service classifications. This implies that work today is distribution and service, not production. For some work is more cognitive and for others it is more boring.

With an understanding of this background, Herzberg questions if man is really motivated primarily by economic considerations.[37] Man, according to Herzberg, strives to enjoy a meaningful existence, one in which there is a balance between his need to realize his potential for growth and perfection and his need to avoid deprivation. An emerging concern is moving beyond the economic considerations. Present achievements have speeded up the rate at which technology creates new designs for living. Scientific progress has outdistanced social progress. We are confronted with the great majority of workers working less hours for higher and higher wages at a steadily lowering standard of workmanship. *Consumer Reports*, in its May and June 1968 issues, notes a vastly increasing number of defects in new cars: "The art of partial assembly" was the heading given to that section of its report. This is only one indication that high pay does not necessarily result in increased workmanship. Economic appeals fall on deaf ears. A meat packing employee, for example, with an annual salary of between $10,000 and $14,000, 20 years on the job, house paid for, family about grown, is not trying to earn more money at his job. What he wants are significant ways of relating to the noneconomic dimension of his life. Thus, vocational education needs to do much more than teach skills or prepare for entry employment. It needs to make a social contribution to the worker's life.

Vocational education at the secondary school level has never attempted to produce graduates with a complete array of skills for highly skilled and technical jobs. Graduates were prepared for entry employment—perhaps

in highly skilled jobs, more generally in low levels of less skilled occupations. For modern American society that modest objective becomes
even more realistic. We need, though, to examine the way we think about
that goal, the way we operate programs to achieve it.

Few vocational educators would dispute the notion that vocational
programs at the high school level have been designed to prepare a youngster for entry employment or for a post–high school vocational-technical
program. Admittedly, the acquired skills may be for very low occupational entry. One way of thinking about the end result is that vocational
education, in its traditional role, has *taught a youngster all about a job*.
This places job skills in central focus. Skill acquisition became our intent
in such a framework. The instructor taught that an arc welder selected
a welding rod, placed it in the electrode holder, turned on the welder,
struck an arc, welded in a variety of positions, and so on. The earning
power of the job was mentioned if the pay was good. The high pay of
computer programmers was pointed out. It was not pointed out in such
programs as farm machinery repair courses that salaries in this industry
may be lower than those for similar jobs in other industries. Follow-up
studies a few months after graduation for these courses found the computer programmer on the job and advancing, while the farm machinery
graduate was likely to be holding a job in another business as in farm
machinery repair the entry wages were just too low.

Another way of thinking about the end product of vocational education at the secondary school level is to consider the social contribution it
can make to the growth and development of young people. Such thinking
would result in teaching what a job is all about rather than all about a
job. The distinction between the two frameworks is great. Teaching what
a job is all about, in addition to the skill component of the job, introduces the young person to occupational classification, employee interaction, job satisfaction, and the style of life associated with the job. Style
of life refers to who the worker associates with, the kind of community in
which he is likely to live, the kind of car he is likely to drive, and related
matters.

The quality and style of life of an occupation mean the degree to
which the job is human. In "human" jobs the worker has some control
over the quality of his existence while working. Some jobs require completely independent action on the part of the worker; others require no
independent action and the worker performs "mechanically." Most jobs
fit on a continuum somewhere between these two extremes.

Did you ever take a group of youngsters to tour an automobile assembly plant, a milk processing plant, a meat packing plant, a cigarette
factory, a department store, or a similar industry after they have studied
it in school? Through careful analysis the group can begin to see the

breakdown of jobs in an industry, the quality of life associated with each type of job, the skills needed to perform each job, the extent to which a job has breadth, the extent to which the job is repetitive. They can talk to workers to discover what and how they think about their jobs, how much contact there is with other workers, whether the worker controls his pace. In such a situation you are beginning to teach what a job is all about. And this is what vocational education must do today.

NOTES

1All figures cited here are reported in *Projections of Educational Statistics 1975–76*; corresponding issues of *Digest of Annual Reports*; *What's Ahead in Vocational Education*; all published by the U.S. Office of Education.

2From "A Republic Task Force on Education and Training (1970)," inserted in the *Congressional Record* and reported by *The Milwaukee Journal*, 3 October, 1971, p. 6.

3Robert J. Havighurst and Bernice L. Neugarten, *Society and Education*, 2nd ed. (Boston: Allyn & Bacon, Inc., 1962), p. 274.

4Louis Fischer and Donald R. Thomas, *Social Foundations of Educational Decisions* (Belmont, Calif.: Wadsworth Publishing Co., Inc., 1965), Chap. 1.

5J. Steele Gow, Jr., Buckart Holzner, and William C. Pendleton, "Economic, Social and Political Forces," in *The Changing American School*, ed., John I. Goodlad, 65th Yearbook of the National Society for the Study of Education, Part II (Chicago: University of Chicago Press, 1966), p. 197.

6W. Vernon Hicks and Frank H. Blackington III, *Introduction to Education* (Columbus, Ohio: Charles E. Merrill Books, Inc. 1965), p. 110.

7Bronislau Malinowski, "Culture," in *The Encyclopedia of the Social Sciences*, ed. E. R. A. Seligman (New York: The Macmillan Company, 1931), p. 621.

8Ralph Linton, *The Study of Man* (New York: Appleton-Century Co., 1936).

9B. Othaniel Smith, William O. Stanley, and J. Harlan Shores, *Fundamentals of Curriculum Development*, rev. ed. (New York: Harcourt, Brace Jovanovich, 1957), p. 6.

10E. Merle Adams, Jr., "New Viewpoints in Sociology," in *New Viewpoints in the Social Science*, ed. Roy A. Price, 28th Yearbook, National Council for the Social Studies, (Washington, D.C.: National Education Association, 1958), pp. 101–3.

11Ellis Ford Hartford, *Education in These United States* (New York: The Macmillan Company, 1964), pp. 46–47.

12This characterization may be too gross in the sense that the entire institution of education is seeking answers to the above questions. See Myron Lieberman, *The Future of Public Education* (Chicago: University of Chicago Press, 1960), pp. 15–33; and Hicks and Blackington, *Introduction to Education*, pp. 93–96.

13Fischer and Thomas, *Social Foundations of Educational Decisions*, pp. 7–9.

14*Ibid.*, p. 8.

15Robert Houston, Frank H. Blackington III, and Horton C. Southworth, *Professional Growth Through Student Teaching* (Columbus, Ohio: Charles E. Merrill Books, Inc., 1965), Chap. 10.

16Charles Morris, *Varieties of Human Values* (Chicago: University of Chicago Press, 1956), pp. 9–12.

17Joseph A. Kahl, *The American Class Structure* (New York: Holt, Rinehart & Winston, Inc., 1957), p. 185.

18For the relation between the community and the schools, see Wilber B. Brookover and David Gottlieb, *A Sociology of Education*, 2nd ed. (New York: American Book Company, 1964) and A. B. Hollingshead, *Elmtown's Youth* (New York: John Wiley & Sons, Inc., 1949), p. 168. For the relation between the community and the labor market, see Sigmund Nosow, "Labor Distribution and the Normative System," in *Man, Work and Society*, eds. S. Nosow and William H. Form (New York: Basic Books, Inc., Publishers, 1962) pp. 117–26.

19Wilbur B. Brookover and Sigmund Nosow, "A Sociological Analysis of Vocational Education in the United States," in *Education for a Changing World of Work*, (Washington, D.C.: Government Printing Office, 1963), Appendix 3.

20A. Salz, "Occupation," in *Encyclopedia of the Social Sciences* (New York: The Macmillan Company, 1937) XI–XII, 424–34.

21Howard M. Bell, *Matching Youth and Jobs* (Washington, D.C.: American Council on Education, 1940), p. 66.

22John Tebbel, "People and Jobs: Why Manpower Is in Short Supply While 3,000,000 Americans Are Unemployed," *Saturday Review*, December 30, 1967, pp. 8–12, 42.

23Kenneth E. Boulding, "Human Resources Development as a Learning Process," in *Human Resources Development*, eds. Edward B. Jakubauskas and E. Philip Baumel (Ames: Iowa State University Press, 1967), pp. 46–55.

24Elizabeth M. Ray, "Social & Philosophical Framework," *Review of Educational Research*, 38, no. 4 (1968), 309–25; Jacob J. Kaufman and Anne F. Brown, "Manpower Supply and Demand," *Review of Educational Research*, pp. 326–45.

25Kaufman and Brown, *Review of Educational Research*, p. 326.

26*Ibid.*, p. 341.

27Garth L. Mangum, *The Manpower Revolution: Its Policy Consequences* (New York: Doubleday & Company, Inc., 1965).

28Nathaniel H. Frank, *Final Report of the Summer Study on Occupational, Vocational and Technical Education* (Cambridge: Science Teaching Center, Massachusetts Institute of Technology, 1965), p. 121.

29*Education for a Changing World of Work, Report of the Panel of Consultants on Vocational Education* (Washington, D.C.: Government Printing Office, 1962), p. 12.

30Jon T. Innes et al., "The Economic Returns to Education: A Survey of Findings," in J. Robert Warmbrod, *Review and Synthesis of Research on the Economics of Vocational Education* (Columbus, Ohio: Center for Studies in Vocational and Technical Education, 1968), p. 4.

31*Education for a Changing World of Work*, pp. 11–12.

32*Vocational Education—The Bridge Between Man and His Work* (Washington, D.C.: Government Printing Office, 1968), p. 168.

33*Ibid.*, pp. 172–73.

34Ray, *Review of Educational Research*, p. 313.

35Edward J. Meade, Jr., "The Changing Society and Its Schools," in *Life Skills in School and Society*, ed. Louis J. Rubin, 1969 Yearbook, Association for Supervision and Curriculum Development (Washington, D.C.: 1969), pp. 35–51.

36W. F. Stewart, "Methods of Good Teaching" (1950), p. 7.

37Frederick Herzberg, *Work and the Nature of Man* (New York: The World Publishing Company, 1966).

2

A HISTORICAL REVIEW
OF SELECTED FORCES THAT INFLUENCED
VOCATIONAL EDUCATION

INTRODUCTION

A history of vocational education in America is one of two complementary forces: the evolution of technology and a changing view of man. Neither could have developed without the other. Technology is man's attempt to sustain the human species in increasing numbers at an increasingly high level of abundance (though, admittedly, the population in America is tending to stabilize). Technology evolved from the application of man's creativity to his never-ending quest for an easier way to a life of abundance and increased leisure time. Man's view of himself changed as increased leisure provided him with more opportunity to study himself and his environment and to speculate on what his possibilities were.

This process of increasing discovery led to technological advancement, which in turn led to an increased need for a new type of education. This new type of education—vocational education—was to increase man's ability to understand and apply his technology. Its primary emphasis was on developing man's ability to perform the physical tasks required to use technology.

In general, each stage in the development of vocational education began with the emergence of a social condition. Philosophical inquiry established a new view of what was possible for man to achieve. Out of a disparity between the social condition (what was) and the philosophical position (what should be) grew recognition of the need to bring the two more closely together. At this point a critical technological advance was made to close the gap between the social condition and the philosophical position. This adjustment led to a new social condition, and the cycle was repeated. As the cycles progressed, vocational education grew discontinuously and was directed and shaped by these changing forces.

THE CHANGE FROM AN AGRARIAN SOCIETY

In early American society, an elite ruled. The elite were primarily owners of property, which was acquired through land grants from the King of England. The history of nearly all the eastern states follows this pattern. Maryland, for example, was chartered in June 1632 from King James I to Cecilius Calvert, the second Lord Baltimore. The ownership of many thousands of acres by an individual gave way to ownership of more manageable tracts of a few thousand acres by larger numbers of the elite. Settlement of our country did not destroy elitism. In fact, it spread with the frontier.

The agrarian society was at first composed basically of self-sustaining family units; that is, families tended to produce their own goods and provide their own services. Education was a service provided by the family. Personal involvement and meaningful interaction among individuals occurred primarily within the family structure. Over the years, the self-sustaining family unit has gradually disappeared. Today, few families produce either goods or services that they personally utilize. The family exists in an entirely different sense, and formal as well as some aspects of informal education occurs increasingly outside of the family unit.

The rural society matured into an industrial society, which gave rise to urbanization, the tendency of families to cluster within a small geographic area. This clustering was based upon the emerging interdependence of people within institutions. Institutions performing both industrial and governmental functions provided employment and tended to give direction to the lives of the masses, while the elite directed the institutions.

The free enterprise capitalist economic system that developed in the United States demanded individually owned businesses in competition with one another. Competition became the motivating force for efficiency, which was conceived as the maximum utilization of resources to produce goods at minimum cost. As industrialization continued, the number of physical resources required to develop economically competitive units increased vastly. To assemble the resources required to maintain a competitive unit, a merging of units occurred. The structure that emerged was corporate enterprise, which developed a bureaucratic system of management.

Urban centers established whole new sets of conditions for the worker. Housing had to be provided. Owner-managers were the only ones who could provide the necessary capital since only they had the financial resources. Owner-managers committed capital to housing with little thought of aesthetics or the quality of life of the worker; their concern was to maintain workers as a resource for the institutions. Hence the adoption of company housing (close quarters, every home alike); the company store; and the use of regulatory group techniques, such as the town whistle signaling when to start work and when to stop.

In the urban society the worker could no longer produce goods for the landlord in return for the right to live on the land. Nor could his family produce all of the goods it needed. The worker needed to receive "something" from his employer that he could use to purchase needed goods and services. Thus a system of payment to the worker for his services was introduced. This enabled the worker to purchase what he needed and in some cases to accumulate monies. It also led to the establishment of a new philosophical position. The thought emerged that all men, not just the elite, had the potential to become property owners.

AN ECONOMIC VIEW OF THE WORTH OF MAN

The history of vocational education is essentially a history of man's efforts to improve his technical competence in order to upgrade his economic position in society. This was accomplished by mastering, shaping, and directing his environment toward economic ends through technology. The accepted man was one who had made an economic contribution. Economics was a measure of power and hence worth. Since an "economic man" was a "good man," he was awarded special privileges that created a very real class cleavage based on the division of labor in society.

In European countries, the King was thought to have power stemming directly from the divinity. Over a period of two centuries the people were able to transfer the "divine right" from the King to the common man. This was undertaken to protect the rising middle-class merchant (the common man) from the omnipotence of the King. If the King were divine he could take all of the property from the merchants. In the classical liberal tradition, property is the key concept. The owners of property, they thought, took all of the risks. They alone had dignity and worth, hence rights. They were freed from control by royalty and could employ any means available to protect their property.

In America, too, the task of the property owner was to employ the propertyless, to plan, to guide society, and to be cultured. The persons employed by the property owner had no rights since they had no property. They were regarded by their employers as machines to perform work. The worker had to be fed and housed. One advantage was that through a rental system he could be responsible for his own housing.

Education for the property owner and his children was socially oriented to help them carry out their "God-given" responsibilities. Education for the worker took the primary form of apprenticeships.[1] This type of vocational education was not regarded as a part of the school curriculum.

During its initial stages of development, vocational education was forced to view man primarily as an economic being, not as a cultural being. Cultural expectations, typified by such expressions as "all men work" and "I know a man by his work," came from this era to reinforce the economic view of man. The greater a person's ability to work, the higher his value as an employee. So education for the worker was strictly a means of increasing his ability to perform work. And as the work to be performed grew increasingly complex, this type of education became more complicated.

The emergence of the philosophical view that all men were potential property owners brought education for culture and education for work into conflict. Evidence of this conflict can be identified in nearly any decade of the history of American education, and at times it has led to a dual system of education. Nevertheless it brought into focus the need for the comprehensive school.

PLURALISM OF INSTITUTIONS

The focus of vocational education has always been toward some concept of the world of work. As each generation added new knowledge to the cumulative experience of mankind, it was only natural that man discovered that some persons could (and probably preferred to) perform some of the tasks of life better than others. Thus, to that person eventually fell the responsibility to preserve the knowledge of that task and pass it on to the next generation.

The process for transmitting specialized knowledge became formalized to the extent that the life's work of the son was usually the same as his father's. The son learned the rudiments (fundamentals) of the job primarily from his father through very informal techniques. These techniques may be called "pick-up" methods and included observation, imitation, and trial and error. In a primitive, static society there was no wealth of knowledge upon which to rely when the boy considered better ways of fulfilling the requirements of the occupation. The major point to remember is that occupations were transmitted from father to son through very informal means. This informal occupational specialization contributed to an understanding and application of technology for early man and is regarded as the beginning of vocational education.

These conditions for vocational training worked as long as a society could be described as one whose institutions—religious, political, cultural, economic, and social—were based on permanence. But in the sixteenth century, a countertrend began to develop: Society and its institutions began their advance toward multiplicity. Multiplicity, accelerating gradually, did not reach its full impact until the late nineteenth and early twentieth centuries. The singleness of institutions evolved into what may best be described by the term *pluralism*. New religious, political, cultural, and economic arrangements developed. Technology, which fostered this change, provided new meanings and made new demands upon the labor force. Change marked the institutions that were to survive in our pluralistic society.[2] This change, which began in the sixteenth century, may be regarded as another era in the development of vocational education. It was during this period that a body of theory and knowledge of a vocational nature was beginning to accumulate, and skill development and transmission of skill to others became more formalized and systematic.

WARS

Shortly after the approval of the Smith-Hughes Act in 1917, the United States became involved in World War I. What was first seen as an educational program geared to the social and occupational needs of the general public had its baptism as a unit of government challenged to contribute its part toward national victory. Other major wars that have influenced vocational education include World War II, the Korean conflict, and the Vietnam war. What was the status of vocational education during periods of war? Has war shaped it or influenced its direction?

Were precedents set and concepts of vocational education ingrained into the minds of the public that have hindered efforts of vocational educators in their communication with the general educator as well as with the public? Here we will consider these and similar questions.[3]

World War I was a war of mechanical forces. It was recognized that in order to fight a mechanical war, trained mechanics, technicians, and highly experienced supervisory forces would be needed in addition to troops. The war effort also created and expanded industries. To produce the necessary equipment and supplies, industry required increasing numbers of trained craftsmen. The War Industries Board and the Federal Board for Vocational Education took the lead in providing this trained manpower. The Federal Board for Vocational Education stated in 1918 that at the request of the United States Army it had "undertaken to aid the Army to secure proper training of conscripted men ... before they are drafted. ... This bulletin is issued for the purpose of supplying information to school authorities who will undertake this work as a patriotic duty."[4]

The Federal Board for Vocational Education worked with the Army to help determine that it needed 200,000 mechanics. In addition, a need for radio operators, radio repairmen, automobile drivers, gasoline engine repairmen, and others was discerned. The Board then formulated a plan to train personnel. Its major effort was to establish classes in specialized subjects for men prior to their induction into service. The men were registered as conscriptees and were waiting to be called to active duty. Training was eventually provided at 125 local induction centers.[5]

Hawkins, Prosser, and Wright list ten benefits from the effects of war training upon vocational education.[6] Among the ten are: (1) The country as a whole became conscious of the need for vocational education. (2) Adults need training even after they are employed. (3) Women can be trained to do men's work. (4) Supervisors need to be trained through short intensive courses. (5) The philosophy was advanced that vocational education was a part of preparation for living needed by all normal individuals rather than a device for keeping youth in school or for taking care of delinquents.

Foreman training was perhaps the largest direct result of vocational education involvement in this war effort.

When America entered World War II, vocational education was again called upon to help face a national problem. The circumstances, however, were quite different. Since 1917, the "regular program" of day, part-time, and evening schools had been in operation, and there was a large pool of trained teachers, supervisors, and administrators of vocational education programs to spearhead the war production efforts. In addition, thousands of inductees were graduates of vocational programs and thus possessed the needed competence. A large number of industrial workers were also graduates of vocational education programs.

The efforts for World War II were largely a matter of expanding existing programs and marshalling the trained leaders. Vocational Training for War Production Workers (VTWPW) and Vocational Education for National Defense (VEND) were initiated to expand the vocational training programs already underway. Distinctions between these two programs are hard to make. VEND, designed to expand the "regular program," was initiated and administered primarily through the same channels as the Smith-Hughes Act. Both the VEND and VTWPW were largely urban centered and operated to train industrial workers. A food production war training program was established in rural areas to train personnel for agriculture and to insure that the nation's food and fiber needs were met. Ten pieces of federal legislation were enacted for vocational training in World War II; these carried a combined total appropriation of over $370 million.

The major effect of the Korean conflict and the Vietnam war on vocational education can be seen by looking at unemployment figures. Large numbers of persons, for example, were drafted in 1965, causing a decline in unemployment. Many persons were employed who might otherwise not have been. In July and August 1967, the unemployment figure rose due to returning veterans entering the labor market and because of a temporary stabilization in the numbers drafted; the net effect was an increased labor supply. Vocational-technical schools, particularly at the postsecondary level, expanded existing programs and created new ones to assist veterans to enter or reenter the labor market. The major effect, then, of the Korean and the Vietnam wars was an alteration of employment patterns and unemployment rates and an expansion of vocational-technical school programs.

During national emergencies vocational education has provided leadership to prepare manpower for the country's needs. In many instances, state supervisors and college teacher-educators have gone directly into factories to teach or supervise classes. Most such training programs were just that—training programs. They were designed as short-unit courses to train production workers to perform single-skill operations. Colleagues of vocational educators involved with such programs often equated single-skill training with vocational education. This explains the roots of many of the stereotypes and misunderstandings that general educators hold of vocational education and educators.

It also affected vocational educators directly in a variety of ways. After World War II, vocational educators were not precise in distinguishing between educational programs and training programs. What had been the regular vocational education programs prior to involvement with war training programs were often referred to afterward as training programs. Needless to say, this did not help to bridge the communication gap among vocational educators or between vocational and general educators.

The development of single-unit courses structured to train production workers in single-skill operations resulted in some trainees of such programs becoming vocational educators. This was the initial experience of many persons who became high school vocational teachers, supervisors, teacher educators. Their orientation toward vocational education was quite different from those who were involved in regular programs prior to World War II and those who entered vocational education after the late 1940s. Many of them perceived vocational teaching as teaching single-skill operations. Relationships between a skill and its theory were not considered important and thus not emphasized in the vocational programs. Skill development was often taught as an isolated activity and as an end in itself. Fortunately, many of these educators did make the transition to differentiating between skill development and vocational education.

Vocational education has also benefited from experiences in national emergencies in refining its teaching methods. Notwithstanding that the teaching was often narrowly conceived, since financial resources were plentiful elaborate procedures and techniques were developed to demonstrate and teach skills in these training programs.

NATIONAL STUDY PANELS

Over the years a number of separate national panels, committees, and commissions have been appointed to study vocational education intensively. Most of these groups were created to find ways of bringing "what is" more into line with "what should be." A social condition existed at the time the panels were appointed that suggested that man had the potential for developing into something that the present structure of vocational education did not permit him to achieve. The panels were to study that condition and recommend what changes were needed. The charge given to the Panel of Consultants in 1961 by President Kennedy, quoted later in this chapter, is a case in point.

Only one of the six panels was not appointed by the President of the United States. The six panels were: (1) Commission on National Aid for Vocational Education, 1914, appointed by President Wilson; (2) Committee on Vocational Education, 1928–1929, appointed by the President of the Department of Superintendency (this committee did not function effectively and it soon faded out of existence); (3) National Advisory

Committee on Education, 1929–1931, appointed by President Hoover and the Department of Interior; (4) Advisory Committee on Education, 1936–1938, appointed by President Roosevelt; (5) Panel of Consultants on Vocational Education, 1961–1962, appointed by President Kennedy; (6) Advisory Council on Education, 1968 (this committee grew out of the 1963 Vocational Education Act and is required by that act to make a report on vocational education every five years). The 1914 and the 1961–1962 reports were credited with shaping subsequent legislation.

Before discussing these national panels, it is important to obtain a perspective of the Douglas Commission, which was appointed in 1905 to examine trade-training programs in Massachusetts. McCarthy comments:

It must be remembered that the Douglas Commission in Massachusetts was created not only because of the inadequacy of manual-training programs in the public schools, but, also because the so-called land-grant colleges failed to serve the needs of agriculture or industry on the workers' level.[7]

The Douglas Commission was very critical of what it found and titled "the trade training," which was offered as "a sort of mustard relish." It recommended a comprehensive program of "instruction and practice in the elements of productive industry." The commission's recommendations resulted in the Massachusetts legislature passing a state law in 1906 to make vocational education a part of the public school system. This was a milestone in the history of education. Thus other states, the early professional associations—particularly the National Society for the Promotion of Industrial Education—and the national study panels had the benefit of this model to guide them.

COMMISSION ON NATIONAL AID TO VOCATIONAL EDUCATION, 1914

This commission grew out of the legislative tie-up over the passage of the Smith-Lever and the Page (a forerunner to the Smith-Hughes Act) bills. From 1906 to 1913, though both pieces of legislation had the common goal of practical education for the workingman, supporters feared that only one would be passed. The National Society for the Promotion of Industrial Education reached an agreement with Senator Smith to support the Smith-Lever Bill if he would see that a commission on national aid to vocational education were created. Such a commission was created in January 1914.

The commission investigated six basic questions, the first being the need for vocational education. Assuming a need for vocational education, was there a need for money? What specific vocational programs required federal money for stimulation? How far should the federal government extend aid for vocational education to the states? How much money was needed? And, under what conditions should the federal government grant monies to the states for vocational education?

The authorization for the commission specified that a report was to be made by June 1, a scant two months after its organization on April 2, 1914. This short time period necessitated that the commission and its staff assemble in Washington to devote full time to their work. In less than sixty days the commission had created a two-volume report of nearly 500 pages on the six basic questions.[8]

The effect of this commission on vocational education was expansive. Its recommendations for legislation became the Smith-Hughes Bill, as introduced in both the Senate and the House. The final Smith-Hughes Law contained only minor revisions of the commission's recommendations. This report also brought vocational education to the attention of the entire nation. Support was consolidated, making vocational education one of the very strong national lobby groups. In addition, it established the general principle of a national board for vocational education, and as a consequence, industry as well as labor and agriculture became articulate spokesmen for vocational education. This legislation paved the way for most high school–level vocational education programs to be integrated into the total "comprehensive" school and not organized as a separate school. There are exceptions to this latter point.

ADVISORY COMMITTEE ON EDUCATION, 1936–1938

This group of twenty-four persons was appointed in 1936 and headed by Dr. Floyd W. Reeves. Within a year the group had its scope enlarged to include all education. It was originally charged by President Roosevelt to study: (1) the experience under existing programs for federal aid to vocational education, (2) the relationship of training to general education and to prevailing economic and social conditions, and (3) the extent to which a need existed for expanded programs in vocational education.

This Advisory Committee made six recommendations: (1) to review the basic statutes with the specific intent of removing restraining provisions, (2) to consolidate all federal funds for vocational education of less than senior college grade into a single fund, (3) that the determination of educational activities deemed vocational be transferred to the states, (4) that plant training programs be continued and expanded, (5) to provide for those states that have separate schools for Negroes to receive a just and equitable share of federal funds, and (6) to establish a minimum age of seventeen for instruction designed to prepare for a specific trade and that the age of fourteen should be established for participation in all special fields of education, but this could be waived for club work for rural boys and girls.[9]

Little credibility was given by vocational educators to the recommendations of this study commission. More often than not the recommendations were condemned. In general, it was regarded as a report prepared by persons who had no experience and little understanding of vocational education and its specific needs.

PANEL OF CONSULTANTS ON VOCATIONAL EDUCATION, 1961–1962

President Kennedy, in a special message to Congress on February 20, 1961, empowered the creation of a panel of consultants to study vocational education. His message said:

The National Vocational Education Acts first enacted by Congress in 1917 and subsequently amended have provided a program of training for industry, agriculture, and other occupational areas. The basic purpose of our vocational education effort is sound and sufficiently broad to provide a basis for meeting future needs. However, the technological changes which have occurred in all occupations call for a review and re-evaluation of these acts, with a view towards their modernization.

To that end, I am requesting the Secretary of Health, Education and Welfare to convene an advisory body drawn from the educational profession, labor, industry, and agriculture as well as the lay public together with representatives from the Departments of Agriculture and Labor to be charged with the responsibility of reviewing and evaluating the current National Vocational Education Acts, and making recommendations for improving and redirecting the program.[10]

This panel of twenty-five consultants was chaired by Dr. Benjamin C. Willis, superintendent of schools for the City of Chicago. Its report, "Education for a Changing World of Work," issued in November 1962 had become a well-thumbed bible for nearly every vocational educator by the mid-1960s. Many of its recommendations found their way into the Vocational Education Act of 1963.

The panel recommended that vocational education must (1) offer training opportunities to the twenty-one million noncollege graduates who would enter the labor market in the 1960s; (2) provide training or retraining for the millions of workers whose skills and technical knowledge must be updated, as well as those whose jobs would disappear due to increasing efficiency, automation, or economic change; (3) meet the critical needs for highly skilled craftsmen and technicians through education offered during and beyond the high school years; (4) expand vocational and technical education training programs consistent with employment potential and national economic needs; and (5) make educational opportunities equally available to all persons regardless of race, sex, scholastic aptitude, or place of residence.[11]

The panel then recommended, as did the Reeves report of 1938, that aid to specific occupational categories be discontinued and support increased for five clientele groups and services: (1) young people in high school preparing to enter the labor market or to become homemakers; (2) high school–age youth with academic, socioeconomic, or other handicaps that prevent them from succeeding in the traditional high school vocational education program; (3) youth and adults who have completed or left high school and are full-time students preparing to enter the labor market; (4) unemployed youth and adults or those working who need training or retraining to achieve employment stability; and (5) adequate services and facilities must be provided to assure quality in all vocational and technical education programs.[12]

ADVISORY COUNCIL ON VOCATIONAL EDUCATION, 1968

The authors of the Vocational Education Act of 1963 recognized the need for flexibility in a rapidly changing society and the difficulties of reorienting institutions to keep pace with new demands. Thus an evaluation system was built into the Act. Part of that evaluative process was the appointment in 1966 and each five years thereafter of a Vocational Education Advisory Council to appraise the results of the act and recommend administrative and legislative improvements. Dr. Martin Essex of Ohio chaired the 1966 twelve-member Advisory Council, and its report was released in early 1968.

The Advisory Council encountered a number of problems. There were actually only two years of experience under the 1963 act to evaluate. This condition resulted primarily from the lag between legislative authorization and the appropriation of funds. In implementing the new legislation, inadequate attention was given to the data and information needs for the council.

To facilitate appraisals at a later date, the council first noted the objectives of the Vocational Education Act of 1963. A fourteen-point program, entitled "Toward a Unified System of Vocational Education," set forth an adequate system of vocational education for achieving its objectives while coping with a changing environment.[13] These fourteen characteristics were:

1. Occupational preparation should begin in the elementary schools with a realistic picture of the world of work. Its fundamental purposes should be to familiarize the student with his world and to provide him with the intellectual tools and rational habits of thought to play a satisfying role in it.

2. In junior high school economic orientation and occupational preparation should reach a more sophisticated stage with study by all students of the economic and industrial system by which goods and services are produced and distributed. The objective should be exposure to the full range of occupational choices which will be available at a later point and full knowledge of the relative advantages and the requirements of each.

3. Occupational preparation should become more specific in the high school, though preparation should be limited to a specific occupation. Given the uncertainties of a changing economy and the limited experiences upon which vocational choices must be made, instruction should not be overly narrow but should be built around significant families of occupations or industries which promise expanding opportunities.

   All students outside the college preparatory curriculum should acquire an entry-level job skill, but they should also be prepared for post-high-school vocational and technical education. Even those in the college preparatory curriculum might profit from the techniques of learning by doing. On the other hand, care should be taken that pursuit of a vocationally oriented curriculum in the high school does not block the upward progress of the competent student who later decides to pursue a college degree.

4. Occupational education should be based on a spiral curriculum which treats concepts at higher and higher levels of complexity as the student moves through the program. Vocational preparation should be used to make general education concrete and understandable; general education should point up the vocational implications of all education. Curriculum materials should be prepared for both general and vocational education to emphasize these relationships.

5. Some formal post-secondary occupational preparation for all should be a goal for the near future. Universal high school education is not yet achieved but is rapidly approaching reality. Post-secondary enrollments are growing, and before many years have passed the labor force entrant without advanced skills gained through post-secondary education, apprenticeship, or on-the-job training will be at a serious disadvantage. Universal advanced training will bring increased productivity, higher standards of living, and greater adaptability, to the profit of the economy as well as the individual. If post-secondary education and training is to be universal, it must be free. Fourteen years of free public education with a terminal occupational emphasis should be a current goal.

6. Beyond initial preparation for employment, many, out of choice or necessity, will want to bolster an upward occupational climb with part-time and sometimes fulltime courses and programs as adults. These should be available as part of the regular public school system. They should not be limited to a few high-demand and low-cost trades, but should provide a range of occupational choice as wide as those available to students preparing for initial entry.

7. Any occupation which contributes to the good of society is a fit subject for

vocational education. In the allocation of scarce resources, first attention must be paid to those occupations which offer expanding opportunities for employment. In the elementary and junior high school, attention can be paid only to groups of occupations which employ large numbers of people, and instruction must be restricted to broad principles, common skills, and pervasive attitudes which will be useful in a broad range of employment. These restrictions are less and less valid as the student goes through high school and junior college, until, in adult education, instruction is justified in even the most restricted field if it is valuable to the individual and to society.

8. Occupational preparation need not and should not be limited to the classroom, to the school shop, or to the laboratory. Many arguments favor training on the job. Expensive equipment need not be duplicated. Familiarization with the environment and discipline of the workplace is an important part of occupational preparation, yet is difficult to simulate in a classroom. Supervisors and other employees can double as instructors. The trainee learns by earning. On the other hand, the employer and his supervisors may be more production than training oriented. The operations and equipment of a particular employer may cover only part of a needed range of skills, necessitating transfer among employers for adequate training. The ideal is to meld the advantages of institutional and on-the-job training in formal cooperative work-study programs.

9. Effective occupational preparation is impossible if the school feels that its obligation ends when the student graduates. The school, therefore, must work with employers to build a bridge between school and work. Placing the student on a job and following up his successes and failures provides the best possible information to the school on its own strengths and weaknesses.

10. No matter how good the system of initial preparation and the opportunities for upgrading on the job, there will always be need for remedial programs. Remedial programs will differ from the preventive in that many of the students will require financial assistance while in training; the courses must be closely oriented to the labor market to assure a quick return to employment; and the trainee will be impatient of what may seem to be the frills of regular vocational programs.

11. At every level from the elementary school through the post-secondary, adult, and remedial programs there will be those with special needs as defined by the 1963 act. For both humanitarian and economic reasons, persons with special needs deserve special help.

12. Many communities are too small to muster sufficient students for a range of occupational offerings broad enough to provide realistic freedom of occupational choice. Potential students, often those with the greatest needs, live in areas too isolated for access to meaningful training, others come from a home and neighborhood environment which makes sound preparation for life and employment difficult. An adequate system of occupational preparation will provide residential facilities wherever their absence presents an obstacle to anyone in need of education and training.

13. The public system for occupational preparation must be supported by adequate facilities and equipment, buttressed by research and innovation, and by the preparation and upgrading of competent teachers, counselors, and administrators. To assure constant improvement, it must provide for constant evaluation and reporting of problems and accomplishments.

14. The system of occupational preparation cannot operate in a vacuum. Data must be made available on public and private training opportunities to eliminate undesirable duplication. Data on supply and demand for various occupations must be available on a broader and more accurate basis. But total training opportunities must be based, not on the number of jobs which are available, but on the number of persons needing training.

Creation of the system of occupational preparation outlined here must be a continuing pursuit. The Vocational Education Act of 1963 and the efforts of vocational educators have carried the Nation a substantial way toward these objectives. Our recommendations which follow will, if adopted, assure further progress. But, they will never end the quest because, fortunately, society does not stand still.

The Council then made twenty-six recommendations: twenty-three for legislation and three to the Commissioner of Education.[14] (a) For legislation that:

1. All Federal vocational education acts administered by the Office of Education be combined into one act.

2. A Department of Education and Manpower Development be established at Cabinet level.

3. Funds and permanent authority be provided for the Commissioner of Education to make grants or contracts to State Boards and with the approval of the State Board to local educational agencies and to other public or non-profit private agencies, organizations, or institutions for planning, development, and operation of exemplary and innovative programs of occupational preparation.

4. Funds and permanent authority be provided to develop and operate new and expanded vocational educational programs and services specifically designed for persons who have academic, social, economic, or other handicaps.

5. The Act provide permanent authority for work-study and include work study and work experience programs in the secondary schools and those at the post-secondary levels related to vocational and technical education.

6. Funds and permanent authority be provided for the Commissioner to make grants to State Boards of Vocational Education and, with the approval of the State Board, to colleges and universities, and/or to public educational agencies, to construct facilities and operate residential vocational schools.

7. The Act provide for at least 25 percent of the funds appropriated for allocation to the States to be used for the intent set forth in purpose (2), post-

secondary schools, and (3), adult programs, of the Vocational Education Act of 1963.

8. The Act include vocational homemaking education in a separate section of the act with specific funding authorization.

9. The Act provide for the distribution of funds to the States on bases which will encourage increased enrollment, attendance, and improved performance.

10. The Act permit matching of the Federal allotment on a statewide basis.

11. Provision be made for States to receive allotments earlier in the calendar year and expenditure of funds be authorized through the succeeding year.

12. The Act provide that salaries and expenses needed for the administration of vocational and technical education be included in the annual appropriation for this Act.

13. Provisions for developing a state plan in the Act provide that a state shall: [submit for approval a legal contract between the Federal and State agencies, and submit a 5-year projected plan with annual updating].

14. The Act recognize the need and provide support for professional and paraprofessional staff recruitment, preparation, and upgrading at all levels, including leadership, administration, teacher education, and counseling and guidance, on a State, regional, and National basis.

15. Twenty-five percent of the funds appropriated for Title IV of the Higher Education Act of 1965 be set aside for opportunity grants for students interested in entering post-secondary technical and vocational programs.

16. Funds be authorized for pilot projects to study the feasibility of reimbursement to employers for unusual costs of supervision, training, and instruction of part-time cooperative students in publicly supported education.

17. Ten percent of the sums appropriated for the purposes listed in Section 4(a) of VEA '63 be used by the Commissioner of Education for the following purposes.

   A. For grants or contracts to colleges and universities and other public or non-profit private agencies and institutions to pay part of the cost of research and dissemination of research results in vocational and technical education;

   B. For grants or contracts approved by the operating bureau for evaluation, demonstration, and experimental programs in vocational and technical education and for dissemination of results;

   C. For grants to States for paying part of the cost of the State research coordinating units, State research, evaluation, demonstration, and experimental programs in vocational and technical education and dissemination of results.

18. The Act provide funds and require the Office of Education to be responsible for collecting data and preparing an annual descriptive and analytical report on vocational education to be submitted to the President and Congress.

19. The Act provide that each State conduct a periodic statewide review and evaluation of its vocational education program.

20. The Act include within the definition of vocational education "pre-vocational" and "employability skills."

21. The Vocational Education Act of 1963 be modified by deleting the word "area" from all designated facilities funded under the construction provisions of the Act.

22. The definition of vocational education in the Act be expanded to include the responsibility of education for initial job placement and follow-up of persons who:
    A. Have completed or are about to complete a program of education;
    B. Require part-time employment to remain in school;
    C. Need work experience which is an integral part of an educational program.

23. To meet the Act's objectives current needs, and contemplated enrollment, an appropriation of $1,565,000,000 per year should be made.

(b) For the Commissioner of Education.[15]

24. There be established two to four centers for curriculum development in vocational education.

25. The Office of Education provide staff for the National Advisory Committee on Vocational Education and establish guidelines for helping the States make more effective use of State Advisory Boards.

26. A Learning Corps be established on a pilot basis to provide improved learning experiences for economically disadvantaged youth, particularly inner-city youth. Such corps would arrange for young people to have the opportunity of living in selected homes in rural, small city, and suburban communities and to enroll in the local schools where skill development for employment would be a part of their educational program.

Seldom have recommendations made by an advisory group found their way into law as rapidly as those of the 1968 Advisory Council. The 1968 amendments to the 1963 Vocational Education Act are in large measure these recommendations. In fact, they were enacted by Congress prior to their official release by the U.S. Office of Education. The rcommendations were formulated very early in 1968 but issued in final form in November of that year. Extensive public review, including Congressional hearings, of these recommendations were made in the intervening months. Congressional leaders liked these recommendations and had the 1963 law amended.

EMPLOYER ASSOCIATIONS AND LABOR ORGANIZATIONS

Employer associations and labor organizations have always shown a keen interest in vocational education that has been primarily self-serving. Much of the advancement or progress in vocational education has been made only with the support of such private groups. Chapter 19 of

Vocational and Practical Arts Education describes these associations and organizations.[16] An inventory of all of the influences of each specific organization is not possible here. Rather, we shall highlight the significant influences of labor, the National Association of Manufacturers, the National Chamber of Commerce, and other organizations and encourage further study on the part of the reader.

LABOR GROUPS

The early part of the twentieth century saw the influence of labor groups on vocational education take the form of their legislative contacts. This affected not only national but also state and local legislation. At the national level, labor groups were involved in drafting the passage of every piece of legislation that has influenced vocational education. Ideas encompassed in the Smith-Hughes Act, for example, were supported through testimony to the congressional committees by labor groups as early as 1908. Views of labor were solicited by the Commission on National Aid for Vocational Education in 1914, and labor groups helped to draft the final version of the Smith-Hughes Bill. Periodically, labor groups have issued statements concerning vocational education. *A Guide for Vocational Education*, for example, was issued by the American Federation of Labor in 1938.[17] Labor used these means to inform legislators, vocational educators, and the general public of its interest, concern, and support of vocational education.

Prior to automation, families encouraged the early employment of their children due to their extremely low family incomes. Each laboring family needed every physically able body working to obtain sufficient funds to maintain an existence. As working conditions improved, wages also increased. At this point labor organizations recognized that an oversupply of labor contributed to low incomes, and they examined ways of limiting the labor force. The obvious solution was to delay entry into the labor force. This would provide increased wages for the adult worker and at the same time improve the condition of his children by letting them get more schooling before going to work.

In Massachusetts, the Douglas Commission was appointed in 1905 to investigate the need to educate for different levels of skill. The commission determined the extent to which the needs of industrial education were being met by existing institutions and considered the new forces that required an educational effort. The commission extended its investigation beyond the actual needs of job training to consider its social and economic aspects. It concluded that public education was narrow and that manual training was inadequate. Most significantly, the report provided an analysis of labor supply as balanced against demand.

It further presented emphatic statements against the use of child labor. The Douglas Commission established a case for the fact that industry could thrive without child labor and that it would derive greater benefits with an educated labor force. Protection against child labor, then, became a goal of organized labor, which worked for the National Child Labor Committee incorporated by Congress in 1907. The early goals of the committee were: (a) to prevent the employment of children under fourteen years of age in gainful occupations, (b) to establish a minimum employment age of sixteen for work done during school hours, (c) to foster vocational education and guidance in public schools, and (d) to promote continuation school education. Organized labor worked for the passage of the Fair Labor Standards Act (1938), which set minimum wages and maximum hours for all workers. This act also considered hours and working conditions for child labor. The latest review and updating of this effort was issued by the Secretary of Labor and took effect in June 1968.

Interest in child labor grew out of the attempt to reduce the labor force, not from a moral conviction that the growth and development of children was stifled by early work. Labor's interest in child labor freed the child from early work so that the public school system could begin to develop systematic instruction in vocational and general education to the children of working-class Americans.

Organized labor has continually sought means to delay entry into the labor force. Consider these statistics: The U.S. Bureau of Census estimates that over four million youngsters annually will reach their fourteenth birthday during the first five years of 1970. In 1970 half of the total labor force will be comprised of persons in the fourteen to twenty-five age group. What would happen to jobs, employment, and wages if no attempts were made to delay the entry of these persons into the labor force? In 1964, Secretary of Labor Willard Wirtz indicated that it would be appropriate manpower policy to increase the average period of a person's education by two years.[18]

One of labor's earlier and more consistent delaying and controlling efforts has been through apprenticeship programs. Local labor groups establish criteria and supervise apprenticeship programs. These criteria dictate the number of persons who can enter an occupation, the type of person who can enroll, the training he is to receive, the length of training, and other details.

Unions use apprenticeship as a means of job and wage control. By maintaining control of apprenticeship, unions are able to standardize the skill content of crafts and protect wage rates. . . . Unions also take an interest in apprenticeship programs as a means to prevent excess use of low-wage apprentices in competition with their journeyman members, as a means of controlling the supply of labor and as a technique for providing job opportunities to friends and relatives."[19]

Marshall and Briggs go on to point out how unions use apprenticeship to keep Negroes out of craft areas.[20] These facts do not negate the primary purpose of apprenticeship; it is a means of providing in an efficient manner the skilled workers needed for an occupational area. At the present time, organized labor strongly supports post–high school training programs. Such programs delay entry into the world of work and protect the jobs and wages of regular workers. In terms of vocational education, the person is available to enroll in vocational education programs. Without the support of organized labor, enrollment in post–high school programs would be substantially reduced.

Organized labor has had a number of other significant influences on the development of vocational education. One of these is labor's willingness to serve in an advisory capacity to various committees and boards, such as the National Board of Vocational Education (discontinued in 1933), state vocational boards, state curriculum committees, and local advisory committees. Labor's involvement in these areas has significantly influenced the development of vocational education.

EMPLOYER ASSOCIATIONS AND OTHER PRIVATE GROUPS

The National Association of Manufacturers, the U.S. Chamber of Commerce, the National Retail Merchants Association, and other groups have generously supported vocational education. In 1916, nearly two years after the report of the Commission on National Aid for Vocational Education, when Congress had not passed legislation for vocational education, the U.S. Chamber of Commerce came to the rescue. Its educational committee favored the Smith-Hughes Bill. The chamber of commerce held a nationwide referendum among its affiliated bodies, which resulted in local chambers of commerce registering action on the bill, which was bottled up in Congress. This broke the congressional stalemate and the bill was signed into law within the year.

These groups were also familiar with the Douglas Commission report, which specified that industry could thrive best with an educated labor force. They have supported training and other programs that have raised the educational level of the worker. These organizations basically seek efficiency and hence view vocational education in economic terms. Investments in vocational education are expected to show an economic return. This consideration is behind much of their support of vocational education. They support vocational education at public expense as it reduces the time needed for training once the worker is on the payroll, and it also saves the private company the expense of full training.

THE DEVELOPMENT OF TECHNOLOGY

From the time man first fashioned a tool, technology has been developing. The use of the club as a lever, the wheel, fire, electricity, and nuclear energy are all examples of technological development.

Technological development has been discontinuous. Many writers equate the development of technology with industrialization and refer to those vast changes in the industrial sector of the world as industrial revolutions. The development of technology brought about industrialization, not vice versa. Technology affected not only industrialization, but also social, economic, and educational institutions as well.

Most early historians of vocational education were concerned with how the Industrial Revolution affected vocational education. This is understandable since they were industrial educators. Such a framework permitted discussion of only the production phase of industry and the design of vocational education programs for production.

In the development of technology it is possible to describe four major phases that occurred during the settlement and growth of the United States. The first permitted the harnessing of power and the bringing of work to machines. The second permitted mass production through assembly-line techniques. The third phase saw automation applied to assembly-line techniques. And the fourth is defined by new materials and new processes. The first phase was of English origin and American adoption. The other phases were of American origin.

FIRST PHASE: APPLYING POWER TO MACHINES

The first phase in the development of technology was characterized by the harnessing of power and the application of that power to machines rugged enough to be driven by forces other than human energy. Inventions such as the loom, the steam engine, and the spinning frame were basic to this era. One of the immediate effects of these inventions was the establishment of a central place for machines where power could be applied—the factory. Thus a stationary machine was created, with work being brought to it. To the factory also went the craftsman, who, until this point, had been responsible for an entire product. Prior to the emergence of the factory, many craftsmen banned together to form a central cooperative workshop to maintain craftsmanship. What the central workshops lacked was the economic ability to purchase the power supply and the power-driven machines. As a factory worker, the craftsman had to sacrifice his pride in his craft, as he typically operated a machine. He was then responsible for only parts of his product.

The factory was not adopted rapidly in colonial America. Goods could be secured with ease from other sources. Americans concentrated on establishing a new government and on expanding the frontiers of the nation. Each family or small town was able to meet its basic needs; and since America was expected to become a great agricultural nation, there was really no reason to manufacture goods. Apprenticeships, it was thought, could provide the basic education for industry.

Once the agricultural myth crumbled, factories were started. They were readily adapted to the natural geographical conditions as there was a ready source of water power along the fault line, which occurs between the coastal plain and the piedmont plateau and has many waterfalls. Technological advancements permitted the development of the American Industrial Revolution; as it grew, it developed the same pattern that was found in England, with exploitation of women and children and the dominance of the profit motive.

SECOND PHASE: MASS PRODUCTION AND ASSEMBLY LINES

The second phase in America's technological development began in the mid-1800s. Population growth and the Civil War placed increasing demands on production facilities. A craftsman, even using a machine, turned out only a single item. Such individual production was too slow and too costly; and each article was accurate only in itself. Manufactured goods increased trade, which in turn created additional demands for improvements and new inventions. Those who controlled industry desired more production as well as an increase in profit, and realized that interchangeability of parts was essential to achieve quantity production. It was necessary, therefore, to refine the power-driven machines to make quantity of production and accurate reproduction possible at lower cost. Thus this second phase developed mass production through assembly-line techniques.

This period is marked by a number of factors that shaped vocational education. With the development of mass production came job opportunities, primarily for unskilled labor. The craftsman who learned his skills through four or more years of apprenticeship saw the need for his skills displaced by machine operators who could be taught in anywhere from two hours to two weeks. If the craftsman took a job as a machine operator, machine operators would become his social and economic equal. So the apprenticeship training that had been so important during the colonial period declined. Why place a child with a master craftsman for long years of training at only a subsistence allowance? The more practical trend was for the child to be placed in a factory under a foreman interested primarily in the repetition of a narrow activity that resulted in production.

Mass production permitted a greater distribution of employment. Those who were unable to develop high-grade craft skills learned to operate simple machines. Economically, the worker's buying power increased, and he became able to enjoy the products of his labor. This era raised the craftsman to the level of a technician. He was then employed to produce parts for machines. Because he was able to build more and better machines, industry was able to produce more and better goods.

Among the disadvantages that technology brought were: (1) increased accidents, (2) poor working conditions, (3) layoffs when production was not in line with demand, (4) blacklisting of those workers who protested the system, and (5) economic chaos for those families who lost their breadwinner. These situations cannot be charged completely to the development of mass production. Rather, they were largely due to the inability of the industrial and political leaders to recognize and to meet the changing conditions of the worker. The dominant value system of our society did not permit recognition of any value above the primary value of economics. The factory owner saw and acknowledged the fact that injustices occurred, but he did not feel a responsibility to correct them. The worker did not have to work for him; he took his chances. If he happened to become injured that was his misfortune.

There was no social consciousness on the part of an employer. Since education was not needed to perform simple work tasks, no "vocational education" was provided to those who performed such tasks, and the employer felt no social responsibility to provide education for anything else. The employer supported apprenticeships, though declining in number, as he needed complex skills performed that required additional training. He did not become concerned about the worker until he became a potential customer. When paid for his services, the worker soon acknowledged the fact that he could acquire property and goods to increase his comfort. Competition and the profit motive demanded that the employer obtain all of the customers that he could for his product. So while, individually, the owner could afford to alienate the worker, he could not afford to alienate the entire group of working-class persons. Here began the development of a social consciousness on the part of employers.

As the employer changed his view of the worker from property to customer, he began to see that his employee, like his other customers, would benefit from such finer things as education. If an employee could be taught to appreciate the "finer things," he would become a better consumer. The employer began to recognize the philosophical position that all men possessed dignity. Consequently he began, in a very limited way, to alter the social conditions of his employees.

THIRD PHASE: AUTOMATION APPLIED TO ASSEMBLY LINES

This phase of technological development is often referred to simply as automation, but it is more than that.[21] Technology had developed to the point where automation could be *applied* to assembly-line techniques. It is hard to pick an exact date to specify the beginning of the era, but Henry Ford is generally regarded as the father of applying automation to assembly lines. And his idea of bringing the work to the worker is one of the early achievements in this phase. Automatic dial and continuous flow were introduced in the 1920s. This development grew significantly during the war production of the 1940s and it had a full head of steam on during the 1950s.

The basic pattern of this era is multiconnected machines. In essence, one machine is used to control one or more additional machines. The facts of automation are well documented in other sources. For our purposes it is sufficient to recall that the critical justification of automation is efficiency. It is the principal avenue leading to the establishment and maintenance of consistent, high-level mass production with maximum accuracy. Automation provides increased flexibility that is basic to efficient production in an age where requirements may change over-night. In light of new technological changes in the physical, chemical, engineering, and space sciences, flexibility is essential. Automation makes it possible to squeeze the most out of a given work space, economizing not only on space but on movement of parts from operation to operation.

Technological advancement has created the myth that automation leads to unemployment. This is not supported by evidence. Automation and electronic controls do not replace the labor force entirely, although there is a considerable savings in terms of man-labor hours and a shift upward in the technical aspects of work. Routine clerical and operative jobs are abolished, to be replaced by new maintenance and technical jobs. A major problem is that often the jobs created by automation cannot be filled by the persons who are replaced by newer machines. Another reason for this myth is the increase in training and education required for many new jobs. This delays entry into the labor force and has the net effect of reducing unemployment for the age groups enrolled in vocational technical programs.

This era produced a number of changes in work and its significance to man. It raised the level of preparation needed by workers, which resulted in more demands for vocational and technical education. Many routine jobs were eliminated only to introduce routine into many other jobs. A worker on an automobile assembly line may perform the same task several hundred times in one day. Another worker may simply watch a set of controls to note any abnormalities. In such situations, the work does very little to stimulate the worker's creativity. Nosow and Form have compiled an excellent set of readings describing these changes in work.[22] The articles entitled "Automation and the Automobile Worker," "When the Computer Takes Over the Office," and "The Machine, The Worker, and The Engineer" are particularly noteworthy as is Chapter 4, "Industrial Change and Occupational Trends."

FOURTH PHASE: MINIATURIZATION

The early 1970s finds us in the midst of a new era. There are really three thrusts being made, and it is difficult to select one to characterize the era. One thrust is the development of new materials; plastics and synthetics are replacing the great majority of materials. Another thrust is in the search for new power techniques. Fluidics is emerging as an engineering science of great promise. In this approach, fluid circuits are being designed to operate machines.

The thrust that may dominate this era is miniaturization, particularly the miniaturization of electronic techniques. It is now possible to reduce the circuits of a twenty-three-inch television set to one square inch. Computers the size of an attaché case are now being built with miniature circuits, and most of that size is taken up by a keyboard. These advances permit the rapid handling of vast amounts of data with greater accuracy and efficiency. They also permit almost instantaneous worldwide communications.

Where will this fourth phase in the development of American technology lead vocational education? One thing is certain: We will have to abandon many of our traditional techniques. Business inventory and marketing practices are a case in point. A large, upper midwestern business with approximately $125 billion in annual sales is headquartered in Minnesota. Once a week on a set schedule each of nearly 500 retail outlets is contacted by telephone and the inventory of over 22,000 different items is computerized. Through the use of electronic equipment, the telephone operator is able to tell the retail store within a few seconds if they have and can ship the quantity of a specific item. If it is not available the retail store manager is able to substitute or back order while he is still on the telephone. As the items are ordered and shipped the computer updates the inventory.

IMPACT OF TECHNOLOGY

There has been an alteration in the demand for skills. Persons engaging in scientific, professional, and technological work have increased in absolute numbers as well as showing a faster proportionate gain in the labor force. Some people mistakenly assume that the introduction of automation in any given work situation results only in fewer total workers. It is true that automated equipment results in a shift in occupations and type of work as well as a possible reduction in the number of persons employed in any specific locality to do a particular kind of work. But the technology also generates jobs, in part through direct creation of tasks of designing, operating, and maintaining new machines, and in part through stimulating economic growth. The 1964 *Manpower Report of the President* states: "According to the record of economic history, the long-run effect of technological advance has so far been to increase employment, and to remove much of the drudgery from work."[23]

The nature of other changes that technology has brought about have been listed as follows:

1. More goods are being produced for more consumers by fewer and fewer workers. The result—fewer jobs in manufacturing, the elimination of unskilled and semi-skilled jobs, the need for better educated and more occupationally sophisticated workers.

2. More food is being produced to feed more people by fewer and fewer farmers. The result—further reduction of an already greatly reduced work force in agriculture.

3. Most jobs will require a higher level of education for entry and for continued employment. The result—more general education preceding specialized occupational education and a higher entrance age for first employment.

4. All workers will have to renew their skills and update their knowledge frequently in order to remain productive. The result—more need for occupational extension education for employed workers.

5. Many workers will find the need to learn a new occupation on one or more occasions during their lifetime. The result—a need for systematic education for new careers for adult workers.

6. More people will find employment in providing services for other people than in producing goods and food for them. The result—a diminishing curricular and program emphasis on the agricultural and industrial aspects of vocational education, and a correspondingly greater emphasis on new and different kinds of occupations in categories other than industry, manufacturing and agriculture.[24]

A variety of additional technical trends have exerted or are exerting an influence on vocational education. Some of these trends are in electronic data processing, instrumentation and control, numerical control, improvements in communications and machinery, mechanization of materials handling, and innovations in transportation and power generation. Each trend is basically substituting physical energy for human labor in the production and service industries. An interesting phenomenon is also occurring among the trends, for we are beginning to see an integration of the items just listed. One illustration is the interplay that is developing between long distance communications, electronic computers, and materials handling equipment. This is resulting in lower inventories, direct factory to customer shipping, and faster service.

The awareness on the part of community leaders that the placement of new firms is related to the general competence of the local population continues. Communities with good schools have the advantage in attracting and keeping firms. Those communities that offer inferior educational programs are suffering. For unless good, well-balanced educational opportunities are available, management is not likely to locate in a community to provide new jobs for its people, new monies to the local economy, and new tax-producing structures.

The most striking thing about the impact of technology on education and vocational education is the pace of these attainments. The dominant fact of the current social scene is change, change at a rate unmatched in all history and one that continues to accelerate. One historian recently commented that mid-nineteenth-century America had more in common with fifth-century Greece than with its own projections into the middle of the twentieth century.[25]

CHANGE IN OCCUPATIONAL STRUCTURE

We have already noted the increase in absolute and proportionate gains in the labor force shown by scientific, professional, and technical workers.

At one point in our history the vast majority of persons were employed in the "heavy" industries. Even right after World War II, manufacturing and trades contributed 28.4 percent and 19.8 percent respectively of the total of our gross national product. These two industries presently occupy the largest contribution to our GNP, but their growth rate is about the same as that for all industries. The fastest growing industries are in the broad category of "service" industries. Some of these have shown growth rates approaching 75 percent from the immediate post–World War II era to the mid-1960s.

The shift in occupational structure in modern America may be seen from another perspective. Table 2 shows the projections for employment in major occupations, including the percent change from 1960 to 1975. Typical blue-collar job categories are fading fast. New jobs in the operatives and laborer categories are just not emerging. On the other hand, white-collar and service categories are showing phenomenal increases in their rates of growth.

TABLE 2. Employment in Major Occupations, 1960–1975

MAJOR OCCUPATIONAL GROUP	NUMBER IN MILLIONS			PERCENT CHANGE
	ACTUAL	PROJECTED		
	1960	1970	1975	1960–1975
White Collar	28.8	37.5	41.9	46
Professional, technical	7.5	10.7	12.4	65
Managers, Officials	7.1	8.6	9.4	32
Clerical, etc.	9.8	12.8	14.2	45
Sales	4.4	5.4	5.9	34
Blue Collar	24.3	27.6	29.1	20
Craftsmen, foreman	8.6	10.3	11.2	30
Operatives	12.0	13.6	14.2	18
Laborers	3.7	3.7	3.7	0
Service	8.3	11.1	12.5	51

Source: Seymour L. Wolfbein, *Employment, Unemployment and Public Policy*, p. 134, by permission of Random House, Inc. Copyright © 1965.

Unemployment is a major factor in our changing occupational structure. From 1954 to 1965, the total economy as shown by the GNP was approximately doubled. The 1967 *Economic Report of the President,* however, indicated that poverty affected nearly 33 million Americans. The unemployment rate for nonwhites has been consistently about double that of the white population. In 1954, for example, 5.0 percent white and 9.8 percent nonwhite were unemployed. In 1958, these figures had changed to 6.1 percent and 12.6 percent respectively, while they were 3.4 and 7.5 in 1966. The under-19 age group also suffers with a lack of available employment opportunity, as 12 percent of this group was unemployed in 1966.

The behavior of women with respect to the labor market has been undergoing a revolutionary change since the onset of World War II. Prior to that time few women sought employment outside the home, and then their contributions were limited to "traditional" women's work. Rarer still was the married woman worker. As we enter the 1970s, there are as many as thirty-one million women who are employed. Regardless of income level, approximately one-fourth or more of a family's income is earned by the wife. Many married women may not be seeking full-time employment, but more and more are interested in working outside the home. They seek employment even when their youngsters are small, and due to early marriages many are looking for full-time employment earlier than their pre–World War II counterparts. It is typical for the married woman today to be seeking full-time employment in her early thirties.

Early marriage has greatly increased the availability of women for work. If we consider early marriage, smaller families, and the wife supporting the family while the husband is enrolled in college or in an advanced degree program, we may safely conclude that in a limited number of specific families the wife may already have passed her husband in the number of years that she will be a productive member of the work force, startling as that may seem.

Automation and other technological impacts have eliminated a great number of clerical and bookkeeping positions, particularly those that women have traditionally filled. And women are seeking jobs in other segments of our economy. The women's liberation movement of the late 1960s and early 1970s, which has very little to do with technology, encourages this trend. In spite of these two forces, the rate at which women are entering occupations once thought to be limited to men is disappointing to some writers in this field.

Poorly educated persons with limited skills are finding it difficult to even secure jobs for themselves. The highly mobile minority groups are finding it difficult to cope with the affluence of our dynamic economy and meeting their new occupational needs is a major challenge.

OTHER FACTORS

This is not a complete history of vocational education, so we have been very selective and have omitted a number of factors that have had a significant impact on vocational education. As a student in this field, you may wish to research some of these factors.

Apprenticeship programs were mentioned. An understanding of apprenticeship is important for a professional in vocational education. When was apprenticeship begun? Why and how did it start? What is the relationship between it and the regular public secondary school? What influence has it had on the total field of vocational education and what has been its influence on a specific field, such as trade and industrial education? How has it been influenced by nonpublic organizations, such as labor unions?

Additional topics worth pursuing include: the influence of state legislation on vocational education; the effects of economic fluctuation on vocational education, including the Great Depression of the 1930s; how vocational education has been shaped by the emergence of pragmatism. Other topics are: the popular press and vocational education; vocational education and professional organizations such as the American Vocational Association; vocational education as a function of the public school system; vocational education as a state's responsibility; worker mobility and its effect on vocational education.

NOTES

[1]Paul H. Douglas, *American Apprenticeship and Industrial Education* (New York, 1921), Chaps. 2, 3.

[2]Grant Venn, *Man, Education and Work* (Washington, D.C.: American Council on Education, 1964), p. 39.

[3]For a discussion of vocational education in World Wars I and II, see Layton S. Hawkins, Charles A. Prosser, and John C. Wright, *Development of Vocational Education* (American Technical Society, 1951), Chaps. 29, 32.

[4]Bulletin No. 2, Federal Board for Vocational Education (Washington, D.C.: Government Printing Office, 1918), p. 3.

[5]*Third Annual Report* (Federal Board of Vocational Education, 1919).

[6]Hawkins, Prosser, and Wright, *Development of Vocational Education*, pp. 439–40.

[7]John A. McCarthy, *Vocational Education: America's Greatest Resource* (Chicago: American Technical Society, 1950), p. 15.

[8]*Report of the Commission on National Aid to Vocational Education* (Washington, D.C.: Government Printing Office, 1914).

[9]*Report of the National Advisory Committee on Education*, 1936–38 (Washington, D.C.: Government Printing Office, 1938), pp. 206–7.

[10]U.S. Congress, *Journal of Proceedings* (Washington, D.C.: Government Printing Office), 107, Part 2, 2391.

[11]*Education for a Changing World of Work* (Washington, D.C.: Government Printing Office, 1963), p. 17.

[12]*Ibid.*, pp. 18–20.

[13]Ninetieth Congress, 2nd Session Committee Report, *Notes and Working Papers Concerning the Administration of Programs Authorized under Vocational Education Act of 1963*, Subcommittee on Education, Committee on Labor and Public Welfare (Washington, D.C.: Government Printing Office, 1968), pp. 50–52.

[14]Ninetieth Congress, *Notes and Working Papers*, pp. 53–54.

[15]*Ibid.*, p. 55.

[16]Roy W. Roberts, *Vocational and Practical Arts Education*, 2nd ed. (New York: Harper & Row, Publishers), pp. 498–525.

[17]American Federation of Labor, *A Guide for Vocational Education* (Washington, D.C.: The Federation, 1938).

[18]Seymour L. Wolfbein, *Employment, Unemployment and Public Policy* (New York: Random House, Inc., 1965), p. 180.

[19]F. Ray Marshall and Vernon M. Briggs, Jr., *The Negro and Apprenticeship* (Baltimore: Johns Hopkins University Press, 1967), p. 13.

[20]*Ibid.*, Chap. 4. Also see Paul H. Norgren et al., *Employing the Negro in American Industry* (New York: Industrial Relations Counselors, 1959).

[21]Walter Buckingham, *Automation: Its Impact on Business and People* (New York: Harper & Row, Publishers, 1961).

[22]Sigmund Nosow and William H. Form, eds., *Man, Work and Society* (New York: Basic Books, Inc., Publishers, 1962).

[23]*Manpower Report of the President—1964* (Washington, D.C.: Government Printing Office, 1964), p. 45.

[24]Gerald B. Leighbody, "Vocational Education," in *New Curriculum Developments*, ed. Glenys G. Unruh (Washington, D.C.: Association for Supervision and Curriculum Development, 1965), pp. 78–80.

[25]Carl Bridenbaugh, "The Great Mutation," *American Historical* Review, 68, no. 1 (January 1963), 316–17.

3

VOCATIONAL EDUCATION
AND NATIONAL LEGISLATION

EARLY LEGISLATIVE ACTS

Vocational educators frequently use the terms "legislation" and "federal aid" synonymously to recognize the many federal legislative acts that have provided funds for vocational education. There has been, however, significant legislation that affected the direction and form of vocational education without providing federal monies directly to education in general or to the school system in particular.

Immigrants to a new nation are seldom dissatisfied with all the conditions of their native land. This was the case with the American settlers. When the early colonists settled in this country, they established many of the same basic institutions that they left behind, and early forms of education were much like education in England.

THE ENGLISH POOR LAW OF 1601

Guilds and apprenticeships were the accepted form of vocational education in Great Britain prior to the time the colonists left. An apprentice was bound to a craftsman (usually a member of a guild) for a minimum term agreed upon by both persons. Guilds were of many types and were regulated primarily at the local level. The Statute of Artificers, passed in 1562, eliminated the local regulation of the apprentices and transformed the apprenticeship to a national system. This statute established uniform standards and regulations for both the apprentice and his master.

Late in the sixteenth century, rising prices and growing unemployment created distress among the poor people of England. A series of "poor laws" was passed to help impoverished families survive the shift from agriculture to manufacturing that was occurring throughout the country. The English Poor Law of 1601 provided that church wardens and overseers could place the children of poor families with an acceptable master until the girls were twenty-one and the boys twenty-four. Its basic intent was to equip the children of poor families with a salable skill. This approach was considered very successful and greatly influenced vocational education in America.

EARLY LAWS IN THE COLONIES

The Church and the Bible were the basic sources of authority for most colonists. Rigidly assigned roles and class distinctions prevented the development of an active minority. All interests were directed toward eternal life in the "other world." The temporal world was considered a place where one demonstrated the piety, works, and material success that entitled him to be a member of the "chosen" and assured him entrance into the other world. Education was viewed as the protecting and sustaining arm of the Church and the State.

In the colonies the authority of the Bible replaced the traditional authority of the Church. Thus, not only did the colonists revolutionize religion, but they revolutionized education as well. The Bible was put into the hands of every individual to serve as a handbook for living. Consequently, if the individual were to make judgments using the Bible as his source of authority, he must be able to read it.

Hence the need to read was universally recognized, and the colonists proceeded to establish schools very early in the settlement of this country. Some schools followed the pattern of the English Dame School; others were maintained by the minister. The Boston Latin Grammar School for boys opened in 1635. The following year Harvard, the first college, opened. Dame schools, Latin grammar schools, and Harvard could provide schooling for the children of the elite, but they could not serve the children of the common man. The resulting need stimulated the early movement toward mass education in America.

Influenced by their English heritage, the colonists believed that the children of the poor should not have access to the style of life produced by a classical education, and an apprenticeship system was encouraged for the children of the common man. Each town or county had its rules and laws governing apprenticeships. The apprenticeship system evolved without the support of guilds and other draft organizations that fostered its development in England.

Two forms of apprenticeships emerged: one voluntary, the other compulsory. In the former case, an apprentice wanted to learn a trade. He selected a master who could teach him and they entered into an agreement. Such an agreement, according to Roberts, was entered into with the free will of the apprentice, thus its reference as a voluntary apprenticeship.[1]

Compulsory apprenticeships were established by the Massachusetts General Court in 1642. The provisions of the English Poor Law of 1601 were adopted, requiring parishes to place the children of poor families with masters in order to teach them a trade. This basic law required parents to see that all children under their control obtained an education that included development of skill in a trade and the literary ability to read, write, and understand the Bible. Any failure to carry out this responsibility resulted in a fine levied against the parents. In the case of many poor families, children were placed with masters against the will of the parent and, frequently, against the will of the child. The parent was usually reluctant to forego the child's contribution to the household in terms of labor and income.

The accepted style of life for the colonists was derived from an individual's interpretation of the Bible, usually consistent with the Puritan ethic of the time. The ability to read and interpret the Bible was a way to deprive the Church of absolute power. Thus a way had to be found to force all individuals to learn to read so they could utilize the Bible themselves rather than rely on the Church to interpret it. This permitted a biblically oriented moral style of life without granting the Church power of absolute interpretation.

The Massachusetts law of 1642 was followed by the Old Delauder Satan Act of 1647, which revealed that education was a universal concern, not only for the elite. Towns were required to establish schools, as an apparent outgrowth of the feeling that the law requiring parents to educate their children could not be enforced unless schools were made available. The Massachusetts General Court required every town of fifty or more families to appoint a teacher to teach reading and writing. Towns of a hundred or more families were required to hire a schoolmaster to give instruction in grammar. Tax monies could be used if, at a town meeting, this method was elected in place of direct payment by parents.

The Church, in its desire for all children to be familiar with its basic doctrines for the "good life," gave the State authority over education. (The State and the religious group were one and the same. The secular state developed later.) Butts comments:

What the New England colonies did was to combine (1) their Calvinist conceptions of education required by state-church and (2) the English tradition of state control over the apprenticeship of poor children, as expressed in the English Poor Law of 1601. The state of New England was establishing its right to require vocational education through compulsory apprenticeship at the same time as it required education in language and reading.[2]

It is apparent that both the direction and form of vocational education were being molded by the prevailing philosophies and actions. And the establishment and maintenance of a dual or differentiated system of education on this continent was one of the effects. Vocational education became the preparation for learning a trade. Students entering the Latin grammar and other types of preparatory schools went on to a profession, while all others were expected to comply with the law and learn a trade. A more subtle effect of these early legislative acts was to insure that the children of the poor were denied access to the style of life of the elite.

SEPARATION OF CHURCH AND STATE

The dominant view of Church and State in colonial life was that they were coterminous corporate bodies. However, a second and equally authentic view was present in America almost from the beginning: the idealistic concept of the separation of these two corporate bodies, which became a majority viewpoint toward the end of the eighteenth century. One of the most effective persons who voiced this concept from the outset was Roger Williams. In his conflict with the Massachusetts authorities, Williams put forth the general belief that conflict between religions could end only when there was essential separation between Church and State, when legal connections between civil and religious authorities were eliminated. The removal of these legal connections directly affected vocational education and its development. Three areas are particularly noteworthy: the rise of secularism, the emergence of public schools, and the framing of the national Constitution.

THE RISE OF SECULARISM

Challenges to the religious and classical foundations of a liberal education began during the eighteenth century. The challenges included the ideal of practical utility with its roots in political ideals, economic motives, and scientific interest.

The demand for attention to these intellectual interests was relatively mild and scattered during the eighteenth century and thus did not meet the religious and classical in mortal combat but rather was often accepted as rounding out a full blown philosophy of education. It was not until the nineteenth century that the utilitarian and scientific challenge achieved the proportions of a head-on conflict with the humanistic and classical traditions. At that time the controversy became shrill and bitter, enlisted vigorous support on both sides, and caused cleavages in the body of education that have not been healed to this day.[3]

A rapid increase in trade and commerce marked the early eighteenth century. New England timber, wood products, shipbuilding materials, fish, fur, grain, and livestock were eagerly sought by other nations. A profitable trade to Europe and the West Indies flourished. New England evolved from a society trading for a living to one living for trade.[4] The property owners or the landed gentry began to be overshadowed by the rising merchant class, who demanded participation in political and economic affairs. A lawyer class, to serve the merchant, also emerged, and was accepted into the style of life of the elite.

The nonproperty owners—increasing in number as the occupations of clerk, fisherman, and sailor provided ready employment opportunities— became resentful of the fact that they had no vote. They experienced discrimination in the laws and courts, as well as in punishments administered to offenders. These nonproperty owners began to feel toward the merchants as the debtors and renters had previously reacted toward the landed gentry. They resented the tax for the established churches, and Butts and Cremin point out that this resentment weakened the hold of the established churches.[5] The nonproperty owners of both the urban and the rural areas saw little need for the classical education provided by the town grammar schools. Residents of rural areas saw no need for any education beyond the rudiments of an elementary education and, in turn, the lower classes demanded training to prepare them to enter the emerging trades.

The Latin grammar schools were structured around college entrance requirements. They were not designed to hear or heed the increasing tempo of practical and intellectual interests that fostered demands for new kinds of education. The English grammar school emerged in response to growing commercial interests in improving trade and commerce by employing properly trained personnel. The English schools popular during the first half of the eighteenth century gave practical and vocational education to young people who desired to enter the emerging occupations. Private in the sense that they charged fees, the English schools often held classes early in the morning or in the late afternoon or evening, and girls were welcome. The subjects were almost entirely of a secular nature, with little attention to religious instruction. In the latter half of the eighteenth century, the English schools gave way to the academies.

A most elaborate plan for a utilitarian education was outlined by Benjamin Franklin in his *Proposals Relating to the Education of Youth in Pennsylvania*.[6] This plan opposed wealth, ecclesiasticism, and useless languages. Franklin proposed that the content of his academy be English, drawing, mathematics, and classics, as optional courses for those who desired it, with required courses in social studies, natural science, and practical experience. His plan was based on the belief that learning and knowledge improved conduct and qualified people to "pass through and execute the several offices of civil life with advantage and reputation to themselves and country." Franklin hoped to enlarge and make respectable a practical education that did not need to rest upon religious institutions or upon the classics. His ideas were not implemented immediately, but they were valuable in indicating what could be done. The influence of secularism continued to affect the development of a vocational type of education.

THE EMERGENCE OF PUBLIC SCHOOLS

An acceptance of the doctrine of separation of Church and State was necessary to facilitate creation of the new society promoted by secularism and democratic concepts. As long as men believed that morality rested upon religious beliefs, the State could not tolerate any dissenters, for to dissent would imply immoral conduct. Philosophically, all men had to be considered capable of moral conduct and good citizenship regardless of religious belief. Granting that good citizenship and morality could be developed by different religious beliefs made it necessary for the Church to provide alternatives to its rigid viewpoint. The Church would still be permitted to control some, but not all, education.

"Public schools" and "free schools" were dominated by governing boards, which were often churches. The word "public" simply differentiated between those schools supported by public monies and those run for profit. Government often contributed monies to the public school for its operation. Movements such as William Penn's in 1682 were initiated to support government control of public schools. It soon became evident that this could not be achieved where mixed religious beliefs developed into hostile rivalries. Many religious groups feared governmental involvement since they believed that "he who pays the fiddler calls the tune."

Charges and countercharges over this point dominated the educational scene for nearly a hundred years. Most efforts were directed toward a public higher education. Thomas Jefferson saw more keenly than most that public schools with aims to serve the whole public must be free from religious or private control. He believed that education under public control must extend from the lowest to the highest levels, from an elementary program to a comprehensive secondary program to a state university. In 1779 he attempted to have the laws of his native state of Virginia changed to provide this kind of education.

The Jeffersonian concept eventually became the most commonly accepted solution for educating a population of heterogeneous background, and it proved to be a distinctively American contribution to the world. During the mid-nineteenth century, the effects of a strong Roman Catholic leadership led many Protestant groups to band together to establish a common nonsectarian public school. Other factors influencing this movement included the varied ethnic backgrounds of immigrants leading to ethnic settlements, the demand for new skills in the industrialization process, and the need to utilize new developments in agricultural science and technology. This continuing controversy reaffirmed the decision to give preference to public education as an agency of national unity. Early in the twentieth century, the U.S. Supreme Court ruled in *Meyer* vs. *Nebraska* (1923) that the state could compel children to attend some school, that it could establish reasonable standards for all schools, that it could determine some of the curriculum, but that it could not interfere with the right of parents to enroll their children in nonpublic schools if they so chose.

Thus public schools became the dominant educational institutions of American society, and it was this climate that enhanced the growth and development of public vocational education. Vocational education would probably never have been integrated into private institutions to any greater degree than it is now due to such factors as cost, lack of tuition monies by many working families, and lack of social acceptance. An alternative form would probably have been separate vocational schools within a federal system.

THE NATIONAL CONSTITUTION

Whether by design or default, the U.S. Constitution makes no mention of education. Apparently most of its framers felt that other matters were of more pressing concern. Many considered education a function of the Church and of local or state governments. Those interested in a strong federal government were not interested in a strong federal educational system. Antifederalists were interested in education for the common man, but they did not support a strong national government.

The right of states to establish and maintain schools is drawn from the Tenth Amendment to the Constitution, which reserved for the states all powers not delegated by the Constitution to the federal government. By ignoring the opportunity for federal support of education, the framers of the Constitution set a precedent, making it difficult for the states to execute their legal right to control education. (The federal government would also experience difficulty in supporting education.)

It was within the framework of secular public schools under local or state control that vocational education was to grow. Significant federal policies, including the interpretation of the Constitution, evolved to make this a reality. The emphasis was on providing the children of the poor, whom authorities considered unqualified to participate in an academic, college preparatory curriculum, with a basic, free education for the jobs that were emerging. Specific skill development was primarily the responsibility of employers. It must be remembered, however, that skill training and other forms of vocational education experienced some growth in proprietary schools. These are run for profit and derive their income from tuition.

THE MOVE TOWARD NATIONALISM

Loyalty to the nation developed gradually. Many people still considered themselves loyal to Great Britain rather than to the newly independent nation. Although Great Britain still dominated much of national life, especially trade, the United States was acquiring a spirit of her own. The nationalistic symbols of flag, song, and holiday proved to be unifying elements. As a public spirit emerged, people began to look inward for leadership and to develop institutions to serve their needs, rather than relying upon distant Britain.

THE MOVE WEST

Nearly a hundred years after the colonies won their independence, and after the Civil War, the westward movement gained momentum. Land had to be tamed and put to use, for some means of feeding the growing population of the eastern seaboard had to be found. The East had a sufficient labor force and there had to be some means to keep it in balance with demands. Vocational education was influenced by the legislation that attempted to deal with these and other problems.

AN AGRARIAN SOCIETY

The years between 1776 and 1865 are known as the expansion years. People moved west to take advantage of open territory, to seek new opportunities for home ownership, to escape undesirable conditions, or to accept the personal challenge of the frontier. Life on the frontier was unique. The people lived off the land and went to town only to trade for the few basic goods and services they could not provide for themselves. This was in complete contrast to the closely knit European village, where people clustered for housing and scattered to their land to work. Roads and other forms of communication were poor or nonexistent. It has been estimated, for example, that only one-fifth of rural New England had access to existing market and trade facilities. The remaining people in the rural areas were almost completely isolated from commercial relations.[7]

The agrarian society functioned with limited technology. Power was available in its crudest forms: Man and animals were the major source. To function in this society only a limited education and certainly a limited vocational education were necessary. Required skills passed from fathers to sons, in the European tradition of a few centuries before. Schools, following the secular trend, were to be basic; the frontiersmen supported the same kind of education as did the eastern, middle-class reformers.

TECHNOLOGICAL GAPS IN THE WESTWARD MOVEMENT

An industrial system had developed on the East Coast to meet its needs in trade and commerce. This industrial system required considerable manpower, manpower that did not need much education. The apprenticeship system provided essential complex skills. One very significant point should be made here: As people moved west, most trained and skilled manpower remained at their jobs. Consequently, the westward movement consisted of basically the unskilled from the East and the farmer from Europe.

The move to the frontier placed new demands on the industrial system. Transportation was needed to move people and goods. Building materials such as wheels, finished wood, and canvas and hardware such as axles, bolts, nails, and hinges were needed by the new settlers. Also, there had to be some way to keep the pioneers informed about relatives, government actions, and political developments. Without a communication system, the country could not build or maintain its concept of unity.

Much of the technological help arrived from England. The East had a Hargreave's spinning jenny by 1775, just nine years after its invention in England and in spite of English efforts to keep it from American shores. The western farmers utilized plant varieties from England. Particularly significant was the animal breeding technology brought to America from England. Thus, gaps in technology existed: American skilled labor was concentrated on the eastern seaboard; the eastern laborer used a machine invented in England; and the western farmer got his best help from England.

CLOSING THE TECHNOLOGICAL GAPS

There had to be ways to encourage continued westward expansion and to channel technology into the West. Frontier life was hard. The self-sufficient, isolated family life and neighborhood communities did not appeal to family men who could find employment in the East. Immigrants, who were relied upon to help settle the West, had to be enticed to go there, for if they stayed in the East, they would glut the labor market. Legislative actions created the Land Ordinances of 1785 and 1787. The Northwest Ordinance of 1787 (providing for the settlement of the present states of Ohio, Indiana, Illinois, Michigan, Wisconsin, and part of Minnesota) stated in reference to schools: "Religion, morality, and knowledge, being necessary to good government and the happiness of mankind, schools and the means of education shall forever be encouraged." These land ordinances provided that the income of the sixteenth section of each township be set aside for a common school when land was sold.[8] Legislative action thus opened the way for family men to purchase western land, move their families, and bring with them technology.

It also assured immigrants that their strong concerns for education would not be ignored. Some of the frontier settlers' basic problems that needed technological answers were how to break the prairie sod, how to make cotton a more profitable crop (since more of it could be grown than could be milled), how to farm a section of ground economically, how to transport produce, and how to move family from home to the town, church, and store. Many persons analyzed these problems and sought solutions. Applying technology to man's problems produced Whitney's cotton gin in 1793, McCormick's reaper in 1830, John Deere's plow in 1837, commercial fertilizer, and the farm wagon. These developments, particularly in agriculture, paved the way for westward expansion. Their influence on the growth of vocational education is immeasurable. They showed that America could create its own technology and could apply technology to its problems, and they testified to the fact that education to help man solve technical problems was in the national interest.

A look at concurrent events within the United States reveals a significant series of incidents during the early years of the nineteenth century, an era that fostered a turning point in the history of vocational education. Congress passed the Embargo Act (prohibiting foreign and domestic ships from leaving port) and the Non-Intercourse Act (prohibiting all foreign commerce by American citizens). These congressional actions were followed by the War of 1812. As a result of these three closely related occurrences, American markets were closed to foreign manufactured goods. American businessmen had noted that domestic markets were dominated by products from England's large-scale production techniques. It was considered too risky to attempt to compete with British products.

America now, in essence, "looked in on itself." It found that it had idle capital and a home market.[9] The impact of urbanization was being felt and there was a growing labor supply. American businessmen now had no competitors. Businesses moved quickly to attempt large-scale production. Fear of financial disaster had been eliminated since domestic products had free run in the market place. The net effect was to promote vocational education or training as national economic policy since it was "to the national good" that a large labor force be effectively utilized to produce goods. It was also to the national good to develop a production system that required the investment of American capital. The cycle of investment, jobs, and profits added to America's expanding gross national product. Vocational education at this point was begun as an institution that could shape pools of manpower toward the end of production. The combined impact of these three events was staggering and their impact on vocational education was expansive.

This was another example, and a most significant one, of federal legislation influencing vocational education without directly referring to or allocating federal funds. Much of the role of federal involvement in vocational education, including legislation, can be considered policy-making, for many basic national policy decisions have influenced the direction and form of vocational education well beyond their original scope and intent.

THE LAND GRANT COLLEGE MOVEMENT

Americans placed little faith in those things that were not practical. Commager comments:

> The American's attitude toward culture was at once suspicious and indulgent, where it interfered with the more important activities he distrusted it; where it was the recreation of his leisure hours, or his women folk, he tolerated it. For the most part, he required that culture serve some useful purpose. He wanted poetry that he could recite, music that he could sing, and paintings that told a story. . . . Education was his religion, and to it he paid the tribute both of his money and his affection; yet, as he expected his religion to be practical and pay dividends, he expected education to prepare for life—by which he meant increasingly, jobs and professions.[10]

Americans had faith in practical education. Colleges such as Harvard and Yale were established to prepare persons for the ministry and other professions. But such education was not viewed as particularly practical by or for the general populace. As they saw it, these institutions, along with the some twenty state universities that had been established by 1860, did not turn out graduates able to address themselves to the practical problems of the day. Agriculture and industry were the two great resources of the nation and technically trained workers were needed to develop their potentials.

It was after 1865 that the machines developed two and three decades earlier came into general use throughout agriculture. In one thirty-year period, from 1860 to 1890, the value of machinery owned by farmers doubled. In the next thirty years it increased 700 percent. Parallel production figures were equally significant. The production of wheat, for example, rose from 173 million bushels in 1860 to nearly 500 million bushels in 1880. As production mounted, prices began a steady decline. Wheat brought $1.06 a bushel in 1866 compared to $0.66 in 1875. Increasing production and declining prices placed the farmer in economic jeopardy and sharpened his desire for attention and help.

One is able to find some demands for the development of vocational education between 1820 and 1860.[11] The agricultural sector of the economy demanded vocational and practical education. The workingman did not want a totally skill-oriented training but, rather, an education more practical than was commonly offered by secondary schools and colleges of the day. If the farmers' problems were to be met, there had to be a "practical" impetus from education. Developing the nation's great agricultural resources required leadership from technically trained persons in public education at the secondary and college level.

Industrial development faced a void of engineers to deal with the more practical problems of plant layout, machine design, and machined parts. Traditional colleges prepared students for the law, medicine, teaching, and the ministry. These four professions would, all told, provide gainful employment for only a small portion of the population. Among America's expanding masses were thousands of young men who could benefit from advanced training but who were not interested in the professional, traditional training available. Congress responded to some of these practical problems by passing the Morrill Act of 1862. Its primary purpose was "to promote the liberal and practical education of the industrial classes in the several pursuits and professions of living."

THE SMITH-HUGHES ACT OF 1917

By the turn of the twentieth century, a genuine community concern had emerged over the fact that the consensus that gave the secondary school a push after the Civil War had not resulted in an institution with clearly defined purposes. Hicks and Blackington describe four well-established categories of potential masters:

1. The *ecclesiastical classicist*, who viewed public secondary school as a necessary evil. His hope was that teachers and textbooks would hold "to the faith" and that the secular instruction would not run contrary to ecclesiastical thought.

2. The *lay classicist*, who viewed secondary education as selection and preparation for college.

3. The *generalist*, who viewed the high school as a source of general education of a terminal nature beyond the elementary level.

4. The *immediate vocationalist*, who viewed the high school as a source of some technical and vocational skills of immediate marketable worth, both to the seller (student) and to the buyer (business community).[12]

Thus, the legitimacy of vocational education in the public schools at this point was contested and vocational education was not to become the dominant purpose of the secondary school. Public vocational education was simply an idea that had not come to full fruition. The famous Committee of Ten, headed by President Charles W. Eliot of Harvard, issued a report in 1893 after an exhaustive study of secondary education. The committee reported the role of the high school as being one of providing an education for non-college-bound as well as college-bound youth. "The secondary schools of the United States taken as a whole do not exist for the purpose of preparing boys and girls for colleges. Only an insignificant percentage of the graduates of these schools go to colleges or scientific schools."[13] However, the committee then proceeded to recommend a curriculum that was almost entirely college oriented.

If professional educators could not agree on the general purposes and priorities of education, the general public could. A growing demand for manual, industrial, and commercial education on the secondary level developed during the last quarter of the nineteenth century. All three types of education obviously stemmed from the increasing commercial and industrial character of the American economy following the Civil War. In rural communities, growing mechanization and commercializing of agriculture placed the skilled worker at a high premium. Trained personnel continued to be needed for the cities. The general public sanctioned classes that had vocational intent. In 1900, a few schools offered classes in "farm and garden" and "sewing and cooking." By 1910, over 20,000 pupils enrolled in agriculture in 965 schools, while nearly 33,000 pupils enrolled in domestic economy in 591 schools. During the same period, enrollments reached nearly 111,000 in commercial education—a growth of 42,000 students.[14] This surge created a demand for more vocational education. It was reasoned that since federal stimulation resulted in the establishment of land grant colleges, federal aid for vocational education of lower than college level would stimulate the public schools and likewise result in the establishment of a vocational type of education. Incorporating vocational education into the public school, with federal aid, became the general goal of a number of diverse organizations, and their combined efforts spanned nearly two decades before fruition.

This proved to be a difficult era for promoters of vocational education. Federal aid to secondary schools would not come easy. The Constitution had clearly left educational matters to the states and local communities. One trend—a tendency toward centralization of American affairs following the Civil War—helped make the efforts of the two decades slightly easier.[15] Prior federal acts, such as the land ordinances and the Morrill Act, were steps toward federal aid to education. However, these were very general (nonspecific) and awarded money to states or townships who in turn used it for education.

AGRICULTURAL AGENCIES[16]

Beginning with the Philadelphia Society for the Promotion of Agriculture, organized in 1785, agriculture has had many supporting organizations. These groups were successful in promoting vocational education at the college level (Morrill Act) and supporting it with basic research

(Hatch Act). Two additional programs seemed imperative to those interested in agricultural education. The first would be designed to educate the adult farmer, the second to educate high school students who might become farmers.

From its establishment in 1888, the Office of Experiment Stations recognized the importance of an organization to disseminate practical results of agricultural experimentation. A $2,000 appropriation was made to that office in 1901 to promote education for the farmer. This group, through its publications and speeches by staff members, supported programs of agricultural education at lower than college level. A part of the appropriation permitted it to act as a clearing house for information, and a section of its 1902 annual report related the progress of secondary education in agriculture.

The Association of Agricultural Colleges and Experiment Stations favored teaching agriculture in secondary schools, and in 1902, it recommended that agriculture be taught in the high school as well as in special agricultural schools. By 1911, the association was supporting federal funding for programs in agriculture, home economics, trades industry, and manual training.

Efforts were made to obtain federal support for both extension work in agriculture and teaching agriculture in the secondary school in the same congressional bill. A bill "making it possible to unite all the forces seeking federal aid for extension, vocational education, and normal schools" was approved and reported out of committee to the Senate on June 22, 1910. The death of its sponsor, Iowa Senator Jonathan P. Dolliver, prevented further action. Senator Dolliver had originally preferred federal monies for vocational education rather than monies for extension and Senator Carroll S. Page of Vermont continued this pursuit. In the House of Representatives the Lever Bill for Extension had emerged in 1911 and was introduced into the Senate in 1912 by Senator Hoke Smith of Georgia. (Senator Asbury F. Lever was from South Carolina.) Before the Congress in 1913 was the Smith-Lever Bill for extension and the Page Bill supporting high school vocational education.

By 1913 three attitudes had emerged. Some people favored the Smith-Lever Bill, others the Page Bill. A third group supported both with a preference for the extension bill if only one could be passed. Most agricultural organizations supported both ideas, but like the position taken by the Agricultural College Association in 1912, they saw greater need for federal funds for extension if both could not be obtained at once. After a series of compromises, including a substitute resolution for the Page Bill, the Smith-Lever Bill for extension was passed in 1914, clearing the way for united support of agricultural organizations in obtaining funds for vocational education in agriculture.

THE NATIONAL SOCIETY FOR THE PROMOTION OF INDUSTRIAL EDUCATION[17]

By the spring of 1906, leaders in practical arts and vocational education were convinced that it was now time to promote trade and industrial education on an extensive basis. Two of these leaders, Professor Charles R. Richards of Teachers College, Columbia University, and Dr. James P. Haney, director of manual training in New York City, assembled a group of thirteen representative leaders at the New York City Engineers Club on June 9. This gathering was followed by another meeting of about 250 persons at the Cooper Union on November 16. At this gathering the National Society for the Promotion of Industrial Education was formed. Its chief objectives were:

To bring to public attention the importance of industrial education as a factor in the industrial development of the United States to provide opportunities for the study and discussion of the various phases of the problem; to make available the results of experiments in the field of industrial education; and to promote the establishment of institutions of industrial training.[18]

The society's membership consisted of educators, businessmen, manufacturers; all persons interested in industrial education were potential members.

State committees for the promotion of industrial education were organized. Through these state organizations, national conclaves, and extensive literature, the society sought to further its purposes. Considerable effort was spent gathering facts concerning the needs and types of organizations for vocational education. The society channeled its activities toward legislation relating to the organization and financing of vocational education in agriculture, in trades and industry, and in homemaking. It had concluded that it would be in the national interest to promote vocational education on a broader basis than its original declaration of purposes defined.

Dr. Charles A. Prosser became executive secretary of the society in 1912. He is considered one of the dynamic founding fathers of present-day vocational education. During the early years of his leadership, public opinion toward vocational education was molded, legislation formulated, and the groundwork laid for extensive federally supported programs of vocational education. As this organization affiliated with other groups, its name was changed to the National Society for Vocational Education, in recognition of its broader objectives and scope.

The National Society for Vocational Education joined the debate concerning federal support for programs in agriculture. Strenuous efforts were exerted to obtain support for the Page Bill, only after it came onto the Senate floor from the hearings committee, having earlier voiced "grave doubts as to whether the bill (combining extension and vocational education) as at present drawn, will accomplish the purpose in view." The executive secretary worked particularly during the congressional session of 1913 to have substitute bills and amendments introduced, all with the general intent of providing separate bills for agricultural extension and vocational education. In 1914, when support for vocational education was not obtained, the society suggested that Congress establish a commission charged with the responsibility of studying the need for national aid to vocational education. True relates this series of events:

Mr. Page offered as a substitute his bill which then had the form of a bill drafted by the secretary of the National Society for Industrial Education.

On the first day of the second session of the 62nd Congress, Senator Smith presented endorsements of the extension bill and a few days later Senator Page presented a memorial in favor of his bill from the National Society for Industrial Education.

Senator Smith also introduced . . . a joint resolution to create a commission to consider the need and report a plan not later than December 1 next for National aid to vocational education. It was not until January 20, 1914, that such a commission was created. The proposition to create it, which was actively supported by the National Society for Industrial Education and other friends of federal aid for vocational education, had the effect of practically postponing further consideration of the Page Bill, thus leaving the way open for the passage of the Smith-Lever Extension Bill.[19]

This resolution of Senator Smith was accepted and created the Commission for National Aid to Vocational Education, which was discussed in Chapter 2. The commission's report was filed on June 1, 1914.

Immediately following this report, two bills were introduced by Senator Smith and Representative Dudley Hughes (also of Georgia), but enactment was slow. Supporters of vocational education were disappointed and alarmed at this delayed congressional action. Since the report had been made within the three-month period prescribed by Congress, many enthusiastic supporters had anticipated that Congress would act on the Smith-Hughes Bill with comparable speed.[20]

The National Society then undertook a massive campaign to win active support of hundreds of organizations—national, state, and local. Such groups as the Department of Superintendents of the National Education Association, the National Association of Manufacturers, the American Federation of Labor, and the United States Chamber of Commerce were involved. President Wilson made three separate appeals for congressional action. He viewed with some consternation the possibility that the United States might become involved in a war and saw the value of a nationwide preparedness program. His third appeal, on December 5, 1916, said in part:

[the bill] is of vital importance to the whole country because it concerns a matter too long neglected upon which thorough industrial preparation for the critical years of economic development immediately ahead of us, in very large measure, depends.

Congress responded promptly to this appeal, and the Smith-Hughes Bill was signed into law by President Wilson on February 23, 1917. At this time the National Society for the Study of Industrial Education was holding its annual convention in Indianapolis. President Wilson purposely delayed signing the bill for a few days so that it could be reported by the society as the highlight of its convention.

The Smith-Hughes Bill provided for vocational education in secondary schools. Specific subjects included agriculture, home economics, and trade and industrial education. In addition, the act provided for the salaries of teachers and supervisors and appropriated $1 million for vocational teacher training. The provisions of the act were very specific. It designated the subjects to be taught, the level at which they should be taught, and who should be taught—students over fourteen years of age but not in colleges. In addition, the act specified that before a state could receive funds it must establish a responsible state vocational board. That board was to develop a state plan that would indicate exactly how the federal funds would be used. This plan would be a legal contract between the state and the federal government. Upon approval of its plan, the state could then expend funds to operate the program.

In essence, the state plan was intended to be developed with local creativity guided by local needs. A set of guidelines, known as Bulletin 1, were formulated to aid states in preparing their plans; these actually evolved into a rigid set of standards. However, since each state developed its own plan, there was considerable variation in the use of federal funds throughout the nation.

States often complained that their plans would not permit them to undertake a specific activity. This was probably true; however, a state plan could be changed when it was renewed, every three years. As it happened, the item of complaint was seldom inserted at that time. State plans thus emerged as very conservative documents that tended not to be evolutionary. In addition, many state departments of education used the state plan as an item of control over local school systems by threatening to reduce or remove federal funds, or even "state approval," if certain state recommendations were not accepted. One state, for instance, set up very specific standards for its class A—best—departments of vocational agriculture. In 1966, a state supervisor, upon exhibiting one of the newest and best facilities for agriculture to a group of visitors, commented that it would never be a class A department. He went on to explain that the overhead door was fourteen feet wide and state standards required a sixteen-foot door in all class A departments.

The specificity of the Smith-Hughes Act was something new in federal-state relationships in education. Prior educational efforts by the federal government offered funds to states with considerable latitude.

The struggle to get direct Federal aid to vocational education involved coming to grips with a number of very significant questions. These included such concerns as states rights, the role of the Federal government in education, the role of industry in providing specific skill training, and unifying educational offerings through an extension system similar to that provided for farmers. Though these concerns were dealt with at that point in time, they did not disappear. States rights and the role of the Federal government in education, for example, continue to be concerns voiced by each generation of educational scholars.

AMENDMENTS TO THE SMITH-HUGHES ACT

Following the enactment of the Smith-Hughes Act there were several amendments, which are summarized in Table 4. Most of them increased the appropriation for various specific services. The original Smith-Hughes law provided funds for agriculture, home economics, trade and industrial education, and teacher education. Distributive education received support in 1937 through the George-Dean Act. The disbursement of monies to the states generally followed the pattern of: agriculture, farm population; home economics, rural population; trade and industrial, nonfarm population; distributive occupations, total population; teacher education, total population.

An additional point of interest concerning the Smith-Hughes Act deserves comment. In the legislative process, two steps are generally required by Congress before funds are forthcoming. First is the act of authorization, which specifies the maximum amount of funds that can be appropriated. The second step actually appropriates the funds. In the Smith-Hughes Act, the authorization and appropriation were together in the original law. This meant that vocational education did not have to appeal to Congress each year for funds. The Smith-Hughes Act is one of the few such bills and the only education bill passed by Congress that is so constructed.

The George-Reed Act (1930–1934) was a temporary measure, with an inclusive authorization of $1.5 million to expand vocational education in agriculture and home economics. This was in addition to the Smith-Hughes appropriation.

The George-Elizey Act (1934–1937) replaced the George-Reed Act with an inclusive authorization of $3 million to be appropriated equally in agriculture, home economics, and trade and industries.

The George-Deen Act (1937–1947) replaced the George-Elizey Act with a continuous authorization for vocational education. Over $14 million was authorized: $4 million each to agriculture, home economics, and trade and industries; $1 million to teacher education; and $1.3 million for education in distributive occupations. This was the first appropriation for distributive education, although a limited number of distributive education students had been provided for through trade and industrial funds prior to this.

The George-Barden Act (1947–1968) replaced the George-Deen Act. Appropriations for vocational education were now authorized at $29 million. One interesting feature of this act was the provision for greater flexibility in the use of funds. No specific funds were allocated for teacher training or for vocational guidance, but each state could write such items into their state plans if they desired. In addition, states were authorized to spend some of the monies for such things as equipment, salary, and travel expenses for the state director, and supervision of FFA and NFA activities.

THE GI BILL OF RIGHTS

In June 1944, President Franklin D. Roosevelt signed into law the Servicemen's Readjustment Act of 1944, better known as the GI Bill. This act was one of the most far-reaching and comprehensive educational acts ever passed by Congress. It was of untold benefit to veterans, educational institutions, and to the country as a whole. Vocational education was an important recipient of its benefits. The number of persons who received an education under this bill approached one million. Of these, approximately 30 percent received college training, 30 percent received on-the-job training from private industry and agriculture, and the other 40 percent were trained in educational institutions at less than the baccalaureate level. An additional impact was the requirement that each school or program had to be approved to participate. This facilitated the expansion of postsecondary education. The impact upon the structure of many participating schools was evident as they modified curriculum patterns, stopped or modified freshman hazing, learned to deal more effectively with student dissent, and learned to deal with the married student in attempting to meet the needs of the GI. In addition to the direct participants in vocational education, a large number of veterans in college majored in vocational teacher education and taught in vocational programs. The bill was a response to the basic recognition that as GIs returned to civilian life, government had a responsibility to help them adjust. A social need existed and government responded. A Korean GI Bill as well as a GI Bill for the Vietnam conflict guarantee to those veterans the same educational benefits received by World War II veterans.

These acts deserve special comment due to their sound philosophy and their impact on vocational education. They contain few stipulations. The veteran who qualifies to receive benefits selects the occupation for which he would like to prepare. If he is unsure of his choice, he can request counseling help. The school or program he wants has only to be legitimate, duly authorized, or licensed to be accepted. Once enrolled, the veteran has only to meet the academic qualifications of the institution to stay in school and receive his benefits. Thus, the veteran selects his school and his major or occupational goal. The Veterans Administration takes the school's word that the student is progressing toward his declared occupational goal. There are relatively few recorded abuses by individuals or institutions.

THE VOCATIONAL EDUCATION ACT OF 1963

The Panel of Consultants' Report of 1962, discussed in Chapter 1, resulted in the passage of the Vocational Education Act of 1963.

Following the panel's report, President John F. Kennedy sent to the Congress an education bill, one section of which dealt with vocational education. Some persons concluded that the bill would not pass that year (1963). Vocational educators marshalled their resources and had the vocational education section introduced as a separate bill. Representative Carl Perkins of Kentucky sponsored this legislative maneuver, hence the bill is sometimes referred to as the Perkins Bill. This strategy assured that the President's bill would not pass and further assured vocational educators a greater opportunity to fulfill their desires. (The essential segments of the President's bill, without the vocational section, became the Elementary and Secondary Education Act of 1965.)

Through a series of rewritings and amendments, the Perkins Bill was shaped. Considerable congressional testimony was heard concerning the relationships between the previous acts, particularly the Smith-Hughes Act of 1917 and the Perkins Bill. Many persons testified that existing policies and programs should continue to function undisturbed by new legislation. Others testified that the new act should be comprehensive and conclusive; it should wipe the old slates clean and start afresh. There was much selfish interest on both sides. This was resolved by having the thrust of the new act focus on new directions. A series of amendments insured that some flexibility would be provided in policies governing existing programs. The specific purposes of the act provide for vocational education becoming available to a wider range of students. Mobley and Barlow write:

[It is the purpose] to maintain, extend, and improve existing programs of vocational education, to develop new programs of vocational education, to provide part-time employment for youth who need such employment in order to continue their vocational training on a full-time basis, to provide instruction so that persons of *all* ages in *all* communities will have ready access to vocational training or retraining which is of high quality, realistic in relation to employment and suited to the needs, interests, and ability of the persons concerned.[21]

The bill was signed into law by President Lyndon B. Johnson in December 1963, when the annual convention of the American Vocational Association (AVA) was being held in Atlantic City, New Jersey. Mayor D. Mobley, executive secretary, rose at one of the functions of that convention to announce the passage of the act. Progressing from $60 million in 1964 an annual authorization of $225 million was to be reached in 1967 and each year thereafter. Section 4(c) reserved 10 percent of the funds for basic and applied research. These funds were distributed by the U.S. Office of Education to universities, other educational institutions, and state boards on the basis of approved research plans.

The Vocational Education Act of 1963 amended existing laws to permit:

1. the transferral of funds formerly earmarked for a special service to another occupational category.

2. the use of funds for agriculture, for vocational education in any occupation involving knowledge and skills in agricultural subjects without directed or supervised practice.

3. funds earmarked for home economics to be used to train for gainful employment in any occupation involving knowledge and skills in home economics subjects, and required 10 percent of the home economics funds to be so spent.

4. preemployment training in distributive education in schools other than part-time or evening schools.

5. the lessening of shop work requirements for some trade and industrial education programs.

6. the use of less than 1.3 percent of the funds earmarked for trade and industrial education for part-time classes.

THE VOCATIONAL EDUCATION AMENDMENTS OF 1968

The Vocational Education Act of 1963 was amended in October 1968; these changes are referred to as the Vocational Education Amendments of 1968. At this time, the guidelines for this act have not been published by the U.S. Office of Education for a sufficient length of time to comment on the specific form and shape that vocational education will take as a result of these amendments. It is clear, however, that the 1968 amendments will affect the future direction of vocational education.

The 1968 amendments narrow the definition of the clientele to be served by vocational education. At the same time, services to these groups will be expanded. One intent of the 1968 amendments is to redirect the priorities for the use of federal monies. Federal funds will be less readily available to support allocation policy programs (specifically aimed at matching men and jobs) and more readily available for employment policy programs (aimed at providing employment opportunities for those willing and able to work).

The first priority will be to support vocational education programs designed to assist the "hard to reach and the hard to teach." Traditional occupational preparation programs will hold second priority.

The 1968 amendments set forth a set of rigid specifications necessary to qualify for the monies allocated. A state will have to meet more specific requirements than have previously been established. In addition, both state and federal governments will exert more direct control on local programs of vocational education than ever before. Section 123, for example, contains eighteen paragraphs of specific details required of a state plan. Among other things, the state must determine manpower needs of each geographic area of the state, the vocational education needs of all population groups, the ability of each local educational agency to pay for education, and excess costs of the program. The state is prohibited from allocating funds to local districts on a uniform percentage basis. Rather, it must use criteria such as the above in distributing funds. One school may receive a greater proportion of the cost of its program from these funds than another. Each school's program will have to be approved on a project-by-project basis. State administrators will be forced to become deskbound, weighing one proposed project against another with little basis for comparison.

There are many positive potentials inherent in all of this detail. Each local educational agency is to prepare and submit to the state a local plan for vocational education needs of potential students in the community or area, specifying the manpower needs of the community and indicating how these needs can be met by vocational education programs. Such comprehensive, long-range plans for a local area will be beneficial and give direction to the local program. Such planning should also result in closer articulation of many educational and community agencies. Another potential benefit is the local innovativeness that should be stimulated.

The 1968 amendments specify a number of new programs: for the disadvantaged, exemplary programs, curriculum development programs, and consumer and homemaking education programs. Homemaking was deleted from the 1963 act, but in the 1968 amendments it was reinstated to receive special funding for three years. Table 3 pinpoints data regarding some of the program areas approved by the 1968 amendments: the authorized appropriation, the budget recommendations from the office of the President, and the actual monies provided by Congress in 1970. The data indicate a painful trend. Vocational education in the years ahead apparently will be charged with more specific responsibilities but there will be no additional funds immediately with which to accomplish the task. This will require withdrawing funds from existing programs, a

TABLE 3. Authorization and Appropriations for Vocational Education for 1970

PROGRAM AREA	AUTHORIZATION	APPROPRIATION
(1) Basic grants to states for administration and basic programs	$565,000,000	$307,497,455[1]
(2) Disadvantaged	40,000,000	17,000,000
(3) Work study	35,000,000	4,250,000
(4) Exemplary programs	57,500,000	6,500,012
(5) Cooperative education	35,000,000	14,000,000
(6) Demonstration residential school	30,000,000	–0–
(7) Grants to states for residential schools	15,000,000	–0–
(8) Dormitories	10,000,000	–0–
(9) Consumer and homemaking education	25,000,000	15,000,000
(10) Curriculum development	10,000,000	–0–
(11) Professional development	35,000,000	–0–[2]
(12) Research	[3]	1,100,000[4]
	Retained by the commissioner	1,700,000[5]
	TOTAL	$367,047,467

[1]Includes $7,161,455 permanent appropriation under the Smith-Hughes Act.

[2]Some $5.5 million was allocated to vocational education by the Professions Development Act.

[3]Ten percent of the basic grant to states is for research.

[4]An additional $5.9 million was allocated for research in vocational education by the Bureau of Research.

[5]Used for administration and the National Advisory Council.

policy that can be beneficial if it stimulates vocational education to reestablish priorities on a more realistic basis.

Categorical federal aid was started in vocational education with the passage of the Smith-Hughes Act in 1917. Definite prescribed proportions of the monies appropriated were designated for agriculture, home economics, and trade and industrial education. The 1968 amendments discontinued categorical aids, so all areas of vocational education must now compete for the appropriated funds. Philosophically this should strengthen vocational education, since special privileges and considerations have now been removed. However, while the 1968 amendments discontinued traditional categorical aids, in their place were inserted such categories as special needs, cooperative education, and innovative programs. In this sense, a set of new categories were simply substituted for the established ones.

The 1968 amendments have recreated a National Advisory Council on Vocational Education. They also require each state to establish a State Advisory Council. The National Advisory Council is composed of twenty-one members appointed by the President. Their duties include (a) advising the Commissioner of Education in terms of preparation of regulations for and administration of vocational education programs, (b) conducting an annual review of effectiveness of vocational education, and (c) conducting independent evaluations of vocational education programs. Just before leaving office in January 1969, President Johnson appointed the national council. This council has been active and has issued a number of reports on the status of vocational education.

OTHER FEDERAL LEGISLATIVE ACTS

A number of other legislative acts that were not amendments to the Smith-Hughes Law were passed by Congress prior to the Vocational Education Act of 1963. These are listed in Table 4. Vocational education received funds for its practical nursing programs, fishery occupations, and area schools.

The Manpower, Development and Training Act (MDTA) of 1962 deserves special comment, as it may be indicative of things to come. This act was intended to alleviate unemployment through the retraining of workers. A unique feature is the provision for payment of subsistence benefits to unemployed workers during training. The original maximum period of retraining was one year; it is now two years, but most programs are considerably shorter than one year in length. Preference for retraining is given to unemployed and underemployed workers who have at least three years experience in gainful employment. Another distinguishing feature of the MDTA is the broad scope of training supported. Courses

TABLE 4. Major National Legislation Affecting Vocational-Technical Education

---

Smith-Hughes Act, 1917*
George-Reed 1929
George-Elizey 1935
George-Deen 1937
George-Barden 1946

Vocational Education Act of 1963
Amended, 1968

National Defense Education Act, 1958

Area Redevelopment, 1962

Manpower Development and Training, 1962
Amended, 1965, 1968

Job Corps, 1964

GI Bill, 1944

Practical Nursing, 1956

---

*Year of initial passage.

can be offered to help the unemployed or underemployed worker find gainful employment in any occupation. The MDTA also requires that the President have prepared and submit to Congress an annual manpower report. These reports, *Manpower Report of the President*, are submitted each March and constitute the best source of information about general national trends in manpower requirements.

Funds for this act are appropriated to the Department of Labor. About one-third of these monies can be transferred to the Department of Health, Education and Welfare for use by state vocational education boards. The local labor representative is responsible for determining if a need exists for a proposed program; without his approval these funds cannot be used. In essence, the local labor representative is a "mini" local board of education. Historically, educational need was to be determined by a local board of education responsible to local communities or elected state officials. Although one act does not create a trend, the direct movement of labor into the field of vocational education is something that must be observed closely in the coming years.

Job Corps legislation was passed in 1964. It was to provide training for school dropouts who lacked a skill, were unemployed, or who had skimpy educational backgrounds. Most recruits came from inner city areas. Contracts for the construction, maintenance, and operation of Job Corps camps went directly to private companies. Vocational educators were forced to sit on the sidelines and watch with some glee the disarray that often passed for education. Often the persons responsible for directing training knew nothing of vocational education for the average pupil. When confronted with the added problems of these trainees, their lack of competence was compounded. The more successful Job Corps camps—such as those at Guthrie, Oklahoma; Lincoln, Nebraska; and Madera, California—involved competent vocational educators and educational psychologists at or near the top administrative policy-making levels.

Perhaps a lesson can be learned by vocational educators through this experience. There is a job to be done in vocational education in selected areas such as the inner city. Vocational education programs, by and large, have not been designed to deal with these problems. Unless vocational educators take the leadership in developing such programs, society will sanction another agency to do the job.

IMPACT OF FEDERAL LEGISLATION

Financial support for vocational education from the federal government was meant to be "stimulating," not "entrenching" legislation. Federal funds were to be used to stimulate the development of new programs, offsetting costs of items such as equipment, which can make the initiation of a new program difficult for local schools. Gradually state and local funds were to be allocated to assume support of these programs. Federal funds would then be available to stimulate similar programs in another area of the state or to broaden existing programs. Fischer and Thomas state:

the Smith-Hughes Act of 1917 responded to the problem of financing vocational training which had been too expensive an activity for some states and communities to provide. Here the federal government intervened financially to achieve a goal local and state resources could not achieve on their own.[22]

This not happened. Once programs were initiated they continued to receive federal funds. Thus, one result of federal aid has been a degree of program entrenchment that has not permitted the degree of local responsibility originally intended.

Some educators maintain that federal legislation has narrowed the offerings of vocational schools. This contention is based on the belief that the programs offered were only those that made available some reimbursement. Consequently, actual community needs have been ignored in these cases, or, at the very least, placed in lower priority.

This contention was and is correct in many communities. However, it does not appear to be the fault of federal aid per se, but rather a failure of the administrators and vocational educators who direct the programs.

It is certainly true that the vocational education programs of this nation have advanced more rapidly with federal funds than would have been possible without them. Mobley and Barlow identify eleven specific impacts of federal legislation.[23] Among these are the promotion of national welfare, development of standards, development of teacher education, leadership development, development of a national consensus on vocational education, and the development of the concept of area programs.

In addition to these factors, federal legislation has generated a significant impact on quality teaching in vocational education programs. Although we know of no research to support the generalization that some of the best teaching at the secondary level occurred in vocational programs, it was frequently noted that, in general, teachers in vocational education were apparently more attuned to the needs of youngsters and used more visual aids and better teaching methods than did their counterpart secondary teachers. This probably remained true until the National Defense Education Act of 1958, which stimulated teaching in the basic sciences and language. Teaching in the humanities is now receiving much of the same kind of attention.

Excellence in teaching was probably the result of the use of federal funds for teacher education programs. Innovation after innovation was introduced at the secondary school level by teacher educators in vocational fields.

Another significant impact of federal legislation has been the stimulus provided for youth organizations in areas of vocational education. The Future Farmers of America (FFA) was organized as a national organization in 1928 to give those students studying vocational agriculture greater opportunity for self-expression and leadership development. Other youth organizations associated with vocational programs include Future Homemakers of America (FHA), Future Business Leaders of America (FBLA), and Distributive Education Clubs of America (DECA).

There have undoubtedly been other influences of federal legislation upon vocational education. Perhaps some of the more subtle aspects should be mentioned. One has been the separation of vocational and general education. A case in point is the separation of the Vocational Education Act of 1963 from the Elementary and Secondary Education Act of 1965. Administrative structures and supporting systems are different. The offerings of public school, general education, and vocational education must be justified on different bases. This is a pervasive problem for all aspects of education. Specifically, a few entire state systems of vocational education have grown and been strengthened because general education did not wish to assume its role. Often, within a specific local school system, vocational education is housed apart from the other facilities and administered as a separate program

Another outgrowth of federal legislation has been a basis for the justification or rationale of vocational education. In 1917, vocational education was charged to construct a program that would result in an educated labor force. This channeled vocational education into a rationale based on economic terms: vocational education was beneficial and approved because it added to the economic well-being of the recipient and his community. This rationale has not been replaced by a more educationally sound justification for too many of the leaders in vocational education. The charge now for vocational education is to construct a program that will enable students to cope with an ever-changing dynamic technology. However, the economic rationale will probably preclude the raising of significant questions and the development of an adequate framework to accomplish this task.

NOTES

1Roy W. Roberts, *Vocational and Practical Arts Education*, 2nd ed. (New York: Harper & Row, Publishers, 1965), p. 52.

2R. Freeman Butts, *A Cultural History of Western Education* (New York: McGraw-Hill Book Company, 1955), p. 251.

3R. Freeman Butts and L. A. Cremin, *A History of Education in American Culture* (New York: Holt, Rinehart & Winston, Inc., 1963), p. 76.

4S. E. Morrison and Henry S. Commager, *The Growth of the American Republic* (New York: Oxford University Press, Inc., 1942), I, 181.

5Butts and Cremin, *A History of Education*, p. 36.

6Carl H. Gross and Charles C. Chandler, *The History of American Education* (Boston: D. C. Heath & Co., 1964) pp. 21–25.

7Butts and Cremin, *A History of Education*, p. 142.

8The land was surveyed into square plots, six miles on a side. This was a township. Each township had thirty-six sections of one square mile each. Thus the sixteenth section was the center one.

9Layton S. Hawkins, Charles A. Prosser, and John C. Wright, *Development of Vocational Education* (Chicago: American Technical Society, 1951), p. 9.

10Henry Steele Commager, *The American Mind* (New Haven: Yale University Press, 1950), p. 10.

11Butts and Cremin, *A History of Education*, p. 214.

12W. Vernon Hicks and Frank H. Blackington III, *Introduction to Education* (Columbus, Ohio: Charles E. Merrill Books, Inc., 1965), p. 82.

13*Report of the Committee of Ten on Secondary School Studies* (New York: American Book Company, 1894), p. 51.

14U.S. Department of the Interior, *Bureau of Education Reports of Commissioner of Education* (Washington, D.C.), 1901, II, 2231; 1911, II, 1194.

15Butts and Cremin, *A History of Education*, p. 425.

[16]Rufus W. Stimson and Frank W. Lathrup, *History of Agricultural Education of Less Than College Grade in the United States*, Vocational Division Bulletin No. 217 (Washington, D.C., Office of Education, 1942).

[17]In 1918 this organization changed its name to the National Society for Vocational Education; in 1926 it combined with the Vocational Education Association of the Midwest to form the American Vocational Association. See F. Theodore Struck, *Foundations of Industrial Education* (New York: Wiley, 1930), Chaps. 8, 9, and A. C. True, *A History of Agricultural Education in the United States 1785–1925* (Washington, D.C.: Government Printing Office, 1929), pp. 358–62.

[18]Struck, *Vocational Education for a Changing World* (New York: John Wiley & Sons, Inc., 1945), p. 193.

[19]True, *A History of Agricultural Education*, p. 109–10.

[20]Hawkins, Prosser, and Wright, *Development of Vocational Education*, p. 85.

[21]Mayor D. Mobley and Melvin L. Barlow, "Impact of Federal Legislation and Policies upon Vocational Education," in *Vocational Education*, 64th Yearbook of the National Society for the Study of Education, Part I (Chicago: University of Chicago Press, 1965), p. 200.

[22]Louis Fischer and Donald R. Thomas, *Social Foundations of Educational Decisions* (Belmont, Calif.: Wadsworth Publishing Co., Inc., 1965), p. 248.

[23]Mobley and Barlow, *Vocational Education*, pp. 192–97.

II

INTERPRETING
THE
DEVELOPMENT

4

ASSUMPTIONS OF
VOCATIONAL EDUCATION

Assumptions are suppositions accepted as truths. Vocational education as a social institution is directed by a set of assumptions. They are the common ground from which its practitioners derive consistency in terms of purposes, guiding principles, and practices of the profession. In short, they are the basis for a philosophy of vocational education in American society.

A PHILOSOPHICAL PROBLEM

All behavior ultimately rests on certain assumptions. If one's assumptions are sound, the resulting behavior will be profitable. But if behavior is based on wrong assumptions, frustration results.

Although assumptions cannot be "proved" in a scientific sense, they need to undergo their own kind of special examination or test. The first test is for *reliability:* Can the belief result in the same outcome time after time? It is likely that some assumptions are held by persons long after their reliability has been disproved. The second test is for *validity:* Does the belief conform to our knowledge and experience? Knowledge continues to expand and these discoveries must modify previously held assumptions. One of the assumptions made in vocational agriculture was that only farm boys could profit from such instruction! Trade and industrial education assumed that every student needed 2,000 hours of instruction to learn a skill. Are these assumptions valid in light of new formulations about the growth and development of students? A final test for assumptions is one of *consistency:* Do the assumptions agree with each other? Some assumptions are made about the way youngsters grow and develop; others are made about the criteria to employ as entrance requirements for a vocational program. How do these two sets of assumptions compare?

Lacking consistency, a person is likely to agree with two or more conflicting views professing one belief while his behavior is determined by forces that bear no relationship to any particular set of principles. Barnes recognized this as the major problem in getting teachers to change their behavior. He noted that they had difficulty in sensing the universal value framework that guided their behavior. When working to get teachers to adopt new ideas, he postulated that "enlightened change can only occur when the objectives on which the proposed change is predicated are consistent with the value system of the person whose behavior is altered by that change."[1]

Venable lists several reasons why belief does not always determine behavior as it should.[2] Among these are (a) a safety in numbers, putting into practice only those things that others have been known to do, (b) emotional satisfaction, and (c) what works. Vocational educators are particularly prone to these three conditions. One reason for this is a lack of direct contact with philosophy. Another results from the fact that many persons have not critically analyzed their basic assumptions about vocational education.

Vocational educators today are faced with a philosophical problem of inconsistency between instrumental and verbal behaviors. That is, we do not guide our practices by our beliefs. For example, we verbalize a belief in individual differences and yet often require the same assignments of all students in a class.

DEMOCRATIC ASSUMPTIONS

Assumptions, beliefs, are frequently expressed as principles. The following is a commonly held belief that is frequently verbalized as basic to realizing the expressed goals of our society.

Every person is important and has dignity, and thus has a right to be educated. Society has a responsibility to give every youngster the opportunity to develop to the fullest extent of his capabilities.

The notion of universal education was born as democracy took root in this country. Jefferson argued that only when all people are educated can tyranny be prevented. A diverse system of education developed to provide universal education. Nevertheless, it was the public school to which Americans pinned their faith and pledged their support.

Thaddeus Stevens, speaking to the Pennsylvania Legislature in 1835, comments:

It would seem to be humiliating to be under the necessity in the Nineteenth Century, of entering into a formal argument to prove the utility, and to free governments, the absolute necessity of education. . . .

If then, education be of admitted importance to the people under all forms of governments; and of unquestioned *necessity* when they govern themselves, it follows, of course, that its cultivation and diffusion is a matter of *public* concern. . . . If an elective republic is to endure for any great length of time, *every* elector must have sufficient information, not only to accumulate wealth, and take care of his pecuniary concerns, but to direct wisely the legislatures, the ambassadors, and the executive of the nation—for *some* part of all these things, *some* agency in approving or disapproving of them, falls to every free man. If then, the permanency of our government depends upon such knowledge, it is the duty of the government to see that the means of information be diffused to every citizen. This is a sufficient answer to those who deem education a private and not a public duty.[3]

Schools that are committed to the attainment of democratic ideals emphasize the importance of individual dignity and promote the development of individual freedom and initiative. But this is not a license to live unto oneself. A complex social order requires a high level of interaction among individuals. Equality in our society does not mean factual identity or sameness. It is conceived to be legal protection of equal opportunity to compete, to rise, or to fall in the social system. What we really mean when we refer to equality of education is equality of opportunity for an individual to develop his potential. In our society the individual's "self" is realized in the social context. The objectives of the American public school have always reflected this democratic concern. In 1938, the Educational Policies Commission described the *Purposes of Education in American Democracy* as self-realization, human relationships, economic efficiency, and civic responsibility.[4]

The history of American education records many groups vying for exclusive control of the means for implementing the public schools' objectives. Many have maintained that it is undemocratic to teach anything except a broad general education, with the rationale that to do so may make a plumber out of a potential doctor. They advocate a general preparatory curriculum to serve all. Others have maintained that all jobs require some preparation and individuals differ; hence there cannot be a single curriculum for all, which would limit the opportunities of those who do not go on to college.

America, with its root theme of individualism in a democracy, has emphasized the attainment of these democratic assumptions but has not achieved them fully. In fact, as Fischer and Thomas point out, two of the assumptions may now conflict.[5] This disparity arises from a changed concept of democracy and the purposes of education in mass society. Democratic individualism, with the twin emphases of liberty and equality before the law, has given rise to modern democracy. Modern democracy values the root theme of individualism—namely, the respect and value of the individual. However, it does not isolate man or set him against the group. Interdependence is a recognized fact of modern life that has to be accepted in creating a life that is conducive to the full development of all members of the society.

The fact that the assumptions set forth here have not been attained to the fullest extent possible and may be in a degree of conflict does not mean that they are unworthy. They may need critical examination by each of us or an increased commitment to their attainment. In either case, if our beliefs are to guide practices, then it is imperative that we discover some of the examples of these assumptions not being achieved by segments of American society. Johnson suggests:

American democracy is not, never was, and never can be a guarantor of equality. On the contrary, it is a guarantor of essential inequality, for its function is to release the talents with which men are endowed; and the moment talents are allowed full play, men become unequal.[6]

The assumption that a youngster must be given the opportunity to develop to the fullest extent of his capacity deserves special attention. A survey in one of our large cities revealed that approximately:

- two out of three out-of-school youth, aged sixteen through twenty-one, are unemployed.
- one out of three unemployed are high school graduates.
- one out of two unemployed completed only the ninth grade.
- two out of three unemployed did not graduate from high school.
- three out of four of those not graduating from high school were unemployed.[7]

Research conducted in a large industrial city illustrates dramatically how the educational system operates to deny opportunity to large segments of that city's children.[8] Where opportunity was not denied, at least access to the opportunity was controlled. The higher the income level of the parents comprising a local school area, the more likely the pupils of that school would attain or exceed grade level, have qualified teachers, and have enrichment programs.

Thus, some of the practices implemented in the schools are in disagreement with a set of beliefs that Americans hold about democracy. The schools are operated in such a way that some members of our society are not educated, that some are denied equality of educational opportunity, and some are considered more important than others.

WORLD OF WORK ASSUMPTIONS

The assumption discussed above is part of a larger group of democratic assumptions held by American educators. Coupled with a group of "world of work" assumptions, they comprise the philosophy of vocational educators. A number of "world of work" assumptions, in essence the basis of a philosophy of vocational education, are examined here.

Traditional vocational education assumptions have centered around concepts of the world of work. In the professional literature these are generally identified as principles of vocational education. Struck, for example, lists thirty-three "Basic Vocational Education Principles and Concepts."[9] Twenty-seven "Principles of Vocational Education" are found in *Vocational and Practical Arts Education*.[10] The world of work assumptions presented here represent the set of beliefs held and expressed by vocational educators. They are not totally discrete categories of beliefs, though they are treated as such here. Each has its area of emphasis; the area of emphasis of the last assumption is evaluation, which continues the economic framework begun with the first one. *Vocational education is economic education as it is geared to the needs of the job market and thus contributes to national economic strength.*

Current discussions of vocational education express this assumption in concise terms, and two sources are quoted here. The first is by Barlow; the second is from the report of the Panel of Consultants on Vocational Education.

A central tenet of vocational education is often expressed by the phrase "to fit for useful employment." This implies an economic future for the individual which will be better than what he might have had without vocational education.

Economic improvement leads toward a better standard of living for the individual, and this in turn becomes a gain for society as a whole. Vocational education has, therefore, been thought of as a "wise business investment" both for the nation and for the individual.[11]

Vocational education programs can help lower unemployment rates by training young people and adults and retraining the unemployed for skilled service, and technical occupations. If national policy requires an increase in labor productivity, vocational education can help produce the desired increase, as it has done before. Most significant, vocational education can help assure that the labor force will in fact attain the 4.5 percent average annual increase in productivity necessary in the present decade to meet the accepted goals for national economic growth.

Vocational education also strives to contribute to the stability and growth of the local, state, and national economies that sustain it. Moreover, vocational education stands to serve the needs of the United States as a major world power in a time of unprecedented peril and change, strengthening its bargaining power in world markets through increased individual productivity, and strengthening its system of national defense through the optimum deployment of manpower resources.[12]

These statements reflect and parallel an economic view of man that is inconsistent with democratic ideals and reflects an economic bias to our culture. Our literature, through the writings of Jack London, for example, reflected this economic view of man. The well-known foundations of the economic system were developed by persons such as David Ricardo and Adam Smith. Each individual, his rights inherent and inalienable, is to pursue his own goals, which will result in what is best for society. Private free competition will produce the best results. The law of supply and demand, functioning in the manner of free competition, will insure the "natural" order of things.

The realization that investment in education contributes to national economic strength has led to a new look at the interdependence of the educational system and the occupational structure of the labor force.[13] Warmbrod comments, "the result is that educational planners and policymakers now place more emphasis than before on estimates of future manpower requirements in determining the need for expansion in education." In other words, if you plan to expand education you look first at the type of people needed by the job market and second to the kinds of educational experience needed to assist individual growth and development toward occupational maturity. In essence, the societal need to further the economic system is the factor that determines the allocation of resources and the type of vocational education programs available. The moment this is permitted to happen—that is, the moment the needs of individuals are placed in a secondary position when determining the allocation of resources—vocational education becomes inconsistent with democratic principles.

Vocational education can develop a marketable man by developing his ability to perform skills that extend his utility as a tool of production.

This assumption is regarded as the basic justification for vocational education, which has been linked with economic theory throughout our history. Vocational education is one of society's social institutions and simply reflects its dominant emphases.

Invention and discovery are continually creating new devices and new processes. These in turn make necessary for their development and efficient use, new tools, new appliances, new operations, and new methods to which both workers and leaders must be continually adapted and re-adapted. This adaptation can be made only as new skills and new technical knowledge can be rapidly transmitted and diffused to great numbers of producers. . . .

As every individual is able to serve to the maximum degree of his capacity, surplus wealth is created, which, if intelligently applied, makes for better living conditions and reduces economic pressure.[14]

The above are comments by Prosser and Allen as they developed "The Economic Theory of Vocational Education." They articulated a relationship between vocational education and the economic foundations of society. The individual must be prepared to earn a living. *Vocational education is the means of acquiring the basic skills essential for equal competition* in the market place. This characterization of economic theory and vocational education has dominated the thoughts of vocational educators during the intervening years. It is thought that each person seeking a job must have a marketable skill: the ability to perform technical functions essential to a job. The content of training programs will include knowledge, skills, and the attitudes needed to perform the job. In this instance a person enters vocational education after he has made an occupational choice. Those persons seeking exploratory experiences are not to enroll in vocational programs.

Many vocational educators accept this assumption without examining it. Real belief in it would cause one to reject many of the economic actions of our government, for the economic foundation of society has evolved as technology has developed. We now, for example, regard full employment as a social responsibility, requiring, if necessary, government intervention. Equal competition by the individual is then removed. An individual's competitor may be in that particular segment of the labor market only because of government action. In addition, the rapidity of advancing technology causes doubt as to our being able to determine accurately the job skills needed very far in the future.

In general, vocational educators recognize the eroding base of this assumption but, while they are discussing training for "clusters" and "common elements" rather than specific skills, they have not examined it philosophically. This is where educators in general have taken vocational education to task and where vocational educators have attempted to justify differences between general and vocational education. For example, the purists claim that practical studies will be debased liberal ones. Instead of being intellectual they will tend to be antiintellectual.[15] Those who oppose an emphasis on vocational education sometimes argue —and this is the one premise on which liberal education is based—that an educated man is distinguished not by his vocational efficiency but by his general intellectual powers.

Vocational educators counter such a charge with a very simple yet accurate response: "Yes, man has an intellect. He also has a stomach. To care for his and his family's basic needs, he must have money, and work is the access to money for nearly all people. Therefore, someone must equip persons with the ability to obtain a job." Operating from that belief, vocational educators develop programs that concentrate on developing marketable skills for their clientele.

Inherent in the two positions is the belief that there is indeed a dualism between vocational and general education. *There need not be a dualism between vocational and general education.* An emphasis on vocational education need not imply a neglect of other essential aspects of a satisfying life that call for intelligence.

What deserves consideration here is the many sidelines of our life, and its complexity. Some educators hope that through education all individuals can achieve integration in the same way. These educators fail to realize that different individuals integrate their lives in different ways. To hope to achieve uniform integration that disregards the individual's way of life is theoretically undesirable and practically impossible. If such hopes were attained, the result would smack of totalitarianism and make a mockery of liberal education. Integration as an educational ideal is achieved not by formulating intellectually a uniform set of beliefs, but by living a life, the various aspects of which are organically related.[16]

Genuine vocational education goes far beyond the caricaturish limitations imposed on it by the educational elite and by the genteel tradition. From the earliest years of an individual through the latest ones to be served by an expanding program of adult education, there can be a vocational approach which will exploit every possible device for making men think, for making them sensitive to authentic and imperative problems, for enriching the making of a living so that it becomes more than a casually neglected instrument.[17]

Vocational education can be more important to individuals if it recognizes that a man's occupation is the greatest factor in determining his entire life-style in addition to earning his living. A means to earning a living is very important to the individual and acquiring skills is a necessary and vital part of one's education. A program that puts nearly all of its emphasis on developing job or intellectual skills is not defensible, as both sets of skills are needed by all citizens.

Vocational education is education for production to serve the ends of the economic system and is said to have social utility.

Placing a major emphasis on production and social utility results in vocational programs that are too narrowly conceived. Developing man as a tool of production becomes more important than developing man as an individual who is important in himself and who can apply his uniqueness to earning his living. The objectives of a program are often permitted to take precedence over the needs of the people enrolled.

Vocational education at the secondary level is concerned with preparation of the individual for initial entry employment.

Vocational education programs tend to be geared to the needs of employers, which does not reflect the notion that vocational programs should be based on the needs of the individual. The assumption suggests that persons who do not plan to obtain a baccalaureate degree are the potential recipients of vocational education. It is not appropriate to prepare a youngster for the entire spectrum of an occupation in high school, but we can prepare him for employment at the entry level. With employment experience and further adult education he can advance.

Entry employment is defined simply as getting a job. Jobs may be obtained in a variety of fashions and thus there has been a reluctance to refine the relationship between vocational education and entry employment. Jobs obtained by secondary school vocational education graduates are expected to be well down in the employment structure. A high school vocational graduate does not enter the job market as an office manager, as a farm owner, or as a sales supervisor. He will enter at a much lower point in the structure and can work up to these positions through ability, desire, and hard work.

This assumption is based on the ideas that (1) There is a hierarchy in each occupation. Some jobs in the occupation require high school preparation and some require more. (2) There is no horizontal specialization function within a given job. All persons with a high school vocational background who become secretaries, for example, will be doing similar work. (3) In order to perform the work at an entry level, skill development takes precedence over other considerations. (4) A person entering employment in an organization is likely to perform a variety of vertical functions that provide for vertical progression in the organization.

The exact nature of the relationship between vocational education and entry employment is unclear, and it is becoming obvious that vocational education at the secondary level must do much more than provide for entry employment. Employers have not been able to tell us what skills and competencies are needed by high school graduates and our research has not identified them with any success. We know that there is a high degree of specialization within a given occupation or business; e.g., there are sales, service, research, maintenance, and other functions all within one organization. Large organizations are now diversified to the extent that few of them provide opportunity for both vertical and horizontal mobility. Movement and progression of employees is likely to be horizontal.

It is no longer likely that a future bank president will start as an assistant teller and progress vertically through the organization to the management level. Managers enter the banking business at the management level with specific educational experiences behind them. A person who starts as an assistant teller in a bank moves horizontally within the banking business: from a small bank to a larger bank, from a medium-sized bank to one with a large volume of business.

One function of vocational education at the secondary level is to provide its clientele with a broad conceptual frame of reference regarding the world of work. It should be related to what an occupational area is all about rather than all about an occupational area. Our concern for entry employment should not be with skills for a specific job, but skills that can be generalized to a life-style.

VOCATIONAL EDUCATION SHOULD BE ORIENTED TO THE MANPOWER NEEDS OF THE COMMUNITY. Vocational education recognizes that everybody must learn to work since eventually everybody must work. It is appropriate to examine "what is" so that one can identify "what ought to be." Work includes what is done by the plumber, the student, the postman, the major, the senator, the PTA president, the Lions Club member, the farmer, the mechanic, the plasterer, the bulldozer operator, and the teacher. We act as though it were true that because these persons have experience, they know what kind of education it takes to become a productive worker at one's job. The task of the school is to prepare children to become the next generation of workers. To do so requires that we keep sharp eyes, receptive ears, and working hands in the community work roles.

This philosophy suggests that the immediate community is reality both now and for the future. Vocational educators are to bring that reality to fruition through the curriculum of vocational programs in the classroom. This can be done through a variety of techniques. Primary among these is assessment of community needs through a community survey, which determines the nature and scope of vocational programs needed, the courses required, the materials and equipment needed, and the time that should be devoted to teaching a particular subject or developing a particular skill. In addition, the survey answers the questions of requirements for entering and being promoted in an occupation.

Another technique in serving the community is through advisory councils or boards. Persons who possess knowledge by virtue of occupational experience or who are in a leadership role or a position of power are asked to join a group to help plan, guide, and implement vocational programs. These boards may be asked to address themselves to many of the concerns raised in the community survey. The advisory committee in technical education has always assumed a stronger role than advisory committees in other vocational programs. In addition to its normal duties, the advisory committee in technical education is usually asked to make recommendations concerning training needs, course content, instructor qualifications, program evaluation, student recruitment, and counseling of students.

Early in our history occupational preparation did not depend on formal programs. A boy learned to farm by imitating his father. An apprentice learned his trade from the master tradesman with whom he lived. Specialization within occupations and dependence upon schools for formal occupational preparation have loosened these community ties. The techniques of community survey and advisory boards attempt to maintain the past relationship between the community and vocational education.

In the past, the community has provided the basis for vocational education curriculum content, method, and teaching process. The community also provided job placement after training. The validity of the relationship between community and vocational education requires a reexamination, for the Commission on Vocational Education, as early as 1914, pointed out that it had undergone change. They said a man may be born in Indiana, trained in Massachusetts, and spend his days as a machinist in California. Iron was smelted in Pennsylvania, made into plows in Wisconsin, and used in Oregon. Community, as traditionally defined by vocational educators, requires two components: territorial proximity and social completeness. These two conditions are no longer present, as Fischer and Thomas point out:

As the metropolis grows, the factor of territorial proximity becomes increasingly meaningless, as in the case of say New York, Chicago, or Los Angeles. Social completeness, that condition when the local community is the source of all the basic functions of human living, departed when suburbia grew like a rust on the edge of the hard core of the city, sapping the heart strength, diversifying the commitment of the city workers.[18]

Community as viewed here has lost its significance as the primary factor in determining curriculum for local vocational education programs. Pumper was able to divide the state of Wisconsin into four separate and discrete areas.[19] These areas varied in agricultural manpower need projections, type of agricultural production, and other economic characteristics. The eastern area of the state had 39 percent of the state's employees in the meat producing industry, while the northern area had no employees in this category. The northern area had 1 percent of the state's employees in the farm machinery industry while the western area had 6 percent, the central area 5 percent, and the eastern area 88 percent. The northern area had nearly all of the state's employees in the lumbering industry. Thus, there were readily discernible differences in types of employment available in communities in Wisconsin where vocational agriculture was taught. Pumper took a random sample of 60 percent of the vocational agriculture teachers in each economic area. He determined the subject matter units taught and the amount of time devoted to the teaching of each. There were 131 subject matter units identified that were grouped to form 16 subject matter areas. If vocational agriculture teachers were indeed basing their programs on local needs, the amount of time devoted to each subject matter area would have been different for each of the four economic areas. Pumper's findings revealed this not to be true. Significant differences in percent of time allotted to teaching a subject matter area varied from one economic area of the state to another in only three of the sixteen subject matter areas identified.

This does not imply the lack of a significant relationship between the community and vocational education. The community does provide an opportunity for students of vocational education to obtain valuable occupational experiences that enhance their vocational development. A high school student may obtain work experiences in landscaping in LaPlata, Maryland. His first job may be with a nursery in Lansing, Michigan. Thus, the significance of the community to the local program of vocational education has shifted from being the site for both training and employment to being primarily the site for training. After these educational experiences are obtained in the local community, employment may be obtained in the much larger community of a geographic area, state, or the nation.

VOCATIONAL EDUCATION SHOULD BE EVALUATED ON THE BASIS OF ECONOMIC EFFICIENCY. The notion of economic efficiency has been with vocational education for a long time and is usually comprised of three subtopics.

VOCATIONAL EDUCATION IS ECONOMICALLY EFFICIENT WHEN IT PREPARES STUDENTS FOR A SPECIFIC JOB IN THE COMMUNITY ON THE BASIS OF MANPOWER NEEDS. The "real job" is what we are looking for. Vocational education is best when it prepares students for real jobs that exist in the community and that they want. The milieu of the job for which the student is to be prepared should be duplicated in the classroom in order to use the equipment and practices identical to that found on the job. Roberts has suggested that it is probably desirable to teach only for those trades and occupations in which real jobs can be provided.[20]

This philosophy requires that vocational education consist of the knowledge, skills, and attitudes the student will be expected to exhibit or perform when he completes his preparation. This can be accomplished only when the vocational educator can identify the specific requirements of the job. The job analysis technique, developed by Dr. Charles R. Allen, becomes the primary tool in making this determination. The extent that the curriculum for the vocational program reflects the performance skills required by present workers in a particular community on a specific job is the criteria for determining efficiency.

VOCATIONAL EDUCATION IS EFFICIENT WHEN IT INSURES AN ADEQUATE LABOR SUPPLY FOR AN OCCUPATIONAL AREA. An expanding economy needs an adequate labor supply. There must be a steady stream of workers entering the labor pool prepared to fill the jobs that exist. There must be a reasonable match between the number of workers who possess a particular skill and the number trained. Too many or too few workers is bad. According to Arnstein, "Vocational education, to be effective, must be related to the labor market. Specifically it must be planned on the basis of labor-market predictions."[21]

Vocational educators drew this relationship between labor supply and demand during World War I. The Smith-Hughes Act was passed by Congress shortly before America's involvement in the war. The first mobilization of vocational education resources was toward the war effort and its first successful venture made trained personnel available as rapidly as the military and industrial complex could use them. The rapid mobilization of vocational education enabled us to convert from a peacetime to a wartime economy rapidly. These efforts reduced the time required to achieve a victory. "In wartime, the war effort comes first" was the slogan of the U.S. Office of Education during World War II, when vocational education was again called upon to mobilize the wartime economy.

An adequate labor supply is necessary during peacetime. Vocational education programs increase the efficiency of modern industry by making available to workers opportunities to acquire additional skills and information.[22] These opportunities provide him with a feeling of security and make him a better citizen. When such opportunities are utilized, they reduce the time required to learn new techniques and decrease the time the worker operates at less than normal efficiency. Given adequate lead time and a system of detecting future needs, vocational educators will have the new worker prepared for employment at the time he is needed by industry. They will also have programs to upgrade worker skills as new technology dictates their need. The ability of vocational education to insure an adequate labor supply and to upgrade the skills of present workers is another criteria for determining efficiency.

VOCATIONAL EDUCATION IS EFFICIENT WHEN THE STUDENT GETS THE JOB FOR WHICH HE WAS TRAINED. "In the opinion of many, the acid test of the quality of a vocational education program is the placement of students in the occupations for which they receive instruction." This could be quoted from almost any early book about vocational education. Follow-up studies have been conducted by all areas of vocational education in an attempt to determine how efficient they have been. The U.S. Office of Education conducts annual statewide surveys to determine the occupational status of those persons who have completed vocational-technical education programs. Often students of vocational education are compared with the students of general education. At other times they are compared with former students of vocational education. The American Institute of Research conducted a comprehensive study of vocational graduates.[23] Their criteria for efficiency was whether or not students of vocational education obtained jobs for which they were trained.

Efficiency has been used by vocational educators in a variety of circumstances. It has been used to answer critics to justify vocational education. It has become a basis for a philosophy of vocational education. This view of efficiency has not shown a parallel concern for the individual. Vocational education is efficient when it develops a worker who reaches maximum production at least cost to employers and with the least waste of national resources. This subconscious and sometimes overt assumption regarding efficiency that has dominated vocational thinking is probably grossly accurate. There are indeed manpower needs for occupational areas that ought to be studied for their implications to vocational education programs.

These original assumptions concerning vocational education and the world of work were at one time accurate. As the guiding principles for vocational education (as it was developing in the last two centuries), they did possess reliability, validity, and consistency. When developed, they were based on a particular philosophy and for a particular social condition. Both man and the social conditions have changed. The central thesis of Venn's writings in *Man, Education and Work* was addressed to this point.[24] He stated that technology created a new relationship between man, his education, and his work. This indicated that the old assumptions needed to be reexamined.

NOTES

[1]Melvin W. Barnes, "Planning and Effecting Needed Changes in Urban and Metropolitan Areas," in *Planning and Effecting Needed Changes in Education*, eds. E. L. Morphet and C. C. Ryan (New York: Citation Press, 1967), p. 204.

[2]Tom C. Venable, *Philosophical Foundations of the Curriculum* (Chicago: Rand McNally & Co., 1967), pp. 10–12.

[3]Thaddeus Stevens, "An Appeal for Tax-Supported Schools," in *Hazard's Registry of Pennsylvania*, 15, no. 18 (May 2, 1835), 283–87.

[4]Educational Policies Commission, *The Purposes of Education in American Democracy* (Washington, D.C.: National Education Association, 1938), pp. 50, 72, 90, 108.

[5]Louis Fischer and Donald R. Thomas, *Social Foundations of Educational Decisions* (Belmont, Calif.: Wadsworth Publishing Co., Inc., 1965), pp. 120–24.

[6]Gerald W. Johnson, "Overloaded Democracy," *Harper's*, 199, no. 1192 (1949), 84.

[7]*Unemployed Out-of-School Youth Survey* (Cleveland: Bureau of Educational Research, Cleveland Public Schools, 1962).

[8]Patricia C. Sexton, *Education and Income* (New York: The Viking Press, Inc., 1961).

[9]F. Theodore Struck, *Vocational Education for a Changing World of Work* (New York: John Wiley & Sons, Inc., 1945), Chap. 7.

[10]Roy W. Roberts, *Vocational and Practical Arts Education*, 2nd ed. (New York: Harper & Row, Publishers, 1965), Chap. 20.

[11]Melvin L. Barlow, "The Challenge to Vocational Education" in *Vocational Education*, ed. M. L. Barlow, 64th Yearbook of the National Society for the Study of Education (Chicago: University of Chicago Press, 1965), p. 5.

[12]*Education for a Changing World of Work—Report of the Panel of Consultants on Vocational Education* (Washington, D.C.: Government Printing Office, 1963), pp. 15–16.

[13]Maureen Woodhall, "The Economics of Education," in J. Robert Warmbrod, *Review and Synthesis of Research For the Economics of Vocational Education* (Columbus, Ohio: Center for Vocational and Technical Education, 1968), p. 4.

[14]Charles A. Prosser and Charles R. Allen, *Vocational Education in a Democracy* (New York: Century Co., 1925), pp. 35, 64.

[15]John S. Brubacher, "Should Liberal Education Bake Bread," *Liberal Education*, 45, no. 4 (1959), 539.

[16]Sing-Nan Fen, "Vocational and Liberal Education: An Integrated Approach," *School Review*, 69, no. 2 (1961), 209.

[17]George R. Geiger, "An Experimentalist Approach to Education," in *Modern Philosophies and Education*, ed. John S. Brubacher, 54th Yearbook of the National Society for the Study of Education, Part I (Chicago: University of Chicago Press, 1955), pp. 153–54.

[18]Fischer and Thomas, *Social Foundations of Educational Decisions*, p. 140.

[19]Fred J. Pumper, "Determination of Subject Matter Units Taught in Wisconsin and the Extent of Contribution Made Toward Meeting the National Objectives of Vocational Agriculture" (Ph.D. diss. University of Wisconsin, 1968), pp. 29, 31, 98.

[20]Roberts, *Vocational and Practical Arts Education*, p. 545.

[21]George E. Arnstein, "The Technological Context of Vocational Education," in *Vocational Education*, ed. M. L. Barlow, p. 54.

[22]Roberts, *Vocational and Practical Arts Education*, p. 531.

[23]Max U. Eninger, *The Process and Product of T & I High School Level Vocational Education in the United States*, (Pittsburgh, Pa.: American Institute for Research, 1965).

[24]Grant Venn, *Man, Education and Work* (Washington, D.C.: American Council on Education, 1964), pp. 1–2.

5

DEFINITIONS FOR
VOCATIONAL EDUCATION

THE ACCIDENT THEORY

A major factor in influencing vocational education in terms of social and philosophical foundations are the definitions that have been applied to it and that have given it meaning and substance. In the history of vocational education a number of definitions have emerged, each with a significant impact. And a series of recurring themes has been apparent through these definitions.

Vocational education as a social institution was formalized and defined in the late nineteenth and early twentieth centuries. Its early definition was guided by a theory that has prevailed throughout much of history: the "accident theory," which was at its peak of popularity when the Smith-Hughes Act was passed in 1917. It holds that one has little control over his environment and therefore must mold his life to what exists rather than attempt to adjust, or modify, or rationally consider his surroundings. The accident theory places major emphasis on environmental forces, which are external to the individual while they minimize the individual. In other words, the environment is an active variable and the individual is a passive variable. For example, it is regarded as a chance or accident if you happened to be born to a dock worker, if you are 5 feet, 8 inches, high, or if you are left-handed. It is simply by chance that you heard that the local baker needed a helper and that you went to see him and got the job.

During this era most people argued that people needed to be "fitted" or "matched" to jobs. Persons from the farm as well as the city were potential workers if they could acquire a skill. It was argued further that the work to be done determined who was to perform it, not vice versa. Any person could be matched to and, therefore, could perform nearly any type of work if he possessed the physical abilities and mental capacities. His interests, level of maturity, aptitudes, and so on had little if anything to do with the type of job that he was to eventually obtain. Primary consideration was given to the fact that one industry needed ten machinists, another seventeen meat cutters, and a third eight bakers. Persons from the pool of raw manpower had to be "fitted" to these jobs. It was simply a matter of accident or fate as to which persons filled which jobs.

Who was to fit these unskilled candidates for the available jobs? Industry could have done the job, but was not prone to assume a social role. The public expressed reservations about entrusting the training of its youth to the captains of industry. Organized labor was fighting for its life and had little time for such matters. The apprenticeship system could have provided the service, but its indenture period was too long for youth as well as their parents. Technological advancements had also provided alternatives to the same jobs. The educational community was apprehensive about vocationalism in the schools: It was considered unwise to recognize vocational education as a necessary and legitimate form of education deserving full status and support. But people refused to take "no" for an answer and continued to urge the public school system to help in the task of "fitting" workers for jobs. One author commented: "If the marriage had to be by shotgun, that was the way it had to be. Vocational education was pushed into the educational system; when it came in, it did so on its own terms." The choices made regarding the philosophy, purpose, and definition of vocational education were more often the product of immediate circumstance than of thoughtful reflection.

In this social climate, the Smith-Hughes Act of 1917 was passed. It was the first national act to designate federal monies directly to vocational education. Here Congress drew upon the prevailing "accident theory" to define vocational education. Sections 10 and 11 of the Smith-Hughes Act stated that vocational education was that education

which is under public supervision or control; that the controlling purpose of such education shall be to fit for useful employment; that such education shall be of less than college grade and that such education be designed to meet the needs of persons over fourteen years of age who have entered or who are preparing to enter work (work of the farm or the work of a trade or industrial pursuit).

The words "fit" and "work" are emphasized in the above definition. Vocational education was to provide a worker with skill so that he would be fit to be employed in a job; he was to be "fitted" so that he better matched the job.

LEGAL DEFINITIONS

There are many legal definitions of vocational education: how vocational education is defined by law. Since the majority of laws defining vocational education are federal, most legal definitions reflect how vocational education is defined by the federal government. These legal definitions are critical since they specify how, for what purpose, and to what extent federal monies may be spent for vocational education. All too often this legal definition is interpreted by state and local officials as the only definition of vocational education.

SMITH-HUGHES DEFINITION (1917)

We just discussed the definition of vocational education in the Smith-Hughes Act of 1917, which stated that vocational education was training of less than college grade to fit for useful employment. The George-Deen Act of 1936 and the George-Barden Act of 1946 did not appreciably change this definition, but did add more disciplines and services. The George-Deen Act specified that federal monies could be expended for distributive occupations. The George-Barden Act added the salaries of vocational counselors and research to this list.

There are a number of reasons, in addition to the prevailing social philosophy, why the legal definition of vocational education was so narrowly constructed in 1917. These reasons are deeply rooted in circumstances of the decades preceding World War I. Venn discusses them as a part of the following concepts.[1]

1. *Uniformity.* At the time the legislation was enacted, few school administrators had any familiarity with what the experienced vocationalists in the National

Society for the Promotion of Industrial Education considered the elements of a good vocational program, and so the vocationalists made sure that these elements were written into the law. The act prescribed what courses were to be supported, and set the conditions under which they must be taught. Thus vocational education tended to become uniform in character throughout the country. More important, vocational education has tended to remain uniform down through the years, as the very detail of the act prevented Federal support for a great deal of possible experimentation with new programs.

2. *Duality.* The historic antipathy of many great educators led the early vocationalists to believe that the integrity and success of a Federal program would depend on its administration by people familiar with and sympathetic to vocational education, and, consequently, the act's administrative provisions were so drawn as to encourage the separate administration of the program.

3. *High School.* The drafters of the act wanted to bring vocational opportunities to the widest possible audience. In 1917, the means lay in putting vocational education in the high school, which for the "industrial classes" served as the capstone of the educational system. The "less than college grade" provision . . . tended to keep vocational education identified as a high school function, one outside the interest or concern of higher education.

4. *Practical.* Out of the old useful-practical concept came provisions in the act that, for example, vocational agriculture students had to participate in at least six months of directed or supervised farming practice, and trades and industry students must spend at least one-half of the instruction time in shop work on a useful or productive basis. The authors of the act, bearing in mind what had happened to the manual arts, took no chance that the utilitarian aspects of the new program were going to be unduly encroached upon by hostile general educators.

5. *Terminal.* The program, with its heavy emphasis on shop-farm experience, was designed to fit its graduates for useful employment, and not for additional study beyond high school. Any vocational program designed for credit toward the baccalaureate degree was declared ineligible for support. The program was to be terminal because it was tailored to fit into an institution, the high school, which in 1917 was the terminal point in education of almost all students the program was designed to serve.

6. *Track.* Despite American abhorrence of European track systems, the practical and terminal provisions of the law meant that the student electing the vocational program after the ninth grade was severely limiting chances for continuing his education beyond high school. But again, in 1917, this could hardly have been considered a problem.

7. *Farm-craft.* The vocational subjects chosen for Federal support were drawn from the particular demands of the contemporary rural and industrial economy.

8. *Shop.* The drafters of the act made the assumption that the student should be taught in a fully equipped school shop by a professional teacher with practical experience. In a period of comparatively slow technological change, it was

valid to assume that the institutionalization of school equipment and teacher experience would present few problems of obsolescence.

9. *Vocation.* The act, with its emphasis on relatively narrow, practical, terminal training, implicitly assumed that student preparation for future retraining was not important, that the training it gives is "vocational" and for life.

As late as 1962 the legal underpinnings of vocational education were still based on the circumstances and assumptions of the nineteenth century. It seems oddly inconsistent that a field like vocational education, closely related to a constantly and dramatically changing world of work, is defined by such outdated circumstances.

VOCATIONAL EDUCATION ACT OF 1963

The Vocational Education Act of 1963 marked the beginning of a broader legal definition for vocational education, but broader in only one sense. It qualified more vocational services to receive federal support and it expanded vocational guidance to support all vocational service areas. The act specified that:

The term vocational education means vocational or technical training or retraining which is given in schools or classes under public supervision and control or under contract with a State Board or local educational agency, and is conducted as part of a program designed to fit individuals for gainful employment as semi-skilled or skilled workers or technicians in recognized occupations (including any program designed to fit individuals for gainful employment in business and office occupations, and any program designed to fit individuals for gainful employment which may be assisted by Federal funds under the Vocational Education Act of 1946 and supplementary vocational education acts, but excluding any program to fit individuals for employment in occupations which the Commissioner determines, and specifies in regulations, to be generally considered professional or as requiring a baccalaureate or higher degree). Such term includes vocational guidance and counseling in connection with such training, instruction related to the occupation for which the persons engaged as, or preparing to become, vocational education teachers, teacher-trainers, and the acquisition and maintenance and repair of instructional supplies, teaching aids and equipment, but does not include the construction or initial equipment of buildings or the acquisition or rental of land. [Public Law 88–210, Part A, Section 8(1)]

In most respects the 1963 act incorporated changes in vocational education. Nearly all of them were in the direction of expansion, but not more flexibility.

1. It permitted instruction in all occupational fields and levels other than those defined as professional.

2. It expanded the clientele to be served as: (a) those in secondary schools, and (b) those preparing to enter the labor market who had completed or discontinued their formal education.

3. To serve the above clientele, vocational education programs were authorized through a wide variety of public institutions (comprehensive high school, area schools, junior and community colleges, and residential schools).

4. It authorized 10 percent of the annual appropriation to be used for research and for experimental and pilot programs.

Though the 1963 legal definition did expand vocational education, it was shaped and influenced by the prior 1917 legal definition. The nine concepts that Venn criticized regarding the 1917 definition could also be addressed to the 1963 definition, but with somewhat less severity.

VOCATIONAL EDUCATION AMENDMENTS OF 1968

In 1968, as the Vocational Education Act of 1963 was being amended, a new legal definition of "vocational" was formulated. It specified that:

The term "vocational education" means vocational or technical training or retraining which is given in schools or classes under public supervision and control or under contract with a State Board or local educational agency and is conducted as part of a program designed to prepare individuals for gainful employment as semi-skilled or skilled workers or technicians or sub-professionals in recognized occupations and in new and emerging occupations or to prepare individuals for employment in occupations which the Commissioner determines, and specifies by regulation, to be generally considered professional or which requires a baccalaureate or higher degree; and such term includes vocational guidance and counseling in connection with such training or for the purpose of facilitating occupational choices; instruction related to the occupation or occupations for which the students are in training or instruction necessary for students to benefit from such training; job placement; the training of persons engaged as, or preparing to become teachers in a vocational education program or preparing such teachers to meet special education needs of handicapped students; teachers, supervisors, or directors of such teachers while in such a training program; travel of students and vocational education personnel while engaged in a training program; and the acquisition, maintenance, and repair of instructional supplies, teaching aids, and equipment; but such term does not include the construction acquisition or rental of land.

This legal definition recognizes "new" and "emerging" occupations (even as late as 1963, the term "recognized occupations" was a part of the definition of vocational education). Another significant feature is its very broad reference to vocational guidance, specifying that vocational education includes "vocational guidance and counseling . . . for the purpose of facilitating occupational choices." Vocational education, as legally defined in the 1968 amendments, is considered appropriate for curricular considerations for junior high school pupils when it is offered to help them make better occupational choices. It is to be noted, however, that the legal definition still emphasizes (1) vocational education primarily as a high school and post–high school function, (2) useful and productive activities, (3) that graduates are expected to enter employment related to their area of training, (4) "tracking" those who elect vocational education, and (5) the institutionalization of teacher experience, school equipment, and school facilities.

DEFINITIONS BY GOOD AND HARRIS

Two standard references in the field of education are the *Dictionary of Education* (1959), by Carter V. Good, and the *Encyclopedia of Educational Research* (1960), edited by Chester W. Harris. Their definitions of vocational education reflect the same theme of fitting a man for work. Good, for example, defines vocational education as: "a program of education below college grade organized to prepare the learner for entrance into a particular chosen vocation or to upgrade employed workers."[2]

The *Encyclopedia* describes vocational education in the following manner:

Vocational education is education for work—any kind of work which the individual finds congenial and for which society has a need. Vocational education is specialized education as distinguished from general education. The American Vocational Association has defined vocational education as education designed to develop skills, abilities, understandings, attitudes, work habits, and appreciations needed by workers to enter and make progress in employment on a useful and productive basis.[3]

These definitions continue the theme of "fitting" man for work. A new dimension was added by Harris: He assumed that if a job were vacant it was needed by an institution in society; the person who filled the job was being useful as well as productive. In addition, according to Harris, the worker should find some happiness, some congeniality, in the job that he has been fitted for.

OBSERVATIONS

The definitions formed when the accident theory was in vogue have continued to dominate vocational education. They give primary emphasis to skills and work and secondary emphasis to the learner by simply ignoring a wide range of individual needs, concerns, desires, and development.

A major focus of the prevailing definitions is toward groups or classes of persons who enroll in vocational programs. This can be noted by such phrases as "persons over fourteen years of age," "who have entered upon," and "to upgrade employed workers." A similar comment is offered in terms of the level at which vocational programs are offered. This point may be noted in references to vocational education that specify "less than the baccalaureate level," and vocational education being for "semi-skilled, skilled, technical or sub-professional workers." Also, vocational education, as guided by these definitions, is limited to existing jobs in preparation for entry or upgrading abilities needed to perform these jobs as well as to "new and emerging occupations."

There is also a major stress on skill development. It is assumed that in order to be a productive and useful worker, skills are more important than individual development. To participate in vocational education programs guided by these definitions one needs to have passed through the exploratory phase of one's career development and be entering or already in the establishment phase.

Associated with this is another area of concern. In the beginning of the twentieth century there was little research and literature dealing with the processes of growth and development. Thus, it was not possible to reflect concepts of growth and development in definitions of vocational education. Now, nearly three-quarters of a century later, there is a significant accumulation of literature concerning human growth and development and how it affects the individual. Vocational education has tended to ignore this body of research.

Perhaps the most striking comment on the established definitions is their total reliance on what has been called "social utility." These definitions require vocational education to fit a man for a job rather than to help him explore and establish himself in a career. In essence, this is a perplexing use of two phrases: vocational training and vocational education.

Vocational training is concerned with social utility; its specific purpose is to fit a man for a job. The individuals undergoing training are channeled into a pattern of similarity by a narrow training program. *Voca-*

tional education, on the other hand, being free of exclusive concern for social utility, should be concerned with the individual's welfare. Its purpose should be to assist him in exploring a career, not in fitting him to a specific job.

ADDITIONAL DEFINITIONS

BARLOW, STRUCK, CONANT

One has to exhaustively search the literature to find definitions of vocational education that escape the somewhat negative aspects of some of the comments we have just noted. Barlow attributes this to the influence of federal participation in vocational education.[4] In the mid-twenties, one writer indicated that "vocational education means getting people ready and keeping them ready, for the types of service we need." He further felt that the term had no limitations as to kind or level of such needed services and that vocational education was good education, good sociology, good economics, and good democracy.

In 1945, Struck offered another broad perspective of vocational education: "Vocational education refers to the experiences that enable one to carry on successfully a socially useful occupation."[5] As a definition, it embraced indirect as well as direct education, out-of-school as well as in-school experiences, and, most important of all, it gave primary consideration to the developing individual and not to the skill he was to learn. The full implication of this definition was lost even on Struck. He later stated that "the central objective of vocational education is to train each person to perform useful work efficiently."

By the late 1950s, some common understandings had emerged in regard to a broader perspective of vocational education. They came from a repeated echoing of such phrases as "a total vocational education program," "serve in-school and out-of-school youths as well as adults," and "prepare for a life of work." Conant, in 1959, was able to formulate the following definitions of vocational education.

The controlling purpose of vocational education programs at the high school level is to develop skills for useful employment. These programs relate school-work to a specific occupational goal but involve more than training for specific job skills.

Vocational education is not offered in lieu of general academic education, but it grows out of it, supplementing and enhancing it. Vocational education is an integral part of the total education program and requires aptitude that students at the lowest academic level do not have.[6]

Most vocational educators embraced this as an accurate definition of vocational education. It encompassed many of the things that they would like to have said about vocational education. Barlow used Conant's views as the primary definition of vocational education in the *1965 Yearbook of the National Society for the Study of Education*.[7]

HAMMONDS AND LAMAR

Hammonds and Lamar have formulated a definition that provides a framework for vocational education somewhat broader than the legal definition. They state:

.The guiding purpose of vocational education is to develop the competencies needed to enter or advance in a vocation. Education should aid individuals in discovering their vocational problems and in developing the specific abilities needed for vocational success—for the sake of the individuals and of society. This is the business of vocational education.

Vocational education deals with the "problems of vocation." They are different from one vocation to another and should be dealt with accordingly. It requires teachers and other educators who can recognize these differences and who are prepared to handle them.[8]

DRAPER

The National Association of Secondary School Principals had a number of questions regarding vocational education and commissioned Dale C. Draper, through its National Committee on Secondary Education, to undertake a fact-finding study. Draper's report, *Education For Work—A Report on the Current Scene in Vocational Education*, was presented in 1967.[9] He did not define vocational education directly, but it was evident from his writings that his definition had a broad perspective. Based on his study, the National Committee on Secondary Education formulated ten conclusions. Examples of these conclusions are:

- A basic obligation of the public school system is the preparation of all young people for effectiveness in the world of work.
- Modification of many traditional definitions and requirements of vocational education is needed to allow for expansion and variation.
- Vocational competence involves much more than what is generally called occupational, vocational, or technical education.
- Too exclusive an emphasis on the building of a specific set of skills must be avoided in vocational education.[10]

This endorsement reflects the committee's enthusiastic response to and support of a broad definition of vocational education.

FRANK

In the summer of 1965, nearly a hundred persons participated in a study on occupational and vocational education. They represented state and federal vocational education offices, technical institutes, junior colleges, industry, university graduate faculties (engineering, education, political science, and design), private foundations, and occupational associations. The group met at the Massachusetts Institute of Technology for six weeks and was directed by Nathaniel H. Frank, a professor of physics. Five subgroups of participants were formed to consider (1) educational goals and structure for vocational objectives, (2) educational design, (3) materials, processes, and systems, (4) teacher education, and (5) the gray area of so-called "general education."

The final report of this conference does not contain a definition of vocational education.[11] The framework within which the study group discussed vocational education was broader than that of Draper. They believe:

• that one objective of education for all youth should be preparation for occupation;

• that pupils at all levels should have some occupationally oriented education;

• that such schooling, part of the core of all education, should touch all of the capacities of an individual;

• that it should be viable in a rapidly changing technological society;

• that it should be open-ended, not terminal; and

• that it should be recognized as providing only part of the total continuing educational input to an occupational career.[12]

To implement this framework the group proposed and designed a totally new curriculum that would be less dependent on the written and spoken word and would be a new vocationally oriented educational path to begin at the junior high level: (a) for those who have not benefited from the traditional curriculum, and (b) as enrichment for academically oriented, high-achieving students.

SUMMARY

The growth of vocational education can be traced through the definitions that have been applied to it. It is difficult to measure the extent to which the various definitions have limited or enhanced its growth. At various points in its history it has been defined in terms of the program utility, the people who enroll, the level at which it is offered, the economic needs of a social system, and the manpower needs of the nation. Usually the current definition reflects a combination of all of these points with one being of major importance. The legal definition—promoting always the manpower needs of the nation—determines how the federal government desires its monies to be spent in developing pools of manpower and usually dwarfs other aspects of the definition. The original legal definition of vocational education was very narrow, forcing it to be monolithic in character and uniform in structure. Recent definitions are essentially more of the same.

Some reports and recommendations stress that vocational education should do something more than build pools of manpower. Hammonds, Draper, Frank, and Venn are examples of those educators who call for a broader perspective in defining vocational education. Frank's report, for example, recommends

that there be initiated a program of development of new curricular patterns and instructional materials for all students beginning with junior high school. In contrast to the traditional overwhelming dependence on the written and spoken word as the road to learning, these new patterns and materials propose to utilize the potential of experimental and investigative activity as a springboard to the acquisition of skills, to understanding and to the development of the ability to think. The intent of this approach is not only to open a new, vocationally oriented educational path for those who have not benefitted from the traditional curriculum, but also to enrich the learning of those who flourish under it.

Vocational education finds itself in a dilemma, even though the 1968 legal definition provides for expansion. On the one hand federal monies are still to be used to shape pools of manpower for employability. The federal government is concerned only with those persons who enter the labor market with less than the baccalaureate degree. On the other hand, it is possible to offer vocational education at the elementary school level when it helps to facilitate occupational choices. Many educators suggest that vocational education, being a part of the public school system, has a basic obligation to aid in the preparation of all youth—even those planning professional careers—for effectiveness in their careers. It seems reasonable to suggest that a vocational educator needs to develop a broad perspective of vocational education, recognizing that the legal definition of vocational education will encompass only a portion of that perspective.

NOTES

[1]Grant Venn, *Man, Education and Work* (Washington, D.C.: American Council on Education, 1964), pp. 64–66.

[2]Carter V. Good, ed., *Dictionary of Education* (New York: McGraw-Hill Book Company, 1959), p. 603.

[3]Chester W. Harris, ed., *Encyclopedia of Educational Research* (New York: The Macmillan Company, 1960), p. 1555.

[4]Melvin L. Barlow, "The Challenge to Vocational Education" in *Vocational Education*, ed. M. L. Barlow, 64th Yearbook of the National Society for the Study of Vocational Education, Part I (Chicago: University of Chicago Press, 1965), p. 5.

[5]F. Theodore Struck, *Vocational Education for a Changing World* (New York: John Wiley & Sons, Inc., 1945), p. 6.

[6]James B. Conant, *The American High School Today* (New York: McGraw-Hill Book Company, 1959), p. 123.

[7]Barlow, *Vocational Education*, p. 6.

[8]Carsie Hammonds and Carl F. Lamar, *Teaching Vocations* (Danville, Ill.: Interstate Printers & Publishers, Inc., 1968), p. 24.

[9]Dale C. Draper, *Education for Work—A Report on the Current Scene in Vocational Education* (Washington, D.C.: The National Committee on Secondary Education, National Association of Secondary School Principals, 1967).

[10]Ibid., pp. 109–11.

[11]Nathaniel H. Frank, *Final Report of the Summer Study on Occupational, Vocational, and Technical Education* (Cambridge: Science Teaching Center, Massachusetts Institute of Technology, 1965).

[12]Ibid., p. 9.

6

A MODEL OF
CONVENTIONAL
VOCATIONAL EDUCATION

RELATING VOCATIONAL AND GENERAL EDUCATION

Many variables must be considered as one thinks about vocational education. These variables can be related conceptually to formulate a model, which helps to present a much clearer understanding of the foundations of vocational education. Vocational education is a great deal more complex than the model shows, and in that sense it is an oversimplification. Some of its dimensions have been excluded so that the basic structure of the discipline may be shown. (This is a totally new venture and is continually being refined; a search of the literature reveals no previous models as such.[1])

A model of vocational education must first relate to the entire field of education. Figure 1 shows the general relationship between vocational and general education. General education begins at kindergarten and proceeds through senior high school into post–high school and adult education. Along the way it loses people. Grade twelve is its most con-

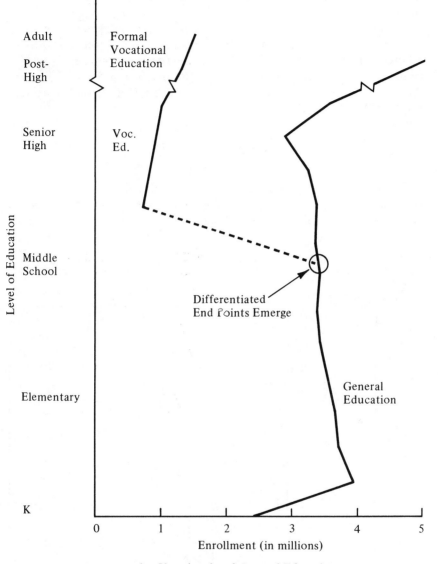

FIGURE 1.   Vocational and General Education

stricted point, after which it experiences an expansion at the adult level.

Vocational education does not appear until the secondary level, for the American public school system has differentiated ends or goals at this point, and vocational education is one of the differentiated goals. Thus, as a student emerges from the junior high level he selects which way he would like to leave the system, through the academic or the vocational exit.

A model of the structure of vocational education that shows a relationship among many variables at the secondary school level is shown in Figure 2. The assumptions or beliefs about vocational education (as discussed in Chapter 4) do not permit vocational education to assist with the growth and development problems of young people at the elementary and middle school levels.

CRITICAL ORIENTATION POINTS

Note that Figure 2 defines five critical orientation components of the vocational model: (1) the marketable skills orientation, (2) the work environment orientation, (3) the orientation of the social base on which

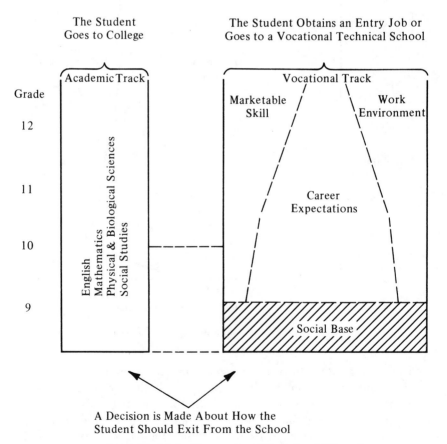

FIGURE 2.   A Model for Conventional Vocational Education

the vocational track is structured, (4) the orientation of the exit point, and (5) the orientation to specific career expectations.

THE MARKETABLE SKILLS ORIENTATION

SKILLS, UNDERSTANDINGS, AND THE LIKE ARE TAUGHT AS SPECIFIC ISOLATES. Vocational education is to fit the student with a specific marketable skill, such as welding, typing, carpentry, bricklaying, farming, shorthand, or selling. The longer a student stays in the vocational track the more likely he will obtain a marketable skill. Instruction at grades nine and ten provides less skill than does instruction at grades eleven and twelve, hence the line widens considerably after grade ten. The teacher determines what knowledge and understandings are needed by a worker to possess the skill to the degree that it can be marketed. The skills for one particular type of training are put together to form a vocational training program. For example, the separate skills needed by a welder (metal selection, amperage setting, etc.) are determined and then form the content of a training program.

Vocational education has abandoned faculty psychology of the early comprehensive school for habit psychology. Faculty psychology held that one possessed general faculties that could be trained by formal discipline into general habits of observation, appreciation, memory, reasoning, and judgment for effective use in meeting situations. Habit psychology promotes the notion that all habits are specific, not general. It further holds that all the habits in which the learner must be trained—his thinking habits, his doing habits, and the habits that enable him to conform to his environment—must be specific in terms of the job and its demands. Prosser and Allen, the fathers of contemporary thought patterns in vocational education, comment:

This being true, vocational education finds it necessary to discard any idea of training in the fundamentals of thinking, or of doing, or of adaptation to environment, even if it be assumed that there are any such things as these fundamentals. Instead it sets up the theory of specific occupational requirements as follows: Each occupation has its own set of equipment habits, doing habits, and thinking habits. These habits carry over very little into other occupations. Therefore, all vocational training must be specific in terms of the particular occupation for which the individual is to be trained.[2]

Thus, the one "equipment habit" in a vocational program is not shown to be related to other "equipment habits." It is specific to that job. You would be unfair to the student to teach relatedness as it would be taking time away from the pursuit and practice of the important "habits."

THE MARKETABLE SKILL IS ACQUIRED WITH A WIDE DEGREE OF PRECISION. Vocational education classes have taught a wide variety of skills. Bookkeeping, shorthand, display techniques, inventory procedures, register checking, welding, soldering, materials fastening, and binding buttonholes are but a few groups of those skills. Within each group there are many "sub-" or related skills. For example, to successfully construct a bound buttonhole, a student has to use the skills of marking, pinning, cutting, basting, folding, stitching, clipping, and making an inverted pleat. Thus, the students acquire not one but many skills as a part of their program.

Each skill is developed to a different degree by each student. This leads to the generalization that the skills are acquired with a wide degree of precision. Shorthand is one of the most "vocational" classes taught at the secondary level, if you use the traditional definition. Even in a second-year shorthand class, whose students are highly selected, the degree of precision has a wide variation. The difference between a top and a bottom student in a typical class may be as much as forty words per minute in the ability to take shorthand. The students are not rewarded accordingly after graduation, i.e., the top student in the class may not acquire the best job. (Top student here means the best student in the total of all the skill areas that go toward making a good secretary, stenographer, or whatever the course objective happens to be.) The student with a much lower ability may land the best-paying job, or the most prestigious job, or whatever other characterization goes toward making one job better than another.

We could rationalize and dismiss this as merely a reflection of individual differences in the students, for they differ in the rate, extent, style, and quality of their learnings. Since they differ individually, they will acquire to different degrees the skills taught them. To dismiss this notion so quickly is to ignore some important characteristics of vocational teaching and vocational programs.

Vocational educators constructed their programs in the early 1900s with the best psychology available. This appears to be one of the last major inputs of psychology into vocational education. Prior to this there was largely a fixed curriculum. Individual differences were taken into account chiefly by eliminating students; students who were less successful dropped out along the way. The programs designed in the early 1900s, when the school began to serve all youngsters, were based on the belief that those students who should not be guided into the academic high school—such judgments being based on intelligence—should be encouraged to try some other types of training. Cronbach identifies this as "adaptation [of the school curriculum] by matching goals to the individual."[3] Those students identified as "less intelligent" or "average" are encouraged to take easier courses, i.e., general mathematics rather than algebra. In effect, this solution is much more than a decision about education; it is a decision about the role, the style of life, and the level of contribution the individual is to make to society as an adult.[4] It was not until the mid-1960s that educators began to seriously implement an alternative. Now much emphasis is placed on all students acquiring an understanding of the basic discipline, even though some go farther and deeper than others. This is accomplished by altering instructional strategies. Some strategies are highly verbal and symbolic while others are more instrumental.

Differentiated goals became a reality within vocational education from the time of its formal entry into the public school. The student who was judged likely to fail in the academic course was given general "useful" courses. Different goals existed for courses within school systems and for individuals when they were placed in one of the two "tracks." Different goals did not exist within a track. The teacher demonstrated a particular skill and with appropriate Thorndikean reasoning allotted a number of hours or class sessions to its practice. The individuals who were able to grasp the skill quickly progressed and acquired some precision in its performance. Those who spent all of the allotted practice time acquiring the rudiments of the skill had no time left to acquire any precision. After the allotted time the teacher moved on to the next predetermined area of instruction. Little attention was really given to individual differences within the class, and the student who had a bare grasp of the fundamentals could gain precision by homework, during study halls, coming back after school, and so on. Once you have fixed instruction within an educational goal, though the goals are optional or differentiated, you discover a lack of a relationship between general ability and learning variables.[5] Individual differences do not account for the gain in performance.

Hence structure of program is at least one variable accounting for differences in performance when fixed time is allocated to the acquisition of a skill.

WORK ENVIRONMENT ORIENTATION

The real world for the vocational educator is the world of work, and an efficient vocational education is tied very closely to the occupational world. The milieu of the job for which the student is to be trained should be duplicated as much as possible in the vocational program. Time spent in the vocational track, particularly after grade ten, increases one's exposure to the work environment.

SPAN OF WORK. A quick look at the general work environment reveals little consistency within industries in regard to the span of work, which refers to the different types of work that are expected to be performed by a worker in the normal performance of his job. When vocational education received its expansive thrust in the early part of this century, there were some workers with an unlimited span of work. Workers were found who performed all the tasks associated with a particular job, which may have included selecting the raw material such as leather, cutting, stitching, nailing, and polishing it to make a shoe. Workers in the same shop would be repeating the same tasks to turn out the same type of product, each one responsible for his particular finished product. Perhaps a more vivid illustration is found in medicine, where the general practitioner or family doctor was the man of the hour. He was likely to perform the tasks associated with the diagnosis and treatment of eye, ear, and throat problems, of appendicitis, of obstetrics, and of pediatrics, as well as taking care of the day-to-day health problems of a family.

At the same time, some workers performed under a much more limited span of work. Some shops could be found where there were several people making one shoe: One cut the body of the shoe, another cut only the soles; one stitched the body, another tacked the soles. Machinists trained for World War I production were generally very specialized persons.

Two generalizations about the span of work are appropriate: One is that the small shops tended to have a wider span of work than did larger shops. This was particularly true of those larger shops run by managers for absentee owners. Another generalization is that the professional worker was likely to experience a wide span of work.

Given a work environment of an occupation that shows no particular pattern as to the span of work, how do you design a vocational program for that occupation? The assumptions of occupational needs and entry employment skills were operationalized. They dictated that in vocational programs the broadest possible span of work be prepared for. This was then narrowed by a consideration of community needs.

The span of work for a worker has undergone considerable change since the early 1900s.[6] Fewer and fewer workers are responsible for the making of an entire product; more and more workers are specialized. The generalization about the span of work that appears to be valid now is: Workers perform in a narrower span of work. Note for example the specialization within the air conditioning marketing field. Even when dealing with a relatively small unit of three to four tons to air condition a home, one company sells it, contracts with a specialized company to install it, who in turn contracts with a third company to maintain it. As companies specialize, their employees specialize. The assumptions of occupational needs, entry employment skills, and community needs do not provide adequate guidance to a vocational educator who is asked to design a vocational program for the home air conditioning field.

CONTROL OF WORK. Another dimension of the work environment is the worker's control of his work. The developments in this dimension parallel those of the span of work. A worker at one point could be described as having semiautonomous control of his work environment. Within reason he could determine how long he would take to perform a car tuneup; another could determine how many engine blocks he would drill in a given day, and both could determine when they might go to the bathroom.

Workers, excepting the professions, now have little or no control of their work environment. Time and pace are controlled by outside factors. The mechanic is guided by reference manuals that say how long it should take him to replace a drive shaft in a car, how long it should take him to replace a windshield, and how long it should take him to give a car a tuneup. An assembly line worker is guided by the pace of the assembly line, which can be speeded up without his consent and against his desire. Even the number of times a worker can go to the bathroom is disputed at contract time.

A large number of jobs are emerging in which the worker works somewhat independently, as in the case of the laboratory technician, the aluminum sider, and the roofer. At first glance it might be supposed that they have control of their work environment, but closer observation does not support this. The laboratory technician is expected to follow a rather detailed set of procedures and his pace is controlled by the number of doctors using the laboratory facilities. The aluminum sider and the roofer are expected to perform at a predetermined rate.

SOCIAL BASE

The third critical orientation component of the model is the social base on which the vocational program is built. "Social base" refers to those experiences, courses, and cognitive styles that supplement technical information and that are designed to teach the social skills and graces needed by the citizen-worker, such as human relations, citizenship, and communications.

Descriptively, the social base of vocational education can be described as being narrow; that is, it does not possess the breadth that it should. Figure 2 shows that the social base did not have any direct relationship with the other program of the school. It was thought that students enrolled in the vocational track needed fewer social skills than other students and that they could not learn academic subject matter to the same extent as other students. Consequently, special sections of English, Principles of Democracy, history, and so forth were credited by school officials for vocational students. The vocational sections were usually taught by the same teachers who taught the academic sections, and this was not necessarily bad. What resulted was bad. The result was a watered-down academic class in which the content was much less inclusive. In spite of the research support for the idea that cognitive styles of students differ, methods have not been questioned. The blame for all failures has been placed on the student.

For instance, somewhere in their program, most vocational students are asked to write a letter, usually to a company asking for information about a product, job opportunities, or to an educational agency asking about post–high school opportunities. When told that they need to write for their own information, a howl of protest is heard. "We can't write letters," they say, "since we are in dumb English. Only kids in smart English get to write letters." The students easily perceive the difference in content between sections.

That social skills are important to vocational students cannot be disputed. Table 5 shows some data collected from seventy-six large corporations.[7] These figures indicate that social skills are needed for workers to advance on the job or even to retain their job. Vocational teachers attempt to fill the gap by teaching some of the social skills themselves. They try to determine some of the basic ones needed and to expose the student briefly to them. Such social skills might include getting along with people, meeting a customer, answering the telephone, personal grooming, and how to conduct oneself during an interview. These activities comprise a very small portion of the teaching time.

ORIENTATION OF THE EXIT POINT

The fourth critical component is the orientation of the exit point. It is assumed that vocational education is designed to develop a specific marketable job skill, one that is oriented to the task of producing a consumer product. That is, the worker would be directly responsible for the production of a consumer product and would use a skill to directly manipulate some object in the production process.

Each act, experience, course, and event is designed to achieve this orientation. It is critical to vocational education, as Brookover and Nosow have pointed out.[8] It is so critical that it often becomes a justification of vocational programs as vocational educators compare their success to the success of other programs. Being so critical, it has become a logical starting point in the conceptual processes of vocational educators, particularly in determining what is to be taught. An idea of the marketable skill needed is obtained; it is then, determined what the student needs to know about the occupational skill and the work environment.

TABLE 5. Reasons for Discharge or Not Getting Promoted[7]

LACK OF SPECIFIC SKILLS	MOST COMMON CAUSES FOR DISCHARGE (PERCENT)	DEFICIENCIES PREVENTING PROMOTION (PERCENT)
Shorthand	2.2	3.2
Typewriting	1.6	2.4
English	1.6	5.2
Dictaphone	1.3	1.6
Arithmetic	1.3	3.0
Office Machines	.9	2.2
Bookkeeping	.6	1.4
Spelling	.6	2.7
Penmanship	.0	1.8
	10.1	23.5
CHARACTER TRAITS		
Carelessness	14.1	7.9
Noncooperation	10.7	6.7
Laziness	10.3	6.4
Absence for causes other than illness	8.5	3.7
Dishonesty	8.1	1.2
Attention to outside things	7.9	5.6
Lack of initiative	7.6	10.9
Lack of ambition	7.2	9.7
Tardiness	6.7	4.6
Lack of loyalty	3.5	4.6
Lack of courtesy	2.2	3.3
Insufficient care of and improper clothing	1.6	3.0
Self-satisfaction	.9	4.4
Irresponsibility	.3	.8
Unadaptability	.3	1.4
Absence due to illness	.0	2.4
	89.9	76.5

Adapted from a study by H. C. Hunt, Meriden, Conn.

CAREER EXPECTATIONS

Vocational education is also oriented to rather specific career expectations. Students are expected to have made a tentative commitment at grade nine or ten to an area of specialization, i.e., agriculture, business, home economics. Exposure to skill courses and work experiences help him narrow his career expectation during grades eleven and twelve. By the end of grade twelve the student should have a specific entry job identified and have the training necessary to get it or to enroll in a vocational-technical school. Vocational education, then, does not help a student explore career areas. It helps him narrow his career expectations within an area to a specific entry job upon high school graduation.

In one sense of the word, that is exploring. The point remains, however, that vocational education does not usually invest its resources in helping students explore alternative career areas.

ANOTHER CONSIDERATION

One final consideration should be made. The vocational track functions alongside the academic track. There is, however, limited contact between the two. Transfer by a student from one track to another is made quite difficult. Students at grade eleven or twelve who desire to transfer from one to the other have to generally go back to grade ten or nine. An eleventh grade academic student, for example, who becomes quite interested in a sales career, finds it difficult to transfer to a vocational business program with sales and merchandising concentration. Transfers of this nature are permitted if the student is willing to go back to enroll in a ninth grade general business course and a tenth grade typewriting course.

SUMMARY

It follows that if a change occurs in the factors that contribute to the orientation of the exit point, changes ought to follow at other critical points. The model presented here is basically an accurate reflection as one thinks about vocational education at the present time. It is not a model of what should be but rather of what is.

One further note of caution. You are urged to study the model in great detail before agreeing or disagreeing with it. Examine the critical stages in the development of vocational education and the model to see if you concur with the author's conclusions. How would you conceptualize the particular set of relationships that make up the complex discipline of vocational education?

NOTES

1Richard's Formula, developed in the 1920s, is not really a model. It stated $E \infty M + T + I$. Efficiency on the job (E) depends upon the possession of the necessary manipulative skill (M), the possession of the necessary technical knowledge (T), and the necessary intelligence (I). See Charles A. Prosser and Charles R. Allen, *Vocational Education in a Democracy* (New York: Century Co., 1925), pp. 42–44.

2Ibid., p. 197.

3Lee J. Cronbach, "How Can Instruction Be Adapted to Individual Differences," in

Learning and Individual Differences, ed. Robert M. Gagné (Columbus, Ohio: Charles E. Merrill Books, Inc., 1967), p. 26.

4Ibid.

5H. A. Woodrow, "The Ability to Learn," *Psychological Review*, 53, no. 3 (1946), 147–58.

6Sigmund Nosow and William Form, *Man, Work and Society* (New York: Basic Books, Inc., Publishers, 1962).

7Paul W. Boynton, *So You Want a Better Job* (New York: Mobil Oil Co., 1955), p. 4. Used by permission of Mrs. Anne Boynton.

8Wilbur Brookover and Sigmund Nosow, *A Sociological Analysis of Vocational Education in the United States, in Education for a Changing World of Work,* (Washington, D.C.: Government Printing Office, 1963), Appen. 3.

III

THE
PRESENT
PROGRAMS

7

THE CONTEMPORARY PROGRAM

INTRODUCTION

The contemporary program of vocational education reflects a cross section of the occupational world of work as it has been divided for funding and supervisory considerations. These divisions are gross categories of functional work areas, which include basic production: marketing, sales, and service; facilitating functions: personnel and public service; and home and family services. A division of vocational education is responsible for bridging the gap between the educational system and its part of the labor market; i.e., home economics education relates people employed or planning for employment in jobs requiring a knowledge of home economics; trade and industrial education relates to such job titles as mechanic, machinist, plumber, and stationary engineer; technical education relates to occupations "requiring applied technical knowledge and applied technical skill," such as engineering aide, computer technologist, and x-ray technician. The divisions of contemporary vocational education working with the functional work areas identified above are agriculture, trade and industrial, technical, distributive, business and office education, health occupations, and home economics. An examination of each division follows. Though brief, it is intended to convey the structure and scope of each division.[1]

Vocational education is administered and supported cooperatively by the local, state, and national governments. After an act has been passed by Congress, it is up to each state to develop a state plan. The U.S. Office of Education develops a set of guidelines for the state plans to follow based on the act and its legal interpretations. These are published in Vocational Education Bulletin No. 1 of the U.S. Office of Education.[2] A state plan designates the legal agency in a state to receive federal funds. This agency is responsible for their supervision and control. In addition, the state plan sets forth the conditions under which the legal agency will allocate funds to local districts, the purposes for which funds may be used, qualifications of personnel involved, cooperative arrangements with other agencies, and provision for a reporting system. Once a state plan has been approved by the U.S. Commissioner of Education, a state can receive monies and allocate them to local districts according to its state plan. In addition to improving vocational education, state supervisors are generally employed to see that funds are utilized according to the provisions of the state plan. Thus, state plans and state supervisors are important elements in the structure of vocational education.

Categorical funding, the practice of identifying or earmarking specific dollars for specific service areas, was discontinued with the passage of the 1968 amendments (see page 79). From one perspective, however, categorical funding was not discontinued. Rather, a set of vertical categories (each service area) was discontinued and replaced by a set of horizontal categories (disadvantaged students, exemplary programs, etc.) that apply equally to all service areas. The U.S. Office of Education, in one of its many reorganizations, deemphasized the service areas by reducing the number of supervisors and moving those remaining lower within the organization. A limited number of states followed this practice.

AGRICULTURAL EDUCATION

Enrollment in agricultural education for 1969 approached 850,705 and represented 10.8 percent of the total enrollment in vocational education programs. Classes are organized for both in-school and out-of-school students. The in-school classes are designed for youth who want to enter production agriculture and who want to prepare for agricultural businesses. Classes for full-time students at the post-high school level are expanding rapidly. These classes prepare students for work in such areas as horticulture, machinery repair, agricultural sales, and forestry. Classes for out-of-school students, always an integral part of vocational programs in agriculture, are usually designated as young farmer classes and adult farmer classes; they are designed for those who are getting established in farming and for established farmers who wish to improve their proficiency. Enrollment figures for all phases of the vocational agriculture program for 1975–1976 are projected to be at the 1,200,000 level, approximately 8.0 percent of the vocational education program.

The controlling purposes of agricultural education have been the occupations associated with farming. The Smith-Hughes Act of 1917 defined agricultural education as fitting for useful employment those who have entered upon or who are preparing to enter upon the work of the farm or the farm home. Seven objectives were identified to implement the aim of training present and prospective farmers for proficiency in farming. They were to develop the abilities to: (1) make a beginning and advance in farming, (2) produce farm commodities efficiently, (3) market farm products advantageously, (4) conserve soil and other natural resources, (5) manage a farm business effectively, (6) maintain a favorable environment, and (7) participate in rural leadership activities.

The Vocational Education Act of 1963 and the 1968 amendments define vocational education as that education designed to "fit individuals for gainful employment as semi-skilled or skilled workers or technicians in recognized occupations." This stimulated state and national leaders to urge the development of agricultural programs that were designed to prepare workers for the nonfarming phases of agriculture, now that it was legal to do so. Long before this, a significant number of vocational programs in agriculture at the local level attempted to meet the needs of those who desired to enter agri-business occupations. These programs were generally not favorably received beyond the local level. After 1963, educational programs to prepare for agri-business occupations were encouraged.

Schools that offer vocational education in agriculture are generally located in rural areas, where the high schools have small enrollments and limited teacher resources. The departments are known as "one-man departments," indicating that most high schools have one teacher of vocational agriculture. In addition, the teacher generally has four grades of high school classes that entail separate class preparations; adult programs; after-school supervision of occupational experience programs; and supervision of a student organization (Future Farmers of America).

Vocational agriculture at the high school level still retains the occupation of farming as its operational arena. Bulletin No. 1[3], which comprises the interpretation of vocational acts and is the guide that must be used for the development and approval of state plans, defines vocational education for those persons "over 14 years of age who have entered upon or are preparing to enter; (a) upon the work of the farm or farm home, or (b) any occupation involving knowledge and skill in agricultural subjects, whether or not such occupation involves work of the farm or of the farm home." Agri-business generally refers to the occupations in the entire food and fiber complex. It is assumed by many educators in agriculture that the best early preparation for the agri-business occupational complex is the same content as that needed for the occupation of farming. Later in high school or at the post–high school level, courses are offered for those students who may be interested in agri-business occupations.

BUSINESS AND OFFICE EDUCATION

Until the Vocational Education Act of 1963, this entire area of occupational education was not supported directly by federal monies, though a few states did include some business education in their federally aided program. Curricula in this area have generally been regarded as being in two categories: general business and vocational. This distinction is not accurate. Business educators suggest that they have three common objectives: (1) vocational, (2) personal use, and (3) the development of economic understanding. The president of the National Business Education Association comments:

With the event of the 1963 Vocational Education Act and the inclusion for the first time of business education for the office occupation for Federal financial support, there has been a sharpening of the differences among the objectives of business education.

There appears to be a tendency on the part of some to identify the objectives of business education with the source of financial support. Some would suggest that "vocational" business education is that which is reimbursed, and if it is not reimbursed it then is "general business education." As any review of the literature will reveal, the primary objective of business education from its very inception in the private business school in the mid 1800's to the present time has been vocational; that is, the preparation of men and women for jobs in business. This objective was not discovered or developed with the event of Federal reimbursement. The objectives of personal-use values and the development of economic understanding have paralleled the vocational objective from the beginning.

Since the present Federal legislation limits financial support to those aspects of the program that are classified as vocational, there is a danger that attempts will be made to divide programs and teaching and supervising personnel into categories of either "vocational" or "non-vocational." This classification just isn't possible since all programs in business education would have the three objectives presented in this editorial. It is recognized, of course, that certain courses within a program would be oriented more toward one objective than the other objectives. It is the thesis of this writer, however, that this grouping isn't desirable or feasible with respect to total programs.[4]

With the event of the 1963 Vocational Education Act, business education has been dichotomized into two categories: "reimbursed" and "nonreimbursed" programs. The nonreimbursed programs are generally sound vocational education programs; they simply do not receive federal monies and are thus not reported in statistical summaries at the state and national levels. Those business and office programs that are reimbursed are clerical and secretarial programs, though many clerical and secretarial programs are classified as nonreimbursed. It is difficult, then, to obtain an accurate picture of the extent of the total business and office education program. The clerical and secretarial programs reported in the reimbursed category reflect only a part of the vocational offerings in business and office education and, further, do not include any of the business programs designed for personal use or for economic understanding.

In 1969, enrollments in reimbursed business and office education totaled 1,835,124 students and comprised nearly one-fourth (23.2 percent) of all students in vocational education. Following the pattern of other vocational education service areas, office education offers programs at the secondary, postsecondary and at the adult levels. Enrollments at the secondary level for 1969 was slightly in excess of one million students. Projected enrollment for the year 1975–1976 approximates 3,250,000 students.

Vocational business and office education had its formative years in less formal, apprenticeship type of programs. When the number of apprentices trained failed to meet the demand of entry avenues to those occupations needing business skills, other techniques were sought. Programs organized in the public schools during the latter part of the nineteenth century provided the major avenue to those occupations. As business and office education programs emerged in the early twentieth century, the phrase "commercial education" became most popular. Some schools still refer to their business and office programs as commercial courses, though the term fails to describe the diversity of these offerings.

Work areas within the category of business and office occupations are quite diverse. Secretary, stenographer, typist, bookkeeper, accountant, office manager, and executive secretary are but a few of the areas classified in the larger category. Diverse programs reflect these differences.

A typical concentration of courses for a medium-sized high school employing two to three business teachers would be as follows:

GRADE	STENOGRAPHIC CONCENTRATION	CLERICAL CONCENTRATION	SALES AND MERCHANDISING CONCENTRATION
9	General Business	General Business	General Business
10	Typewriting I	Typewriting I	Typewriting I
11	Bookkeeping Shorthand I	Bookkeeping	Bookkeeping
12	Shorthand II Typewriting II*	Typewriting II Clerical Office Practice*	Salesmanship and Merchandising*

ELECTIVES

Consumer Economics
Advanced General Business
Business Law
Salesmanship
Personal Typewriting
Personal Shorthand and Note-Taking

*Whenever possible, an Occupational Experience Program is planned and conducted in connection with these senior courses.

Graduates of business and office education programs at the secondary level go on to postsecondary programs or enter the job market.

DISTRIBUTIVE EDUCATION

Enrollment in distributive education for 1969 was 563,431 and represented 7.3 percent of all students enrolled in vocational programs. Classes are designed for in-school youth as well as out-of-school youth and adults. The in-school program is designed for students in the eleventh and twelfth grades. The out-of-school programs are provided during or outside of normal working hours for employed youth or adults; they comprise over 70 percent of the enrollment in distributive education. Distributive education enrollment is expected to continue its present growth and should total approximately 1,350,000 by 1975.

Education for distribution is a program of instruction largely related to principles and practices of marketing and distribution. It is defined by Beaumont as a program of instruction in marketing, merchandising, and management with emphasis on training required for career development.[5] Three basic goals of distributive education are developed: (1) to offer instruction in marketing, merchandising, and management, (2) to aid in the improvement of techniques of distribution, and (3) to develop an understanding of the social and economic responsibilities associated with distribution in a free, competitive society.[6] In implementing these objectives, programs in distributive education are generally designed to develop social and salesmanship abilities, product knowledge, and merchandising techniques in students. Each of these areas may be offered through an entire course.

While in school the student enrolls in basic courses such as English, mathematics, and history. Nearly all schools utilize a two-year sequence of training for distributive education. Sanders and Beaumont identify three organizational patterns that are typical in high school.[7] In grade eleven enrollees acquire depth in subject matter that is common to all distributive occupations. This also prepares them for job possibilities, acquaints them with the world of work, and serves as a screening device for the following year. In grade twelve a related class is added that teaches the student about the specifics of a job. It is here that the student relates class assignments and job experience.

Practice in an employment environment is an integral part of distributive education programs. A job is usually obtained during the twelfth grade and entails an average of fifteen hours of work per week during the school year. Students work at all types of entry jobs. They are salespeople, stock boys, clerks, cashiers, and waitresses. Employers include retail stores, restaurants, motels, hotels, hardware stores, and pharmacies. A training agreement is usually developed to insure that the student is exposed to work in many departments of the business. Office and maintenance work areas are reserved for other programs. The teacher of distributive education is charged with the responsibility of coordinating the student's job. This entails supervising the student on the job to insure that he get adequate educational experiences. Usually a teacher needs an average of a half hour per week of coordination time for each student enrolled in the cooperative (related) class.

Approximately 70 percent of the persons enrolled in distributive education classes are out of school and are generally of two age groupings: the post–high school age group (out of school and under twenty-five years old) and the adult group (aged twenty-five to sixty-five). The former group usually is enrolled full time in some post–high school institution; the latter group holds jobs or has some other condition that prevents full-time school attendance. Goals of distributive education programs for these two groups are similar to those identified for the high school group, but are adjusted to meet the needs of out-of-school youth and adults.

HEALTH OCCUPATIONS

Occupations in the area of health are expanding rapidly, for a team concept has evolved. The previous single category of nurse—professional and registered—has given way to a variety of persons comprising a team. Now the professional nurse is supported by technicians of many types; practical nurses, and nurse's aides. Each category of worker has its own set of responsibilities, and each category below the level of professional nurse comprises an area for different training programs in vocational education. Enrollment in health occupations for 1969 was 175,101 students and comprised only 2.2 percent of all of the students enrolled in vocational programs. Enrollment statistics projected for the year 1975–1976 call for 450,000 in health occupations, approximately 3.2 percent of all vocational students. Writing in *Today's Health*, Wilber projects a need for nearly double the U.S. Office of Education projections.[8] He indicates that the health occupations will need an additional 750,000 trained persons by 1970.

Preparation for health occupations occurs at the high school and post–high school levels and includes full-time and part-time students. However, the majority of health occupations programs are at the post–high school level for full-time students. Of all these programs, practical nursing programs for in-school youth have the longest tradition and the largest enrollments. They are generally one year long and require approximately 2,000 hours of instruction.[9] The first four months are generally offered in a classroom setting, with the remaining time consisting of much supervised hospital experience and some classwork. Classroom work includes community health, conditions of illness, the human body, nutrition, geriatric nursing, and personal relationships. Upon completing a training program and passing a state examination, one is licensed to be a Licensed Practical Nurse (LPN).

In addition to practical nursing, programs are designed for medical assistants, medical laboratory assistants, dietary technicians, dental assistants, dental laboratory technicians, X-ray technicians, occupational therapists, physical therapists, operating room assistants, and nurse's aides. Training periods for these occupations may vary from a few weeks to three years. One trend in health occupations is the expansion of nurse's aide programs at the secondary level; many high schools are beginning to offer such a program in the twelfth grade.

HOME ECONOMICS EDUCATION

Enrollment in home economics education for 1969 total 2,449,052 students and represented 30.9 percent of all enrollment in vocational programs. Classes are organized for in-school as well as out-of-school clients; however, the vast majority of home economics education is offered at the secondary level to in-school youth. Classes at both high school and post–high school levels prepare students for homemaking and wage-earning occupations. Enrollment figures projected to the year 1975–1976 call for 2,100,000 in home economics programs, approximately 15.0 percent of all students enrolled in vocational programs.

Home economics education may be vocational in one of two senses. In the traditional sense it prepares students for homemaking by teaching those understandings, abilities, and attitudes that contribute toward effectiveness in homemaking. Confusion enters the definition at this point. Some states differentiate this objective by referring to those programs which do not request federal funds as being nonvocational. Those programs that do request federal funds are hence vocational. The other definition refers to those programs that prepare students for wage-earning occupations. This may be accomplished (a) by preparing young people to enter those service occupations that are related to home economics, (b) by helping girls to be wage-earners as well as homemakers, and (c) by helping girls achieve employability through human relations skills and work habits.

Basic to the homemaking objective is a belief in the importance of family life. The family unit possesses the potential for growth, development, and change, and it is assumed that education can enhance that inherent potential. Education for homemaking programs embraces the study of many phases of family living, including home management and family economics, family health, family and social relationships, child development and care, family nutrition, clothing and textiles, and family recreation.

Preparation for wage-earning occupations through home economics programs recognizes the dynamic changes that are taking place in the occupations of women. Some facts are: Nine out of ten women will work at paid employment sometime in their lifetime; women comprise 35 percent of the labor force; 37 percent of all women fourteen years of age and older are working; over 50 percent of all individuals enrolled in vocational education courses are women.[10] Programs for wage-earning occupations identify a particular job such as food service and commercial sewing. Students study the basic content of the job and the social ability associated with it. This latter category includes work habits, personal traits, finding employment opportunities, and securing a job.

The home project and occupational experience programs are essential to home economics instruction. Associated with the purpose of homemaking, the home project consists of undertaking a group of related activities such as child care and clothing construction. The teacher visits the home to supervise phases of the project and to assist the student who may have some difficulty with a particular skill. Summer employment of the teacher may be possible for this purpose. Occupational experience in wage-earning programs is similar to occupational experience programs in other areas of vocational education. Students obtain a job and are given some released school time to work at the job for which they are receiving training. Teachers are given time to supervise the students on the job.

TECHNICAL EDUCATION

Enrollment in technical education for 1969 totaled 315,311 students, making up 3.9 percent of all students enrolled in vocational education programs. Approximately 88 percent of these students were beyond high school. Nearly equal numbers were enrolled in postsecondary and adult programs. By 1975–1976, technical education is expected to experience a growth of 350 percent, with total enrollment projected to be 850,000.

Technical education programs prepare students for a variety of specialty and technological areas. They function as technical workers, technical specialists, manufacturing technicians, and engineering technicians. Jobs for technical education graduates are in business, industry and government, where they perform activities in maintenance, operation, construction, manufacturing, research and development, and sales.

Technical curricula are based on technical and practical knowledge requirements as well as basic mathematics and science. Instruction is usually offered in broad areas of technology such as electronics, mechanics, chemistry, aeronautics, production, instrumentation, data processing, and computer programming. These broad occupational areas represent a cluster of specific occupations.

TRADE AND INDUSTRIAL OCCUPATIONS

Enrollment in trade and industry programs for the year 1969 was 1,720,859 students and represented 21.7 percent of students enrolled in vocational education. Classes are organized for both in-school and out-of-school students, but nearly three out of four students are at the adult level. Postsecondary programs enroll only 8 percent of the trade and industry students, with secondary programs enrolling approximately 20 percent. Enrollments projected to 1975–1976 establish 4,850,000 enrollees in trade and industrial programs, which would comprise nearly 35 percent of all vocational students.

The major objective of trade and industrial education is to prepare workers for entry employment at a productive level with the necessary educational background to move ahead within the occupation and its related areas.[11] Such preparation includes occupational skills, technical knowledge, safety attitudes, work attitudes, and occupational practices. This area is thought to be the broadest of all vocational education service areas. Bulletin 1, U.S. Office of Education, indicates this area of vocational education as:

(1) Any craft, skilled trade, or semiskilled occupation which directly functions in the designing, producing, processing, fabricating, assembling, testing, modifying, maintaining, servicing, or repairing of any product or commodity.

(2) Any other occupation including a service occupation, which is not covered in sub-paragraph one (1) of this paragraph, but which is usually considered to be technical, or trade and industrial in nature.[12]

A variety of organizational patterns are employed in trade and industrial programs. They include shop and academic subjects, cooperative programs that combine supervised skill development on the job with shop and academic classes at school, and specialized occupational curricula in trade and vocational-technical schools. Apprentices are usually included in the third organizational pattern. Approximately 15 percent of the enrollees of trade and industrial courses are apprentices. Most apprenticeship programs are registered and operated under a state apprenticeship law, a state apprenticeship agency, or by the U.S. Department of Labor Bureau of Apprenticeship.

OCCUPATIONAL EXPERIENCE PROGRAMS

All students enrolled in vocational programs for which federal funds are used must have on record an occupational objective in a recognized occupation. This requirement is a part of the Vocational Education Act of 1963. It was also a significant part of Smith-Hughes Act and other federal legislation. The occupational objective may either be for a specific occupation or for a cluster of closely related occupations in an occupational field. The student is not left to his own devices to wonder what is a recognized occupation. Rules and regulations for vocational education specify that a recognized occupation "means a lawful occupation that the commissioner [of education] finds is identifiable by employers, employee groups, and governmental and non-governmental agencies and institutions concerned with the definition and classification of occupations."[13] This ties vocational education to an immediate present orientation.

Occupational experience was initially required of students in vocational programs for a number of reasons. Vocational educators believed that the student should apply what he learned in the classroom to real-life situations. By being employed he could find out what it was like to work at the job for which he was being trained. Participation was another reason for requiring occupational experience programs. Students learn best when they are active in the process, when they are asked to assume responsibility. Also, on-the-job training may be required when, due to expensive equipment, large space requirements, or lack of qualified technical teachers, it is unwise for the school to undertake that phase of the instructional program.

Occupational experience is required of all vocational students. Each service area of vocational education, following the general guidelines of the U.S. Office of Education, may specify in its state plan how it chooses to implement this phase of the program. Thus occupational experience requirements vary by area of vocational service and by states.

One pattern of occupational experience programs deserves special attention: This is the cooperative method and is highly developed in distributive and office occupations. Mason has defined the cooperative method as a vocational education plan organized by the school in cooperation with qualified local business. Classroom instruction is directly related to their chosen part-time occupations.[14]

A cooperative program between the student, his parents, the school, and an employer is developed. The student becomes a learning worker. In the senior year of high school and in post–high school programs the student is given released time to work at a job. At school, related instruction is provided in a special class. Units of instruction for the related class in cooperative office occupations include office relationships, good grooming, using communications techniques and devices such as the telephone, human relations, and the operation of specific machines.

A teacher in such a program is known generally as the coordinator. It is his function to organize and conduct the total program. For example, he must disseminate information, select students, arrange for related classroom facilities, requisition teaching materials and supplies, survey and select possible training stations, place students at training stations, visit parents, develop training agreements, and follow up graduates. Released time is provided for the coordinator to perform most of these functions away from the school.

An important feature of the cooperative education method of occupational experience is the development of a training agreement. Such an agreement indicates what is to be learned by a specific student and whether it is to be taught in the classroom or on the job. The training agreement includes:

1. Background data: the names of all persons involved, addresses, name of business, and so on.

2. Length of training period: starting and ending dates.

3. Pay: starting wage and increases.

4. Hours: during school hours, weekends, and evenings.

5. Occupational goal: a statement by the student specifying the skills and attitudes necessary for him in that specific occupation.

6. Job activities: those activities to be provided on the job that will lead toward the occupational goal.

7. Related class: an outline of what will be taught about the job by the coordinator in the related class.

8. Responsibilities: what the employer, student, and the school will be expected to do.

9. Signatures: the employer, the student, the parents, and the coordinator sign and retain a copy of the training program.

Through this training agreement each person is informed of the activities that he is expected to perform. The employer accepts a "student-learner" and not a "student-worker"; the student goes to his classroom away from school rather than getting away from school; the parents know it is more than a job; and the coordinator has a model to which instruction and job performance may be related.

Basic to occupational experience programs are national and state child labor laws. These laws designate the ages at which a young person can obtain a job, what he can do, how long he can work, the total number of school-work hours that he can have each week, wages, and his working conditions. Jobs where there are motors, moving machines, running or sliding equipment, where the worker has to lift moderately heavy weights, are classified as hazardous and are not open to students under the age of eighteen. The laws of each state differ and need to be investigated for their implications to occupational experience programs in that state. It is possible to obtain an exemption for students in some states.

Occupational experience programs should not be confused with work experience programs. The former are for those students with an occupational goal. The latter are designed to (1) keep over-age pupils in school, (2) assist maladjusted pupils with personality and behavior problems, and (3) provide a way for some students, particularly potential dropouts, to earn money while attending school. In work experience programs the school does not help locate a job for the student and does not coordinate the school activities and the job; the job is not likely to be related to the future goals of the student. The student does one phase of the job and is not likely to be intentionally rotated so that he learns all phases, and the job is usually open to any student who requests it in addition to those who are assigned to it. This is not to say that work experience programs are bad. They simply have a different form and function from those of occupational experience programs.[15]

YOUTH ORGANIZATIONS

Each of the vocational service areas, with the exception of health occupations, has a youth organization associated with its program. These youth organizations are generally affiliated with those programs that qualify for reimbursement under provisions of the national vocational education laws and are considered an integral part of the vocation curriculum of the school. Their primary purposes are leadership and character development and promotion of scholarship, citizenship, service, and professionalism. Many have a national organization with affiliated state organizations that are comprised of chartered local clubs. National and state conventions are held annually.

The Future Farmers of America (FFA), is associated with high school vocational agriculture programs and is the oldest of the youth organizations.

It was early recognized that some of the goals of vocational agriculture could best be promoted through an organization in which students had primary responsibility. Following the passage of the Smith-Hughes Act of 1917 and prior to 1928, many local clubs were organized to give students enrolled in vocational agriculture programs an opportunity for self-expression and leadership development. These local clubs were advised by the teacher of agriculture. The pattern that developed in Virginia became the national pattern. The first national FFA convention was held in 1928, with representatives from eighteen states.

As vocational agricultural programs have evolved to diversified occupational student goals, the name Future Farmers of America has been retained. In 1968 at the national convention it was proposed to drop the name and retain the letters FFA, but this idea was rejected by the delegates. However, in 1971–1972 the National Board of Directors ruled that state and local units may use the letters FFA if they so wish. At the 1969 national convention, the membership was opened to girls for the first time on the national level. An official magazine, *The Future Farmer*, is published by the organization. Other youth organizations have patterned much of their organizational structure after that of the FFA.

Between 1938 and 1942, local clubs such as Future Retailers, Future Merchants, and Distributive Education Clubs became affiliated with emerging distributive education programs. State organizational efforts emerged from 1942–1946. Under the leadership of representatives of the U.S. Office of Education and state supervisors of distributive education, a national conference was called in 1947 and organized the Distributive Education Clubs of America (DECA). An adult DECA, Incorporated, was also formed to be responsible for the legal and financial activities of the student organization. The primary purpose of DECA is leadership development. Its membership is usually confined to students enrolled in cooperative classes in vocational distributive education. The local distributive teacher serves as adult adviser to the local DECA chapter.

Associated with home economics programs is the youth organization of Future Homemakers of America (FHA). FHA was organized nationally in 1948. From 1917 to 1944, local and state clubs were organized around home economics programs. In 1945 the name Future Homemakers of America was selected and a provisional constitution adopted, leading the way to its first national convention. As with FFA and DECA, the local teacher serves as adviser. Students enrolled in home economics classes at either the junior or senior high school levels are eligible for membership in FHA, whose primary purpose is to develop cooperative and intelligent leadership.

Sponsored by the National Business Education Association, the FBLA (Future Business Leaders Association) is the national organization for students enrolled in business subjects. Chapters of FBLA are found at local, state and college levels. They select and carry out projects designed to increase both student and public understanding of the business education program and to help individual students make intelligent choices of business occupations. Chapter projects include planning and sponsoring exhibits and demonstrations of business machines and equipment; visiting various business offices to observe workers, study procedures, and inspect equipment; and interviewing or conducting discussion with community business leaders. Business teachers, as do the advisers of all youth organizations in vocational education, find that the leadership experiences and projects encourage scholarship, promote school loyalty, and strengthen the confidence of young people in themselves and in their work.

Another organization in this field is the Future Secretaries Association (FSA), sponsored by the National Secretaries Association. Chapters of the FSA are found in high schools, junior colleges, and four-year colleges and are open to business students interested in the secretarial field. The objectives of FSA are to stimulate interest in the secretarial profession, to develop an understanding of the profession and its responsibilities, and to upgrade secretarial opportunities.

Another youth organization, the Future Data Processors (FDP), was founded in 1964 by the Data Processing Management Association. Its objectives are similar to those of FBLA and the FSA.

The three business education youth organizations—FBLA, FSA, and

FDP—were all founded by special interest groups and do not serve the entire field of business and office education. A new youth organization, the Office Education Association (OEA), was formed in 1967 to serve all business and office education students. OEA is designed to develop leadership abilities, interest in the American business system, and competency in office occupations within the framework of vocational education. Students who are members of FBLA, FSA, and FDP may also be members of OEA.

Local and state clubs are also associated with vocational programs in the trade and industrial and technical areas. These have been known under a variety of names, such as T and I Clubs or Future Tradesmen. The purpose of these clubs is similar to those of the youth organizations associated with other vocational service areas. In 1936, a trade school in Oregon led an attempt to form a national organization of students in vocational industrial education. This attempt was not successful due to questions raised by organized labor about apprentices and other employed workers belonging to a national organization.[16] In May 1965, the Vocational Industrial Clubs of America (VICA) was formed for youth who are enrolled in trade and industrial programs. National membership in 1972 totaled 120,519 students.

NOTES

[1]All figures cited here are reported in *Projections of Educational Statistics to 1975–76*; Corresponding Issues of *Digest of Annual Reports; What's Ahead for Vocational Education*; all published by the U.S. Office of Education, Division of Vocational and Technical Education.

[2]*Administration of Vocational Education-Rules and Regulations*, Vocational Education Bulletin, No. 1, U.S. Office of Education (Washington, D.C.: Government Printing Office, 1966).

[3]Ibid., p. 43.

[4]Russell J. Hosler, "Objectives of Business Education," *The Balance Sheet*, 50, no. 6 (1969), 243. Used with permission from Dr. Hosler.

[5]John A. Beaumont, "The Emerging Program of Distributive Education," in *Implementation of Vocational Education in Distribution* ed. Harland E. Sampson (Madison: Department of Curriculum and Instruction, University of Wisconsin, 1967), p. 9.

[6]Ibid.

[7]George Sanders and John A. Beaumont, "Organizational Patterns in Distributive Education," in *Implementation of Vocational Education in Distribution*, pp. 36–44.

[8]Dwight L. Wilber, "Wanted: 750,000 Humanitarians," *Today's Health*, 45 (1) (January 1967), p. 88.

[9]Margaret D. West and Beatrice Crowther, *Education for Practical Nursing* (New York: Department of Practical Nursing, National League for Nursing, 1962).

[10]Sylvia L. Lee, Louise Vetter, Kathleen M. Howell, and Patricia Smith, *Implications of Women's Patterns for Vocational and Technical Education* (Columbus, Ohio: Center for Vocational and Technical Education, 1967).

11John P. Walsh and William Selden, "Vocational Education in the Secondary School," in *Vocational Education*, ed. M. L. Barlow, 64th Yearbook, National Society for the Study of Education, Part I (Chicago: University of Chicago Press, 1965), p. 93.

12*Administration of Vocational Programs*, p. 46.

13Ibid., p. 6.

14Ralph E. Mason, *Methods in Distributive Education* (Danville, Ill.: Interstate Printers and Publishers, 1964), p. 105.

15See Ralph E. Mason and Peter G. Haines, *Cooperative Occupational Education* (Danville, Ill.: Interstate Printers & Publishers, 1965), Chaps. 3–5 for a discussion and comparison of these two types of programs.

16Roy W. Roberts, *Vocational and Practical Arts Education*, 2nd ed. (New York: Harper & Row, Publishers, 1965), p. 309.

8

CURRICULA FOUNDATIONS

The long and arduous search for occupational competence in modern American society has included a variety of approaches. Generally, though, the means to occupational competence have too often been based on a narrow concept of the individual seeking the competency as well as a narrow concept of the world of work. The general assumption was that to obtain ideas about what is needed for occupational competence one looked first at the work being performed by a worker. This led to a philosophy of "matching" the man to the job. This included finding out what job was needed and what was needed to do the job. Did the job demand a tall or short person, left- or right-handed, stooping or sitting? What about finger dexterity, manipulation of tools? Following this, a list of potential workers was examined for a person who possessed all of the needed attributes. When one was found, the job was his—it was regarded as a perfect match. It was not regarded as an attempt to fit square pegs into round holes, for the educators involved were convinced that they had found a square peg for a square hole. Hence one following this practice could not imagine that the match was not ideal, that man changed as a result of the work that he did. Unfortunately the manpower programs and many technical programs still function with a "matching" philosophy. The following extract is quoted from the 1966 *Manpower Report to the President* and sums up this position rather clearly:

The likelihood of experiencing shortages in individual occupations and areas becomes greater as growth continues at a high rate and full employment is approached. The need for preparing against this eventuality has been recognized as an essential element of any program which aims at achieving and maintaining full employment. It is this challenge which the Nation's manpower policy has undertaken to meet.

Operating alongside and within the framework of overall economic policy, the special contribution of manpower policy lies in reducing waste in matching workers and jobs through development of worker capabilities and improved adjustment between industry needs and available human resources. In a broader sense, manpower policy embraces both social and economic goals, since it deals with human beings and aims at raising their productive abilities, promoting their full employment, and raising their levels of living.[1]

In other words, those without jobs are to be matched to industry needs as efficiently as possible. If an unemployed person lacks the competence to perform a work role, he is to be taught a skill that industry needs and then offered a job of the same type for which training was received.

Such a philosophy suggests that man does not change as a result of his work and that he does not use his interests and other personal variables in finding the kind and level of work that he would like to pursue. There is sufficient observational and research evidence to suggest that work changes the worker. Waller, for example, has a penetrating analysis into the way teaching shapes and changes the teacher.[2] This suggests that current manpower policy has a very narrow criterion of what constitutes occupational competency and who should be offered training for a job. Such a criterion is not likely to be of much help in developing occupational competency in a society that exhibits rapid technological obsolescence and that is founded on democratic principles.

WHAT CONSTITUTES OCCUPATIONAL COMPETENCY

OCCUPATIONAL FLEXIBILITY

In order to be occupationally competent in modern American society, a worker needs at least (1) occupational flexibility, (2) to expect and to know how to seek new employment when his present job becomes displaced, (3) an understanding of job relationships, (4) social compatibility, and (5) a skill that is needed at some place in the world of work. The need for occupational flexibility is well recognized. The worker now outlives his job. Seymour L. Wolfbein, U.S. Department of Labor, indicated as far back as 1965 that workers were expected to hold several jobs in their lifetime.[3]

ACCEPT NON-PERMANENCY OF SKILL

The occupationally competent worker must also know that his current skill may not be permanent. The check-writing staff of the Treasury Department has been reduced from 400 to 4; 40,000 elevator operators were recently displaced in New York City, and farm jobs were reduced in one California county from 25,000 to 17,000.[4] Thus, large segments of the labor force can depend only on a limited degree of permanency. Our techniques of preparing a worker for occupational competency must prepare him to accept that fact.

In nearly every industry that one studies the same thing is discovered: in order to survive in an occupational area, a worker needs to acquire skills on an evolutionary basis. Michael suggests that bricklayers may eventually be replaced if the building trades become automated.[5] "Buildings would be redesigned so that they could be built by machines." Occupations in the bakery field are another example, for few of the traditional jobs in a bakery are surviving. In the larger bakeries, machines have taken over for the craftsman. Quantities of the desired materials are measured out by machines (computers), kneaded or mixed, measured by weight into baking utensils, and fed by conveyor into the oven. Specialized machines, such as pie crust—making machines, are now commonplace. An interview with the owner of a chain of five small, independent bakeries in Rhode Island indicated that he had recently installed a pie crust machine. On weekends his twelve-year-old son made all of the pie crusts for the coming week. These were frozen and the supply for each day thawed. The quality of the pie crust remained consistently high. No longer, for this bakery, is there an occupation called pie baker or "pie man."

JOB RELATIONSHIPS

The need for occupational competency to include an understanding of job relationships is also evident but not always recognized. A recent interview I had with the manager of a small, light industry (a manufacturer of traverse rods) brings this point into sharp focus. The company distributes nationally and has a large sales force. The plant layout is flexible and permits the operation of three to five assembly lines. The manager was asked how, who makes, and how often are decisions made relevant to changes in the production schedule that necessitated adjustments in the number of lines operated. A summary of his comments follows:

Our whole operation is controlled by a computer. As sales orders are taken anywhere in the nation, they are immediately relayed to us here. This permits a constant and daily updating of inventory and order information in the computer. The girl who occupies this position (pointing to a chart) is the key person within the plant. Each morning she checks orders and inventory and decides how best to get the desired quantity. Her alternatives include the speed of the lines as well as the number of lines to operate.

The same observations may be made in a variety of industries. When you go through a cigarette factory, ask about the worker (usually a woman) who sits high above the general floor operation and who observes and controls the entire operation of several packaging lines. She stops, speeds up, or slows down the assembly lines depending upon a variety of conditions. She observes the relationships between packaging machines, conveyor belts, packages of cigarettes, cartons, and cases. She has to anticipate bottlenecks and control the work environment to such an extent that bottlenecks do not occur.

Thus far, our examples describe the situations where one worker controls the environment of many objects and workers. An example of the interrelationships between workers is in order, and may be observed in a poultry processing plant. The plant is in continuous operation for a day. Each small group of workers punches in and out at different times. No shutdowns occur for breaks or for lunch. What one individual worker does influences many or all of the other workers in the plant. Trucks with live poultry back up to a door, live chickens are placed on a track, and that track takes the chicken through all of the slaughtering steps. The person who removes the chickens from the truck and places them on the track is scheduled for lunch first, followed in turn by each small group of workers. He resumes his work approximately twenty-eight minutes later when the last chicken is ending its final processing step.

Each small group of workers follow him back to work. What happens if he decides to take twenty minutes for lunch? Every worker has to take twenty minutes or there is no one on the line to perform the jobs on the chickens passing their work stations on the track. If he takes forty minutes for lunch, everyone has to take forty minutes for lunch.

The point of these examples is that each worker cannot function as an independent being: What he does drastically influences every other worker. He needs to understand relationships between the work performed by the total plant and how one operation is phased and coordinated with another. A failure to check inventory may result in too many traverse rods and add to inventory which is costly to a business; a failure to anticipate shortage of materials on the cigarette packaging line results in wasted products, lost man hours, and materials; a failure to take the specified time for lunch may result in live chickens entering the scalding vat, which makes expensive waste for the plant.

SOCIAL COMPATIBILITY

A worker's social compatibility—his ability to get along with fellow workers—is also an important ingredient in his occupational competency. Table 5 (Chapter 6) shows the results of a study of seventy-six corporations. The study revealed a relatively low incidence of inadequate skills and technical knowledge as reasons for lack of success of workers. Lack of skills was given as a reason for failure to promote in 23.5 percent of the cases and as a reason for discharge in 10.1 percent of the cases. On the other hand, unacceptable character and behavior traits were frequently responsible for workers not being promoted or for being discharged from their job. Some 76.5 percent of the cases not promoted lacked needed character traits, while 89.9 percent of the persons discharged lacked the needed character traits. This does not infer that character traits are more important than technical skill. The implication is rather one of equal importance and suggests that vocational education programs have been less successful in preparing workers in areas that enhance their social compatibility.

A NEEDED SKILL

A final point of what constitutes occupational competence is having an occupational skill. At selected points in this book some of the approaches and traditions in vocational education have been questioned. One area receiving careful analysis is the set of relationships that have emerged between vocational education and the present job market.

Vocational education should be designed to help people grow and develop in relation to the world of work. An occupational skill includes much more than the technical component of the world of work that vocational education has always emphasized to the exclusion of other important considerations. It includes an understanding of the industry, how one functions in that industry, how one can contribute to the industry, and how the industry contributes to society. Brookover and Nosow, after noting that the needed skill in vocational education has traditionally emphasized manual and technical skills, has traditionally been terminal, and has traditionally been first job–oriented, comment:

> The most valuable vocational training that can be provided in the elementary and secondary school for most youths is, therefore, in the basic general education program which has not previously been identified as vocational education. . . . This suggests that the major part of our education for vocations should not be oriented to training for a specific occupational career. Rather, the vocational education program should be designed to prepare youth for a continuing program of continuing education throughout life. Vocational education which is designed to prepare an individual for a particular occupation before he completes his pre-service education may serve as a handicap rather than an advantage to a large segment of the working force.[6]

The needed skill must exist in an occupational area, it must not be terminal, and it must be more than first job–oriented.

APPROACHES TO CURRICULUM

The primary way to influence the development of occupational competency is through curriculum. "Curriculum" has taken on different meanings and connotations throughout the history of formal schooling. One of the older and more persistent meanings identifies curriculum as subject matter content. This understanding can be traced back to the schools of ancient Greece and Rome and the *Seven Liberal Arts* that give the so-called "solid" subjects this orientation. Algebra, physics, chemistry, logic, and grammar illustrate the solid subjects.

Curriculum may also be viewed as a course of study. A teacher who holds such a view considers his curriculum as being an outline of topics covered in the class.

A central concept developed by Caswell and Campbell broadens the definition of curriculum to consider pupil experiences.[7] Professional educators and curriculum workers generally accept a refined version of the Caswell and Campbell concept as the best definition of curriculum. Anderson defines curriculum as the interacting forces of the total pupil environment and the pupil's experiences provided by the school in that environment.[8] This definition awards the school moral responsibility in situations over which it has little or no control. Experiences occur on school buses and in school lavatories. Having little or no control over either, most teachers are not willing to accept the responsibility for the quality of experience a pupil has in those environments even though they are provided by the educational system.

Curriculum as defined here concerns itself with objectives, content, and methodology and is planned to lead to the students' growth and development. Vocational educators have developed a variety of approaches to determine what should be taught and how it should be organized. Some of these are narrow and consider only content and content objectives. Others are more comprehensive and deal with the five constituents of occupational competency identified earlier.

FACTORS THAT HAVE INFLUENCED CURRICULUM DEVELOPMENT IN VOCATIONAL EDUCATION

CHANGES IN OCCUPATIONS. Prior to the rise and development of the factory system and modern industry, men were self-employed for the most part. In modern American society—except for small businesses, professional workers, and farmers—most people gainfully employed are employed by others. Such persons are wage-earners and depend upon a regular cash income. Occupational changes such as the broad one sketched here are important to curriculum workers in vocational education. One especially difficult problem is to identify emerging occupations. Some industries and occupational areas expand rapidly. Health occupations are an example. The passage of the health acts (Medicare, Medicaid, etc.) has created many jobs in hospitals, nursing homes, and in private home care. The industry was demanding trained workers long before facilities, staff, and curriculum were organized to meet this demand.

CHANGES IN TECHNOLOGY. Most changes in occupations are brought about by changes in technology. One change in technology has created a sophisticated division of labor. The specialized production system progresses with workers who have highly developed skills and is coordinated by engineers and business managers. The skilled worker may make a small part of a single product that he never sees as a whole. Technicians possess specialized knowledge in such areas as fluid power, solid state transistors, and conductors. Professional workers are specialists not just in law but in civil law, corporation law, criminal law, and so on. The curriculum worker in vocational education has to be aware of how technology creates these specialized workers and must plan a curriculum to prepare them.

Technology also influences the employment and employability of workers. The dominant theme of technology seems to create conditions where a worker needs adjustments in his skills rather than the total acquisition of new skills. Automobiles, for example, are built with different specifications and tolerances each year along with variations in basic skills. Mig and tig welding are now employed in some parts of the assembly process. A welder who had learned and practiced basic arc or oxyacetylene welding had to acquire the new techniques associated with mig and tig welding. The phase of vocational education important to such an established and mature individual is retraining. Curriculum workers, then, need to construct curricula that help him maintain and improve his skills so that he can remain gainfully employed.

On some occasions new technology actually phases out the need for a particular skill in a particular industry. One illustration is in the case of telephone operators. A large manufacturing firm in Detroit had approximately 200 operators on the company switchboard. A direct dial system was installed, resulting in a need for only a very few of the operators. Further, these remaining operators had to acquire new skills if they wished to stay with the company. After some retired and some sought employment with other companies, a block of approximately 140 former switchboard operators had to be retrained. This was when data processing was being introduced into the company, and most of them were retrained as key punch operators.

CHANGES IN COMMUNITY. One central concept of vocational education already discussed is that it serves the needs of the community. This presented no particular problem to the curriculum worker when small communities prevailed and the mobility of people from towns to villages to cities was very slight. In today's urbanized and highly mobile society, the curriculum worker is left with a number of perplexing problems, all of which stem from the basic question: What is a community? If a boy lives in a small town and desires to be a diesel mechanic, which would necessitate him working at least fifty miles from his home, what responsibilities do the local school officials and taxpayers have for providing him with the beginning of such training? How do you identify the experiences and content of a curriculum that is to prepare workers for jobs not located in the school district? Procedures to arrive at answers to these and other questions are not very well developed.

PROCEDURES OF CONTENT SELECTION

As the curriculum worker develops a curriculum, he needs a set of procedures to identify and verify its content. In most cases the worker is confronted with several choices, each of which has some validity. Choices of
particular contents must be consistent, educationally sound, and compatible. In vocational education, curriculum workers have looked to
specialists and practitioners for help. The procedures developed to
identify and verify content may be discussed under four headings: judgmental, experimental, analytical, and consensual.[9]

JUDGMENTAL PROCEDURE. This procedure is loosely defined and
can be described only in broad outlines. Consequently it places great
demands for intellectual honesty upon the curriculum worker. His judgment must be from a broad perspective.

If his social perspective is narrow, and his ideas and prejudices are too little
affected by democratic ideals and too closely identified with the interests of
special social groups such as industrial managers, business organizations, labor
unions, farm organizations, or academic groups, or if he is so occupied with the
past that he cannot appreciate the present nor see its potentials for the future,
the curriculum worker's judgment will hardly lead to the best selection of
subject matter.[10]

There are three phases in the judgmental procedure: The curriculum
worker must (1) identify the educational and social objectives that
should be accepted, (2) determine the conditions under which these objectives are considered desirable and in which they must be realized, and
(3) select the subject matter that best satisfies those objectives under
these existing conditions. The professional literature contains many answers to these procedures. Judgmental procedures require a fairly consistent curriculum development process. A change in personnel or conditions requires a reexamination of conclusions reached earlier.

EXPERIMENTAL PROCEDURE. The experimental procedure determines by actual field trial or pilot test whether the curriculum satisfies a particular criterion. The criteria may be: Is the subject matter
interesting, do students learn, do adults like it, do workers get jobs? Field
tests must be as rigorous and as controlled as possible. Errors due to personal values and outside conditions are reduced to a minimum.

Scientific techniques are followed in this procedure. Subject matter is
first selected according to various criteria. Hypotheses are then formed
suggesting that the tentatively selected subject matter is interesting, results in learning, or otherwise meets the conditions of the criteria. Spe-

cifying and prescribing the experimental conditions is the third step. Here the number of schools, number of groups, size of groups, sequence of experiences, and so on, are established. In the fourth step the objective techniques for determining the results are specified. These may involve a pre- and posttest and a control group, interviews with the respondents, or an analysis of performance and records. The final step is to check the results against the criteria.

ANALYTICAL PROCEDURE. This procedure is widely used and well known. Job analysis developed and refined in vocational education is a widely used analytical procedure. In general, it consists of analyzing the things people do in order to discover the subject matter content of a particular activity.

Data about an area of human concern or a specific occupation are gathered by one or more of six techniques: interviewing, working on the job, analysis by the worker, questionnaire, documentary analysis, and observation of the worker.[11] After one obtains what the worker does, the activities must be ordered in terms of importance. Frequency of occurrence is a common standard. That is, those things done most frequently are judged to be more important than those things done less frequently. The curriculum worker is still left with some alternatives in selecting content. If the curriculum constructor discovers that a worker selects one type of metal from among the five available, provisions will be made in the curriculum to teach the characteristics and uses of these five metals so that the correct type can be chosen by the worker when he must make his choice.

A curriculum worker employing analytical procedures needs to be aware of two inherent dangers. An analysis of what the worker actually does in no way infers anything about what he *should* do. And the technique is concerned with present, not future, conditions. These two factors cause the analytical procedure to identify content that supports the status quo. The second inherent danger is that the technique does not concern itself with objectives. It assumes that the curriculum worker has formulated objectives and the analysis, then, identifies content or subject matter to be used in realizing those objectives. Care must be exercised so that the curriculum worker is aware of what a particular analysis is for and is sure that it is sufficient for the purpose.

CONSENSUAL PROCEDURE. The consensual procedure is a way of collecting people's opinions about what they believe the curriculum should be.[12] A "jury of experts" is asked its opinion. Results are reported in terms of the proportion of experts in a particular community or group that believes a specific item is important in a curriculum. The jury of experts may be professional people, leaders of industry, community leaders, or any other group whose position, education, or background gives it more specialized knowledge than that possessed by the average person. The stages of the consensual procedure are very simple. First a jury of experts is chosen. This is followed by collecting their opinions—probably the most difficult step—through questionnaires, interview schedules, or group conferences. The wording and phrasing of the data-collecting instruments must be carefully worked out so that the opinion of the expert is gathered without influencing him. The final stage is the tabulation and interpretation of the responses.

When used alone the consensual procedure is subject to vested interests and occupational biases. For this reason the narrower the field of study the more alike are the experts and the greater likelihood of obtaining satisfactory results. The procedure results not in consensus but rather in a tabulation of votes. There is no opportunity for group deliberations. This has led many curriculum workers to use the consensual procedure with the judgmental procedure.

EXAMPLES OF CURRICULAR APPROACHES
IN VOCATIONAL EDUCATION

We shall now discuss curriculum approaches that are in practice in vocational education. These are related to the four procedures discussed above and provide examples of them. Some of the approaches use more than one of the four procedures; curriculum development in vocational education is getting more sophisticated. Writing in the *Review of Educational Research*, Phipps and Evans conclude:

Since 1962, the interest in curriculum development research has increased and there has been a large number of studies completed. Much of this recent research was more soundly designed than were earlier studies. Many innovative data collection and analysis techniques were utilized; factor analysis, analysis of variance and covariance, Q-sort, and many other procedures were incorporated into research designs in meaningful ways. Because of the complexity of the problems involved in curriculum development research, however, investigators must continue to be increasingly creative regarding designs and the adaptation of statistical tools. Less and less curriculum research can be justified that depends completely on simple opinion surveys.[13]

Sophisticated research techniques do indeed continue to be used. Most of these advanced techniques are used in conjunction with the four basic procedures already discussed and in the examples that follow.

INTEGRATED APPROACH TO CURRICULUM DEVELOPMENT

The major thrust for vocational education to become one of the parts of the secondary school offerings as well as a differentiated end for the public school system occurred between 1905 and 1920. An *integrated* or *cross-sectioned* approach was one of the earlier curriculum techniques developed in vocational education. In such an approach the plan cuts across all divisions of subject matter within a given field of study and is then integrated in a sequence to match the background, maturity, and competence of the students. Agricultural education developed this technique; it is a good example of this approach in operation.

As agriculture was introduced into the high school curriculum, it was customary to teach a different subject each year: Crops and Soils the first year, Animal Science in the second year, Farm Mechanics in the third year, and Farm Management in the fourth year. All of a student's knowledge about crops and soils was to be acquired during his first year of agriculture, usually grade nine. This four-year sequence was typical. However, each school determined from its own community needs exactly what four courses were needed and what content should be built into each course. Eaton surveyed seventeen states in 1917 and reported a tendency for first-year agriculture to include soils and vegetable gardening, the second year to include farm crops and fruit production, the third year to include animal husbandry, and the fourth year to include farm management and farm mechanics.[14] The major point was that subject matter was identified by courses and taught in such a way that it isolated agricultural subjects. This was the conventional or traditional sequence, followed by English and other established academic subjects.

Hamlin identifies three additional reasons for agricultural subjects being taught as whole-year courses: (1) the organization of subjects in colleges of agriculture was transferred to high schools; (2) textbooks were written about a particular subject and teachers relied extensively upon textbooks; and (3) the earliest agriculture courses were in the first two years of high school and, as later courses were added, the content of the first two years was left undisturbed.[15]

It became difficult to confine actual farm problems to particular bodies of material. Many of the practices recommended by the teacher to his students were at cross purposes. The teacher recommended that students plan realistic farming programs that increased in size and scope as the student progressed through school. Farm ownership was the student's occupational goal, and farming programs were an important instrument for that purpose. As a tenth-grader he might add a bred gilt to his farming program. His problems two years later—when his animal units may include ten sows, a boar and over a hundred pigs—are different from his problems faced with one bred gilt. What should the teacher do? Should he tell the student to ignore his animal units and concentrate on farm layout or some other phase of farm management? The reverse was also true. Few problems identified for study were "pure" problems; that is, the solution to the problem required cutting across subject lines. Teachers began to introduce relevant data to the problem regardless of subject.

The integrated agriculture curriculum eliminated traditional subjects and designated the successive years under the nondescriptive titles of Agriculture I, II, III, and IV. This swing from four one-year courses in agriculture to four years of integrated content was well underway by 1927. The rationale for such a shift was formulated by Hamlin and Sanford. They specified that farming involves the integration and skills from all the specialized areas of agriculture. A program training for farm ownership must include the same problems faced by practicing farmers. As pupils seek solutions to actual problems they must not be bound by an artificial structure of subject matter, thus the abandonment of the four traditional subjects.[16]

Following the integrated plan of curriculum organization, a Maryland high school in the mid-1960s offered the following units for Agriculture I:

DAYS	TOPIC OR UNIT
5	A History of Southern Maryland Agriculture
5	Occupations in Agriculture
15	Judging (Poultry, Livestock, Public Speaking, Agricultural Mechanics, and Dairy)
19	Understanding the Future Farmers of America
51	Agricultural Mechanics Instruction
25	Selecting and Planning a Supervised Occupational Experience Program
14	Introduction to Poultry and Poultry in St. Mary's County
9	Introduction to Dairy and Dairying in St. Mary's County
3	Introduction to Beef and Beef in St. Mary's County
4	Introduction to Swine and Swine in St. Mary's County
12	Introduction to Horticulture
8	Introduction to Agronomic Plants
10	Examinations, etc.
180	

Even within this diverse listing of topics all of the time allocated to each unit may not have been utilized consecutively. For example, the history and purposes and organization of the FFA was taught in the fall, when the students were deciding whether or not to join the organization. FFA officer responsibilities and leadership were taught in May, just before the new FFA members were to help elect new officers.

The integrated approach to agricultural curriculum offered a number of advantages to the competent teacher.[17] A major one was flexibility. The teacher could now teach together those things that belonged together. Planning a crop enterprise could include, in addition to the crop, a consideration of how the crop would be used, soil, machinery, harvesting alternatives, and the best use of alternative resources. The teacher could also meet student needs associated with farm problems. A boy might bring to class the very real problem of how to prepare his sow for farrowing. Assuming this problem is likely to be faced by a large number of the students eventually, the teacher can let them help solve a very real problem.

The integrated approach also better serves the maturity of the class members. Students mature at different rates, and class instruction should be geared toward the general maturity level of the members. Ninth-grade boys are fascinated by how things work and how things grow. Thus they enjoy learning about basic mechanical skills, the operation of basic machinery, and how seeds sprout. Eleventh-graders are likely to be bored by such activity. Conversely, ninth-graders find the traditional teaching of balancing rations and other nutritional problems too complex. The integrated approach permits a gradation and distribution of course materials as students gain maturity and experience.

A third advantage is that continuity of learning is secured. One item, such as a field with appropriate fertility practices and another without, may be studied over a four-year period rather than in one season. Also, concepts of an important enterprise such as tobacco may be introduced each year to provide continuity and sequence. Each time the student studies the concept, his learning builds upon preceding study to go more broadly and deeply into the concept.

A fourth advantage concerns student interest. Boys primarily interested in one phase of agriculture know that they will get to study it each year. The school can also approximate the farm as a whole. The student can then learn about farming the way proficient farmers farm. He thus gains, from his first formal exposure to the study of farming, an integrated understanding of the complex interrelationships of the activities in a well-planned farm business. His interests and motivation are maintained as he sees the relationship between what he is studying and his occupational goal of farm ownership.

A final major advantage of the integrated approach concerns the use of facilities. Agricultural mechanics facilities are used every year by all classes. It is possible to design a curriculum so that at least one agricultural mechanics class is scheduled every day in the shop. This particular advantage is also viewed as one of the disadvantages, to be discussed in the following pages.

A modified integrated pattern was also developed by a large number of high schools. In such a pattern a major unit for each year is identified. For tenth-graders it might be plant science. The instructor would add to this a limited number of other units. In this way most of what the students learned about plants in their study of agriculture would be acquired in Agriculture II, though some complex areas might be delayed a year or two.

Any particular pattern has its disadvantages or inherent weaknesses. The major weakness of the integrated pattern is its formlessness. When particular units are allocated to a particular spot in the four-year sequence this weakness is avoided. However, as Hamlin points out, some teachers, instead of planning a four-year sequence, plan from day to day.[18] Some important subjects are likely to be neglected and the teacher's favorite subjects overemphasized. Students may become dejected in these cases, as they lack a clear perception of the entire field of agriculture and fail to see that they are making progress toward their occupational goal.

A related weakness is that no guarantee can be provided that a four-year course, though put on paper, is more than a hodgepodge of unrelated units. A curriculum whose horizontal relationships are not clear is said to lack integration. Such a curriculum would develop students who lacked thorough learning in important phases of agriculture and would be handicapped in advancing toward their occupational goal of farm ownership. A third weakness concerns transferring students. Since the content of Agriculture III is not likely to be the same for even neighboring schools, pupils who transfer from school to school may miss an important phase of instruction.

A fourth weakness concerns facilities. The integrated pattern requires expansive facilities that are often not used. Administrators see an agricultural mechanics shop used one or two periods a day and empty the rest of the school day while other shop classes are overcrowded. At the present time this is one area of the agriculture program at the secondary level that is under serious scrutiny by school administrators simply because of pressing space needs. The trend now is to open the agricultural mechanics facilities to other classes when not used by the teacher of agriculture. This forces the agricultural teacher to offer all the mechanics instruction in separate classes, thus departing from the integrated approach.

A final weakness of the integrated approach to curriculum development mentioned here is the noncompatibility with diverse occupational goals. This approach was developed when students enrolled in agriculture had the common occupational goal of farm entrepreneurship. Now agricultural students have a wide variety of goals. Some are planning for farm ownership, some are planning for post–high school education, some are interested in sales, others are interested in agricultural service occupations. An integrated curriculum drawing the content for such diverse occupational goals lacks the thoroughness of a sound vocational program. As classes with diverse occupational goals become more typical, alternative curriculum patterns are emerging in agriculture.

OCCUPATIONAL OR JOB ANALYSIS

Job analysis is one of the narrow curricular approaches identifying only subject matter content; it was developed by vocational educators during their participation in World War I training programs. It was initiated by trade and industrial educators but has been used very extensively in technical education, rather extensively in business and distributive education and agricultural education, and less extensively in home economics education. Dr. Charles R. "Skip" Allen is generally regarded as the major developer of the job analysis approach, but many other persons have also contributed significantly to it.

This curricular approach follows the analytical procedures for content selection. The technique tries to determine the teaching content in programs that are designed to prepare workers for specific occupations or trades. Information is obtained from current workers in the occupation, from supervisors, and from instructors who are occupationally qualified. This technique, then, requires the cooperation of persons who are thoroughly familiar with the various operations and aspects of the occupation. Job analysis, as a technique, is occasionally used also to determine the general education content of a training program. This involves an analysis of the worker's activities when he is not on the job. Included are civic, recreational, home, health, and cultural activities. Much of Allen's original work was published in bulletins when he was with Federal Board for Vocational Education.[19]

Present-day vocational educators prefer the term "occupational analysis" to the terms "job analysis" or "trade analysis." Occupational analysis is defined similarly to job analysis, and grows out of the history of job analysis. Illustrations of the development of occupational and job analysis are taken from job analysis in trade and industrial and technical education.

Job analysis and trade analysis are slightly different terms, though the same process is used in each. Job analysis is an analysis of unit-skill jobs that are typically highly specialized and require a few days, a few weeks, or perhaps two years to learn. Trade analysis is an analysis of a trade that usually requires an extended period of training by students who are preparing to enter that particular trade. The term occupational analysis can be used to include both job and trade analysis.

The two outstanding systems of occupational analysis are those of Dr. Allen and Dean Robert W. Selvidge.[20] Dr. Allen takes the complete job to be done by the worker as the basis of his analysis; Dean Selvidge takes as his basis the operations composing the job.

"Analyzing a trade simply means listing out all the things that the learner must be taught." In the process of doing the analysis, Allen followed four basic steps:

1. What to teach? List all the jobs performed by the worker along with all of the special terms, and related knowledge needed to perform these jobs.

2. Classifying the teaching content. An analogy for this step described by Allen was to label a set of pigeon holes and sort articles according to the labels. The content may be classified as forming, shaping, assembling, etc. jobs. Trade drawing, trade problems, trade terms and trade mathematics were also included as were occupational dangers and care of tools and equipment.

3. Blocking. A block is a group of or unit of jobs involving the same sort of learning. Blocks may be based on operations performed, materials used or construction skills. Blocking is not necessary on all jobs particularly it is not needed on unit-skill jobs.

4. Arrangement of blocks. Following the listing of jobs in each block, the blocks are arranged in order of learning difficulty or some other logical arrangement that is suited to teaching-learning conditions.

A set of cards was developed by Allen on which were recorded the general information about the job, an analysis of the job, auxiliary information needed for proper job performance, technical information needed, and applications and correlations to be developed by the instructor. Later large sheets were used to show the trade analysis graphically. Such a graphic presentation helps to reveal relationships that are hard to see when small cards are used.

The method of teaching and the sequence of learning activities were highly developed by Allen. Each job analyzed was characterized as being complete and detailed. Instructional units and job sheets were developed. The order of teaching the units was specified. Job sheets became the basic link between student, instructor, and the trade to be learned. Each job sheet was developed in great detail, explaining how a complete job that usually involved several operations was done. The student was expected to do what the job sheet directed him to do and to perform the operations in the predetermined sequence. Instructors provided help at any point of difficulty and checked on quality of performance.

This heavy reliance on the system of job sheets caused some criticisms: Pupil initiative is reduced, pupils who are poor readers suffer, the pupil is not required to think the problem through, the instruction becomes routinized, and the instructor tends to become lazy and is not challenged. These criticisms are offset by the following claims: New pupils can enter a class at any time, the pupil progresses at his own rate, each pupil is striving for the same perfection, and less variability between classes is achieved.

Selvidge made some major changes in occupational analysis. His four basic steps are:

1. Make a list of unit operations (a group of skills or manipulations occurring together).

2. Give specific and concise directions on how to perform the operations.

3. Prepare a set of information sheets. An information sheet gives information about machines, parts, tools, and materials and provides some other types of background information. Information sheets might be prepared on how to adjust a lathe, characteristics of plastics, how to pack a cast iron joint, or how to use a slide rule.

4. Inventory any related mathematics or science that needs to be mastered.[21]

Among the advantages of the Selvidge plan are: The problem is stated definitely, the pupil must plan his work before he undertakes it, it helps to develop the ability of analyzing, the order of teaching units is not considered and is left to the instructor, and much of the general nature of the analysis is left to the knowledge of the instructor.

These basic methods are compared by Friese and Williams.[22] Basically, the Allen method analyzes the complete job; the student is given a set of sequential operations that he is expected to master. The Selvidge method analyzes basic unit operations in the trade. The student is given broad trade analysis sheets with definite instructions and references but he is expected to set up and solve problems associated with the trade.

The trade or occupational analysis approach to curriculum development originated by Allen, modified by Selvidge, Bowman, Haynes, and Nichols, is an excellent method of describing or identifying the *present* activities of a worker.[23] It also permits the identification of related content. That is, the method identifies the mathematical skills and the scientific reasoning that the worker uses when performing a particular job. These skills and reasonings are then introduced to the trainee. An advantage to teaching inherent in occupational analysis concerns the way in which the resulting course of study is organized. In order to prepare the trainee for his potential work, the course of study is divided into short, complete units. These units then permit the trainee to advance through the work at his own rate if the instructor would permit such to occur.

The occupational analysis technique intends to identify exactly what the master worker does so that these actions may be imitated by the trainee. This technique obviously cannot prepare the trainee for the future changes in his occupation. He must go through an intensive process of upgrading every time a new change is implemented. In an era of rapid technological change, this is a serious handicap. Another disadvantage lies in the inability of the method to permit transfer of learning from one operation to another. Occupational detail was provided to the trainee without always having him understand why this was a necessary step. In learning the chucking operation of a lathe, for example, the trainee was told that it was necessary to take off the face plate, put chuck on spindle nose, and so on. He understood and could perform what was to be done, but he could not always tell why the task was necessary. Lacking this type of occupational understanding, transfer of the skill to other situations was left to chance or to the intelligence and initiative of the trainee.

CLUSTERS, FAMILIES, OR COMMON ELEMENTS OF OCCUPATIONS

With a diversity of student occupational objectives particularly at the secondary level, vocational educators reasoned that some way had to be found to meet these individual needs. Out of a group of a hundred students in a high school who desired vocational education, it might be that they identified with fifty specific occupations. It would be tutorial education to organize fifty classes averaging two students each, and the public school is not intended to provide this. Vocational educators sought ways of grouping those fifty specific occupations, and one thought was to form a cluster, or family of occupations.

Following a modified analytical procedure and consensual procedures on occupational analysis performed on each occupation, occupations are then grouped around what is common to them, based on the degree of similarity in knowledge and abilities that are required by workers in these jobs. Figure 3 schematically shows the common elements of a series of seven jobs that represent one family. The shaded areas are common to more than one job in that family.

Maley has researched the cluster concept for its application to industrial education.[24] Within the construction family he clustered jobs such as carpenter, mason, plumber, electrician, and painter. Within the electromechanical installation and repair family, he clustered the jobs of business machine serviceman, home appliance serviceman, radio and television serviceman, and air conditioning and refrigeration serviceman. For examples of the cluster concept applied to other areas in vocational education, see Baker (agriculture), Schill and Arnold (technical), and Whitmarsh (child care).[25]

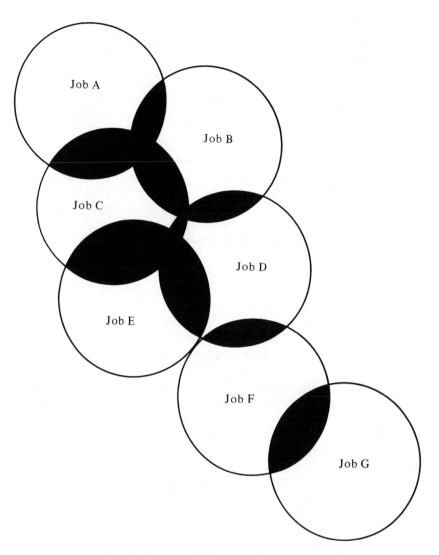

FIGURE 3.   Common Elements of a Family of Jobs

The cluster concept overcomes two major problems faced by vocational education at the high school level. One problem is whether to prepare highly skilled students for employment in a specific occupation or to prepare generalists for a wide variety of occupations. The cluster concept is aimed at a middle ground, where specific job entry skills for a cluster of occupations are developed. The second problem concerns population mobility and a definition of community. Many high school graduates migrate to work in another community. Having been prepared for a family of occupations, the graduate is more likely to find employment opportunities as he migrates.

Unfortunately, several serious errors in logic are made in the cluster concept approach. A logical assumption is made that what is common to a family of occupations is what is important, which leads to the further assumption that what is unique about a family of occupations is not important to the entry worker. Similarly, another error is made when what is unique about an occupation is assumed to be more technical than what is common to an occupation and hence should be taught at the post–high school level. These logical errors are serious. Sociological analyses reveal that persons in a profession within a family of jobs identify with what is unique in that family. Also, a more thorough approach to occupational analysis would reveal that what is unique to a job is not necessarily highly technical.

FUNCTIONS OF INDUSTRY

Many curricular approaches in vocational education take the job title of the worker as the basic unit. Parts man for a farm machinery dealer, diesel mechanic, and key punch operator are examples of job titles. Clark, working in the discipline of agricultural education, found that job titles do not really describe what a worker does.[26] In one instance a parts man at a farm machinery dealer inventories stock, waits on customers, and gets parts for mechanics. In another instance the individual with the same job title waits on customers but also delivers new machinery to customers' farms. In a third instance the parts man was a mechanic who was also responsible for keeping the parts bin in order. Thus tasks performed by workers with similar job titles in similar business varied considerably. A conceptual framework was sought by Clark and approximately ten doctoral students that would overcome this and other obstacles. The conceptual framework that evolved was called the functions of industry. Bateson and Stern were developing this approach for industrial education at nearly the same time.[27] The two research efforts moved forward independently with no cross-fertilization until 1966.

The functions of industry approach combines the judgmental and consensual procedure of content selection. Basically, it does not attempt to prepare workers for a specific job. Rather, it is intended to prepare workers for functions that are performed at various levels within the industry. Gleason defines a function as "a process which requires the performance of closely related activities to achieve a desired outcome. It may or may not be identical with a job title or job description."[28] A job (the work load of a single worker) may be composed of portions of several functions, or several jobs may be required to complete a single function. The functions approach is process-oriented in that it focuses on the purposes of the industry rather than upon particular activities performed by an individual. Regardless of variables such as location, size of industry, numbers of employees, and specialization of service, specific functions require the performance of an identifiable group of activities to successfully carry out each function. That is, sales as a function within an industry may be carried out by persons performing a group of very closely related activities. It is reasoned that the areas of competency required to perform specific activities essential to a function should provide a basis for curriculum development. Clark analyzed the feed industry for its functions. He discerned the nine functions of processing, sales, service, office practice, public relations, purchasing, transportation, research, and maintenance.[29] Stern developed the functions concept as it applies to industrial education.[30]

The functions approach has not been widely researched beyond the two series of investigations cited above. There is much to suggest that it will serve as a curriculum technique and will be widely employed in years to come. It escapes nearly all of the problems of the job title, cluster, and competency curriculum techniques. It prepares the worker to perform within a functional area at many levels within an industry. A great deal of stress in education is placed upon team teaching and cooperation between vocational services. Much of the early work by Clark indicates that many workers in the nonfarm agricultural occupations need competencies that cut across traditional vocational services. The functions approach identifies for the curriculum developer what a worker needs to be able to know and do if he is to perform the sales function in a particular industry. The curriculum developer then utilizes various vocational areas to prepare the worker to perform the function. As a curriculum technique, then, it offers an excellent model for team teaching and cooperation between vocational services.

THE CONCEPT APPROACH

Jerome S. Bruner opened new paths to teaching and learning with his publication of *The Process of Education*. Here he makes a case for an examination of the structure of subject matter:

The main objective of this work has been to present subject matter effectively—that is, with due regard not only for coverage but also for structure. . . . What are the implications of emphasizing the structure of a subject, be it mathematics or history—emphasizing it in a way that seeks to give a student as quickly as possible a sense of the fundamental ideas of a discipline?[31]

"Grasping the structure of a subject," according to Bruner, "is understanding it in a way that permits many other things to be related to it meaningfully. To learn structure, in short, is to learn how things are related."[32]

Seeking an understanding of relationships becomes the objective of the concept approach to vocational curriculum. Technological advancements, labor-saving devices, automation, and sophisticated electronic equipment all lend support to an expanding world of knowledge. The shell of man's environment becomes more closely knit and interrelated. With an incomprehensible array of facts available, some way must be found to permit man to understand and direct his environment. One way is to discover larger units of knowledge to use as structuring reference points. Understanding a small number of reference points enables one to comprehend a vast quantity and quality of one's environment. The industrial environment as it interacts with society is one environment that needs to be and can be understood by all citizens, by recognizing selected reference points called concepts. A concept was identified by Thompson as having at least five constructs.[33] These constructs view a concept to be: a psychological construct; of functional value to guide an individual's thinking or behavior; derived from experience; fixed by a name, a word, an idea, or phrase; and a kind of learning.

This approach follows primarily the judgmental procedure of content selection. An example of a concept-based curriculum in vocational education is the American Industry Project developed at University of Wisconsin, Stout, in Menomonie, Wisconsin.

It is also apparent that students are affected and must understand those forces which influence their lives. American industry has been identified as one of those forces and must be studied in order that students have an adequate understanding of their environment.[34]

A conceptual structure of the American Industry Project is presented in Figure 4. Fourteen concepts were identified as the structuring points for American industry: production, management, marketing, industrial relations, procurement, research, property, finance, public interest, transportation, communication, energy, processes, and materials. The curriculum is designed at three levels. Level one (grade eight) attempts to develop a broad foundational understanding of industry; the second level (grade ten) is an in-depth study of the major conceptual areas; and the third level (grade twelve) allows the student to do research and experimentation in one or more of the conceptual areas. The details of level one are shown in Figure 5 (p. 174).

An illustration of the content may be helpful. All forms of fastening can be categorized under three major concepts: fastening by adhesion,

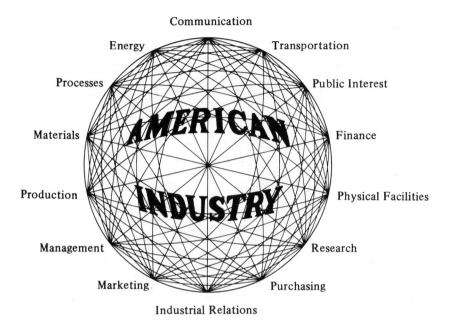

FIGURE 4. A Conceptual Structure of the Knowledges of Industry. By permission of the Stout Foundation.

cohesion, and by mechanical linkage. In the American Industry Project, a student would be concerned with developing an understanding of the basic attributes of fastening. He would learn fastening by mechanical linkage, for example, rather than learning how to fasten with wood screws. The student who understands the basic attributes of fastening by mechanical linkage stands in a better position to make a reasoned choice of fasteners when dealing with a variety of materials other than wood.

POSTSCRIPT

The examples in this chapter have included a variety of curricular approaches that vocational educators have used and are using to develop occupational competency. If the list of five constituents of occupational competency is at all accurate, then two of these curricular approaches will become very important in the future of vocational education: the functions of industry approach and the conceptual approach. They permit occupational experiences to be planned for the trainee so that he has a needed skill as well as the other factors that comprise occupational competence.

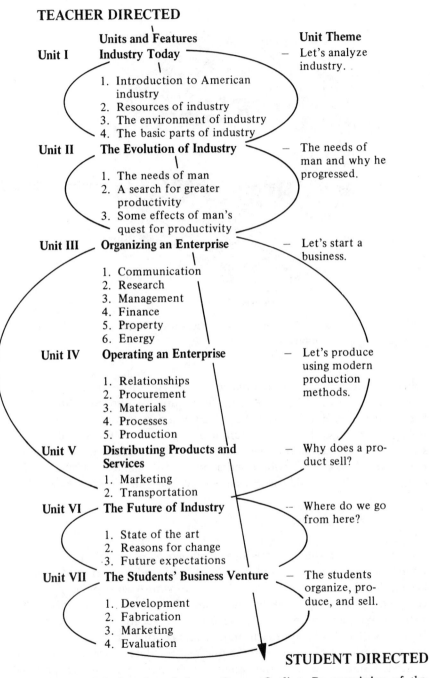

TEACHER DIRECTED

Units and Features | Unit Theme

Unit I — **Industry Today** — Let's analyze industry.
1. Introduction to American industry
2. Resources of industry
3. The environment of industry
4. The basic parts of industry

Unit II — **The Evolution of Industry** — The needs of man and why he progressed.
1. The needs of man
2. A search for greater productivity
3. Some effects of man's quest for productivity

Unit III — **Organizing an Enterprise** — Let's start a business.
1. Communication
2. Research
3. Management
4. Finance
5. Property
6. Energy

Unit IV — **Operating an Enterprise** — Let's produce using modern production methods.
1. Relationships
2. Procurement
3. Materials
4. Processes
5. Production

Unit V — **Distributing Products and Services** — Why does a product sell?
1. Marketing
2. Transportation

Unit VI — **The Future of Industry** — Where do we go from here?
1. State of the art
2. Reasons for change
3. Future expectations

Unit VII — **The Students' Business Venture** — The students organize, produce, and sell.
1. Development
2. Fabrication
3. Marketing
4. Evaluation

STUDENT DIRECTED

FIGURE 5. Level I—American Industry Course Outline. By permission of the Stout Foundation.

NOTES

[1]*Manpower Report of the President, 1966* (Washington, D.C.: Government Printing Office, 1966), p. 33.

[2]Willard Waller, "What Teaching Does to Teachers," in Maurice Stein, *Identity and Anxiety* (Glencoe, Ill.: The Free Press, 1960), pp. 329–51. The entire book is devoted to the general topic of the worker seeking and changing his identity in an occupational setting.

[3]Seymour L. Wolfbein, *Employment, Unemployment and Public Policy* (New York: Random House, Inc., 1965).

[4]Grant Venn, *Man, Education and Work* (Washington, D.C.: American Council on Education, 1964), pp. 4–5.

[5]Donald N. Michael, *Cybernation: The Silent Conquest* (Santa Barbara, Calif.: Center for the Study of Democratic Institutions, 1962).

[6]Wilber Brookover and Sigmund Nosow, *A Sociological Analysis of Vocational Education in the United States* (Washington, D.C.: Government Printing Office, 1963).

[7]Hollis L. Caswell and Doak S. Campbell, *Curriculum Development* (New York: American Book Company, 1935), Chap. 4.

[8]Vernon E. Anderson, *Principles and Procedures of Curriculum Improvement* (New York: Roland Press, 1956), p. 9.

[9]B. Othanel Smith, William O. Stanley, and J. Harlan Shores, *Fundamentals of Curriculum Development*, rev. ed. (New York: Harcourt, Brace Jovanovich, 1957), Chap. 7.

[10]Ibid., p. 153.

[11]Ibid., p. 162.

[12]Ibid., p. 166.

[13]Lloyd J. Phipps and Rupert N. Evans, "Curriculum Development," *Review of Educational Research*, 38, no. 4 (1968), 377.

[14]Theodore H. Eaton, *A Study of Organization and Method of the Course of Study in Agriculture in Secondary Schools* (New York: Teachers College, Columbia University, Contributions to Education, no. 86, 1917), p. 70.

[15]Herbert M. Hamlin, *Agricultural Education in Community Schools* (Danville, Ill.: Interstate Printers and Publishers, 1949), p. 226.

[16]Herbert M. Hamlin and Charles W. Sanford, *The Place of Agriculture in the Secondary School Program* (Urbana: The University of Illinois Bulletin, 41, no. 12, 1943), p. 15.

[17]George P. Deyoe, "The Cross-Sectioned Course in Theory and Practice," *Agricultural Education Magazine*, 12, no. 4 (1939), 64–66.

[18]Hamlin, *Agricultural Education in Community Schools*, p. 229.

[19]For example, see Federal Board for Vocational Education, Bulletin 52, *Theory and Practice, Outlines of Instruction in Related Subjects for the Machinist's Trade* (Washington, D.C.: Government Printing Office, 1919).

[20]Charles R. Allen, *The Instructor, the Man, and the Job* (Philadelphia: J. B. Lippincott Co., 1919); Robert W. Selvidge, *How to Teach a Trade* (Peoria, Ill.: Manual Press, 1923).

[21]Ibid.

[22]John F. Friese and William A. Williams, *Course Making in Industrial Education*, 3rd ed. (Peoria, Ill.: Charles A. Bennett Co., 1966), p. 117.

[23]Clyde A. Bowman, *Graphic Aids in Occupational Analysis* (Milwaukee: The Bruce Publishing Co., 1924); Merritt W. Haynes, *Teaching Shop Work, Unit Three, Trade*

Analysis (New York: Ginn and Company, 1924); Frederick G. Nichols, *The Personal Secretary: Differentiating Duties and Essential Personal Traits* (Cambridge: Harvard University Press, 1934).

24Donald Maley, *An Investigation and Development of the "Cluster Concept" as a Program in Vocational Education at the Secondary School Level* (College Park: University of Maryland, 1966), p. 135.

25Richard Baker, "Curriculum for the World of Work," *Agricultural Education*, 39, no. 1 (1966), 6–9; William J. Schill and Joseph P. Arnold, *Curricula Content for Six Technologies* (Urbana: Bureau of Educational Research, University of Illinois, 1965); Ruth J. Whitmarsh, "An Exploratory Study of Knowledge in Child Development and Guidance Needed by Mothers and Workers in Occupations Related to Child Care" (Ph.D. diss., University of Illinois, 1966).

26Raymond M. Clark, *The Need for Training for Non-Farm Agricultural Occupations* (East Lansing: Michigan State University, 1959).

27Willard M. Bateson and Jacob Stern, "The Functions of Industry as the Basis for Industrial Education Programs," *Journal of Industrial Teacher Education*, 1 (1963), 3–16.

28William E. Gleason, "Functions of Industry Approach to Curriculum for Vocational Education" (Ph.D. diss., Michigan State University, 1967), p. 17.

29Raymond M. Clark, *Vocational Competencies Needed for Employment in the Feed Industry*, Educational Research Series no. 22 (East Lansing: Michigan State University, 1965), p. 5.

30Jacob Stern, "The Functions of Goods–Production Industrial Establishments: A Validation of Selected Elements in a Definition of Industry as a Framework for Curriculum in Industrial Education (Ph.D. diss., Wayne State University, 1964).

31Jerome S. Bruner, *The Process of Education* (Cambridge: Harvard University Press, 1960), pp. 2–3.

32Ibid., p. 7.

33John F. Thompson, "Is A Whale A Fish?—Working With Concepts" (Seminar paper, University of Wisconsin, Department of Agricultural and Extension Education, 1968).

34Richard H. Gebhart, *Developing American Industry Courses for the Secondary School* (Menomonie, Wis.: Stout State University, 1968), p. 2.

IV

THE
EMERGENT

9

THE CHANGING
EDUCATIONAL SCENE

INTRODUCTION

American education is emerging as a new frontier. The school is confronted with a bulging and diverse student population. Along with large numbers is the contemporary demand for quality. Old solutions for new problems will not suffice. Eurich writes: "show me a school which is not experimenting with new ways of improving education, and I will show you a school which is likely slated for decline. Today good education is in large part synonymous with innovative education."[1]

A number of new programs, new theories, new practices, and new structures are being tested within the school environment. Continuous reform has led to the belief that if the schools are to be significantly better, they will have to be substantially different. This belief is moving the schools toward a new standard of education dedicated to the high purposes of freedom and opportunity for all of its clients. We may refer to these forces as the reform movement.

THE REFORM MOVEMENT

BSCS, SMSG, PSSC, CHEMS—these are examples of the new alphabet soup of American education, and they are indicative of the curriculum reform movement that has affected education in the last two decades. The reform movement within education is not grass-roots inspired, as local, state, and national public school leaders have had little influence in its initiation. The leaders of these reforms have been largely university professors in the academic disciplines corresponding to the secondary subjects. (The college physicists became involved in the reform of the high school physics curriculum, etc.) Those charged legally with the responsibilities for determining what to teach were largely bystanders. Also influencing the reform movement have been a number of variables outside the school environment. We may, then, group the factors directing the reform movement under two broad categories: implosions and explosions.

IMPLOSIONS

Education does not exist apart from other institutions in our society: It is guided and shaped by societal forces, and often can exert little influence on them. Education often must sit back as a force batters it; at other times it can respond while the force is operating. We refer to these outside forces as implosions.

MAN IS CONCERNED WITH SETS OF EVENTS. First, we ought to recognize the fact that a new view of man's surroundings, the world, has emerged. A world viewed in a cultural relativism framework and with pessimism no longer exists. Nor are the components of the world any longer viewed as fixed structures. The modern view of the world holds new promises for each person and segment of our society. It also poses a new set of problems for each and every world citizen. The new view regards change as the rule rather than the exception. Modern man is

concerned with sets of events, not with fixed and immutable structures, nor with processes the direction of which is predetermined and unchanging. He orients himself to probabilities, not certainties, thus facing up to the fact that man is compelled to make responsible decisions in the face of uncertainty. He recognizes that certainty is unattainable in any field of human knowledge or of belief.[2]

This new view carries with it parallel views about man and society, as well as a need for new symbolic systems for analysis and expression.

Modern man, then, needs to be equipped to live with and fashion change.

A new working conception of the individual in the context of his society has emerged as man himself has become an object of close scrutiny. Man knows that human experience and truth depend on the perspective of the observer; they are not absolutes in themselves.

The view of man as a "rugged individualist," popular in the era when American industry was being built, is now regarded as naïve. During that era any state or political organization was viewed as a threat to one's individual initiative. The new individualism, based on the humanistic world-view, expresses a concern for the responsibility of society to its members and of the citizen to his state. The state, political organizations, and social institutions (such as schools) are viewed as positive forces when they are used to provide equal opportunities for all children, to overcome discrimination, and to protect the individual.

MATHEMATICAL AND SCIENTIFIC ILLITERACY. By the early 1950s, some scientists—particularly the School of Mathematics Study Group (SMSG)—had concluded that high school graduates possessed extensive mathematical and scientific illiteracy. These scientists were outside of the formal school setting. The SMSG was concerned by the fact that each year high school seniors and college freshmen scored in lower percentiles in the science and math sections of various standardized tests. Their concerns were largely ignored by other groups. General educational and public concern and action materialized only after the launching of the first Russian satellite, Sputnik, in October 1957. The general public could not understand how our "perfect" educational system could permit the Russians to be first in anything. First scorn, then encouragement, and finally support was given to education. This placed education at the core of the nation's malaise. Consequently education was seen to be at the core of the nation's welfare.

PROSPERITY. An economic depression was predicted for the early 1950s. When it did not occur in 1952, it was predicted for 1953, then 1954. . . . It never materialized. A large segment of the American population, particularly the expanding middle class, knew greater prosperity and higher standards of living at an earlier age than ever before. This class of people knew that education was the way to a good life for their children, a better life than they had had. It was imperative that their children get into college.

The doors of the prestige colleges were barred to many students as they were faced with an increased number of applicants and an inadequate number of places for new students. Parents turned to the public school again and demanded that the school do its job—get the high school graduates into college. The reform movement and demand for action came first from suburban communities where the middle class had gone to rear its children.

CONCERN FOR ALL STUDENTS. Shortly after the so-called Sputnik era, the educational resources devoted to selected science-based programs increased. This happened when the schools were experiencing both a sharp rise in the percent of school-age youngsters and the effect of the war babies. These were more school-age youngsters and more of them were seeking school diplomas. School dropouts became more noticeable.

It soon became apparent that an increased commitment of resources to the sciences had permitted a basic problem in the school offerings to become manifest. (Some writers have termed this an overcommitment to science. If this is true, it is an overcommitment in only one aspect: that being insufficient resources devoted to other areas and programs of the school. It was not an overcommitment to science per se.) Parallel improvements were not made in equipment, materials, and methodology for other curricular areas: English, social studies, vocational education, history. With such a gap in its offerings, the public schools simply could not meet the needs of all of its youngsters.

But not all the youngsters were planning to go to college, and many of these students could find little in the secondary school to help them. The schools were being operated on the philosophy that education was for the future, which was adequate for those planning to go to college. Those youngsters not planning for college began to urge the school to do something for them. This movement was supported very strongly at various points by a number of organizations: The American Junior College Association, The Panel of Consultants for Vocational Education, The United States Congress, The National Association of Secondary School Principals, The American Vocational Association. It was recognized that the secondary school system must provide a meaningful education to that proportion of its students that were preparing for careers that did not include or need a four-year college preparation. A significant response to this recognition was to offer sound vocational education programs at the secondary and post–secondary school levels.

This called for the close scrutiny and revision of vocational educational offerings. Vocational education had come to occupy a special place in the secondary school; sometimes it was appropriate to refer to it as an "institution" within an institution. It had, in some cases, operated with special rules and special dispensations. Arnstein commented after the President's Panel's Report in 1962 that vocational education "seeks to enlarge the scope of the programs and to claim that it is a part of general education but it is not willing to have it become a *real* part of the general education program."[3]

VALUES. Groups in America have always been chipping away at the prevailing value patterns. These groups were always at the periphery and were few in number. After World War II and with postwar prosperity, the chipping away at the prevailing value patterns moved to the center of the social fabric. College and job opportunities took many young people away from the stable communities of their early youth to newer, more transient communities. Unemployment was also a threat as job obsolescence was a possibility. As young people they had heard their parents say, "If we can't pay cash, we can't afford it." Now, as young married couples, they discovered that if they waited to pay cash for an item it cost much more than it did when they started to save for it. Time payments became a way of life for young couples. These forces combined to promote a new cultural value pattern stressing uncertainty, adaptability, and rationality.

KNOWLEDGE EXPLOSION. Should the school and the teachers be affected by the knowledge explosion? Large segments of education were built around the concept that education "was for the future." Educators planned programs on the assumption that a person was able to acquire and store up knowledge during his early life, which included his formal education, and spend the rest of his life using those stored facts. Incredible speed characterizes the change that is taking place in modern society. Society is advancing so rapidly that new knowledge and technology confront its members before they fully understand past achievements. Keeping abreast of developments requires one to run fast just to keep up.[4] This is an indication that now "people outlive facts." That is, so much of what we will need to know ten years from now is not available today. Clearly, an educational system designed to prepare the pupil for a future of recalling facts is not appropriate when the task of the educator shifts to being one of preparing students so that they may fashion change.

LEISURE. Today the American people stand on the threshold of an era that will bring them more leisure than has ever been available to any other people. Profound ramifications and implications of this are apparent. Should persons be educated to new work and new leisure? At one point in our history the majority of persons worked directly to produce goods. Work was from dawn to dusk, from Monday morning until Saturday night. Hard work was virtuous. Life was difficult, but meaning was seen in its rhythm and naturalness. Now work takes less and less of the average man's working day, and today the average American spends about 35 percent of his time in leisure activities. Economists have shown that the American economy has historically absorbed about two-fifths of its increasing productivity in more leisure time rather than in more goods.[5] As the productivity of the American economy continues it is only natural that leisure be increased.

Work has been shown to have an intensity of meanings and has at least five functions for man: It (1) produces an income or a means to a livelihood, (2) regulates life activity, (3) provides a person's identification, (4) provides an opportunity for association, and (5) furnishes many meaningful life experiences.[6] Can man find some of these functions in leisure? Research seems to indicate that at present he does not.[7] Thus, we need to educate the population for all aspects of leisure. It should be pointed out here also that the new leisure time does not affect all types of work; the professional and managerial work classifications have less leisure time.

This increased free time presents a challenging educational problem. Many Americans have not been "educated" to use free time and consider "time on their hands" as wasted time. Leisure time can be a burden as well as a blessing if one has not developed any productive outside interests. One out of ten Americans lives in poverty and cannot afford the minimum essentials of life, much less any leisure-time activities.

Education for leisure has opened avenues for the student to develop an interest in recreation. This interest cannot be pursued and refined in adult life unless adequate recreational areas are provided at the local, county, state, and national levels. Housing, industry, and highways have taken precedence in areas ideally suited for recreation. This stresses the fact, first of all, that recreation is not considered an important dimension of human needs. Secondly, it ignores the significant economic impact of the recreation industry. In 1969, recreation was an $83 billion industry, with an increase of 42 percent over what was spent in 1965. The largest item in the recreational budget is for equipment.

Additional attempts to meet the challenge for an appropriate use of future leisure have come in increased emphasis given to the fine arts: Schools are giving some attention to improving art, music, and literature. Eurich comments:

We are well into second, third, and even fourth "generations" of curriculum reform in math and science—each building on the achievements (and striving to remedy the defects) of the ones which came before. Now it is time for a strong shift of focus. . . . The new frontier, I believe, lies in the humanistic area of the curriculum. In this chapter I shall attempt to appraise the present state and to discern the immediate future of the humanities in public education, in the light of a new climate of opinion almost comparable to the impact of Sputnik on the American mind: the so-called "cultural explosion."

We must account for two contrasting sets of facts. First, *the American people are today concerned with humanistic and cultural matters to a degree unpre-cedented in their history.* And, second, far from reflecting this new concern with humanistic and cultural matters, *the schools of the nation have let the humanities and arts languish.* I do not believe we can long permit such a dis-crepancy between what people want, and very badly need, and what the schools offer. Educators must stake out a role in the forefront of the new American concern for the intellectual, aesthetic, and spiritual dimensions of life.[8]

Alvin Toffler deserves credit for bringing culture to the attention of the persons with leisure through his book *The Culture Consumers.*[9] Facts that point to the consumption of culture include: more art galleries in New York City today than there were in the entire country in 1950, increase of LP record sales, a paperback revolution in printing and pub-lishing, library circulation increasing faster than the population, growth of educational television, and twice as many persons at concerts and recitals as at major league baseball games. A Stanford Research Institute report in 1962 pointed out that consumer spending on the arts rose by 130 percent from 1953 to 1960. This was twice as fast as spending on all recreation and better than six times as fast as outlays for spectator sports or admission to movies.[10]

In 1965, a congressional act established a National Endowment for the Arts and also encouraged the development of state art councils. In 1950, there were eight local arts councils in the country and almost no state or-ganization or statewide coordination. In 1969, there were more than 1,500 local councils and a state council in each state. These councils seek to foster an active concern for the community in enterprises dedicated to art and try to add arts dimensions to present private and public agencies.[11]

URBANIZATION. Since 1940, the population of the United States has increased by some 70 million persons—from about 132 million to slightly above 200 million. This increase has resulted in a more dense habitation of the land mass; that is, more people now live in each square mile of our country than ever before.[12] As some people indicate, this is not as significant as the changing distribution of the population. In 1940, about 56 percent of the American population lived in urban areas; that figure is now approaching 80 percent. Most of the increase in the urban population has been in the suburbs. From 1950 to 1960, for exam-ple, the population of the central cities increased by 11 percent, while the suburban population increased by 49 percent.

It is no longer possible to deal with the urban problem as a simple juxtaposition of urban and rural, and in that sense the above figures only hint at the magnitude of the change. The urban way of life has invaded the rural areas, making them more complex and more influ-enced by national forces. Electricity, radio and television, and roads and automobiles account for most of the urban influence on the rural community.

EXPLOSIONS

The nation is experiencing profound social changes. From the Sputnik era education has been seen as the core of the nation's malaise. Education is being called upon to perform more roles and more tasks and to achieve for every child a quality education. A number of forces within education—explosions—are at work directing and shaping education as it adjusts to its new roles.

NEW INSIGHTS INTO LEARNING. For many years intermediate educational objectives were implemented by a methodology that stressed the known. We knew that the world was round, that gravity affected objects, how to weld, how to "sweat" a joint of three-quarter-inch copper pipe, how to raise children, and we even knew how to learn. This educational methodology was based on the general assumption that the teacher had a series of facts about each and every known and his task was to get these facts to the pupil. The pupil was not educated until he knew the facts and could recall them in various ways and forms and under a variety of conditions.

This method was based on a variety of learning principles characterized by such phrases as reward-punishment, and stimulus-response.[13] Learning was conceived by psychologists and educators as restricted to building a connection to elicit a specific response; hence learning was practice in making the appropriate response to the specific stimulus. The appropriate methodology was to teach each skill and concept as a separate entity. Each key on the home row of the typewriter was learned. After the home row was mastered another small segment of the keyboard was introduced to the pupil.

We have no idea of what kind of society will evolve in which present students will spend their adult years. We do believe that change will be a significant aspect of it and that isolated facts will not prepare pupils to deal with the changed society. Allport summarizes this inadequacy:

Our emphasis has been on learning by drill and by reinforcement. Such *"habit acquisition"* receives all the emphasis. But the learning theory involved postulates a continuing dependency relation (extraneous reinforcement). When the relation terminates, the habits of study simply extinguish themselves.[14]

We know that learning is much more than the association of a stimulus-response connection.[15] Gagné is one of several researchers who have made significant contributions toward new approaches to learning by extending the forementioned framework. He has developed a hierarchy of behavioral categories that are preconditions to make learning occur with optimal effectiveness.[16] This hierarchy of behaviors and varieties of learning may be explained as follows:

TYPES OF LEARNING

PROBLEM SOLVING: A kind of learning that requires the internal events called thinking. Two or more previously acquired rules are somehow combined that produce a new capability.

Requires the Pre-learning of:

RULE LEARNING: A chain of two or more concepts.

Requires the Pre-learning of:

CONCEPT LEARNING: The learner acquires a capability of making a common response to a class of stimuli that may differ from each other widely.

Requires the Pre-learning of:

DISCRIMINATION LEARNING: The individual learns to make n different identifying responses to as many different stimuli.

Requires the Pre-learning of:

VERBAL ASSOCIATION: The learning of chains that are verbal.

Requires the Pre-learning of:

CHAINING: What is acquired in a chain of two or more stimulus-response connections.

Requires the Pre-learning of:

STIMULUS-RESPONSE LEARNING: The learner acquires a precise response to a discriminated stimulus.

(May) Require the Pre-learning of:

SIGNAL LEARNING: The individual learns to make general, diffuse response to a signal.

Children learn in different ways, at different rates, and with different motivations. Much research suggests that the "dull" student—to use a prevailing but inappropriate label—can learn as much as the "bright," though his learning is in a different style and at a different tempo.

Man must build his relationship with the world into which he was born. He must learn to relate to nature in such a way as to survive and continually transcend his biological beginnings. Such learning is a three-step process and is of two types. Man must first learn what he is, then what he can become. This is known as intrinsic learning. Finally, man learns how his becoming can be achieved. This is known as instrumental learning. Intrinsic learning involves taking on goals and purposes and giving direction to one's general motivation to survive and to find satisfactions. Instrumental learning involves skills and knowledge that make psychological growth possible. Intrinsic learning becomes the criteria, then, for selecting the instrumental learning to be achieved.

The phrase *cognitive organization* sums up the new insights into learning, which draw their major strength from cognitive field theory.[17] Cognitive field theory postulates that the individual's behavior is completely determined by his perceptual field, that he always perceives and behaves in such a way as to maintain the organization of his perceptual field. An individual's perceptual field is organized so that outside events and objects are always perceived in the way that will cause the least change in the field. Behavior is a way of changing the field or "decreasing the dissonance" to get better organization. Behavior is changed only after a change in the perceptual field. More efficient behavior—that is, learning—results when the learner discovers aspects of his situation that enable him to reach the goal he is pursuing at that time. From this point of view, learning is an active process of discovering.

THE DISCOVERY METHOD. As an outgrowth of this new learning theory, educators have rediscovered the discovery method of teaching. Contemporary learning theory emphasizes the individual and his learning. A premium is placed on the learning impetus that students derive from their innate tendency to explore unknown situations, to seek challenges in which they try out their newly won skills, and to gain pleasure from the active pursuit of learning. The mature student is involved in intellectual activities that arouse his curiosity and force him to confront the challenging and the unknown.

The student is at the heart of the discovery method. It is assumed that the student ought to acquire significant information by himself by a process that is useful to him in a variety of situations. The method does not imply that a student must learn all of his information by the discovery method.

What it does imply is something profoundly important in learning: that periodically the student ought to use his aggregation of data, however accumulated, in attacking problems so that he gives meaning to his information and order to his conceptual understanding and his rational insights.[18]

As a student learns to be responsible for taking the initiative and for carrying out his own learning, his whole point of view changes. Before this he may have been a passive recipient. The teacher decided what he was to learn, made the assignments, chose not only the questions to ask but also of whom to ask them, and at stated intervals made up a test to see how much each had "learned." The student could make only minor modifications in the process. A self-directed learner becomes involved in the purposes of his study, grows aware of the value of his learning, and sees how it makes a difference in his day-to-day living. Many of the new curriculum reforms are based on the discovery method and help students achieve self-direction. They provide for the student to inquire into phenomena, to experiment with unknowns, and to utilize one level of knowledge as a springboard to more knowledge at a higher level.

INSTITUTIONAL CHANGES. There are two institutional changes occurring in education at the present time. One is in the design of facilities, the other the growth of two-year colleges. A significant number of schools being built today at the elementary and secondary level follow the "open design," with an instructional materials center, a learning center, or a resource center as the core of the building. The instructional materials center combines the resources of the traditional book-oriented library with the newer media of the audio-visual aids center. It is larger than both departments were when separate and it is characterized by activity and diversity. Its staff serves both in the old role of helping students with their classroom assignments and in the new roles of remedial work, counseling, and supervising students in their learning activities. Students can type, read, listen to tapes, make tapes, carry on group work, lounge, and listen to recordings. The instructional materials center is the heart of the school, and the other parts of the school as well as the learning activities radiate from it.

Community colleges, junior colleges, and technical institutes—each a different type of institution with a different philosophy—have been around since the early 1900s and were regarded as the step-child of higher education for nearly fifty years. Now the two-year colleges have emerged to claim a distinct place in the educational picture. They enrolled relatively small numbers of students until 1960. In 1961, there were 678 two-year colleges in operation, enrolling approximately 750,000 students. By 1969, the number of institutions had increased by 372 to 1050, with an enrollment of over 2,000,000 students—nearly triple that of 1961. The increase is expected to continue by the American Association of Junior

Colleges. It predicts 200 more two-year colleges, with enrollment approaching 3,500,000 by 1973.

The growth of the two-year colleges has been brought about by a number of factors. Not all high school graduates are able to get into a four-year college and thus begin to explore alternatives. Also, many high school personnel are advising students to seek additional educational opportunities before they enter the labor market. Perhaps the major reason for the growth of the two-year colleges is the increased technology associated with many jobs. A worker on a job simply needs to know a much more complex technology about that job than did the person who held that job even a few years ago. The level of technological attainment possible by the time of high school graduation is not sufficient to obtain many of the jobs available.

METHODS OF INSTITUTING CURRICULUM CHANGE. For nearly its entire existence, the school has developed its own curricular materials. Textbooks were about the only outside material that was tolerated. If a new course was to be instituted, a group of teachers who would be likely to teach the course would start its development. They would meet for as long as a year or two, counseling with other teachers and administrators and examining a textbook here and there.

Such a practice, in general, is no longer practical. A school system cannot afford the time as well as the personnel costs of developing most of its own materials. Soon after a need for a course is discerned it must be ready for introduction into the curriculum. School systems are turning more and more to commercially prepared materials and instructional systems. Once a set of materials is found, the local system must adapt it to its needs.

A major problem of the school system is how to pick and choose among available commercial instructional packages or systems. The Association for Supervision and Curriculum Development constructed "A Model for Curriculum Development Decision Making" to aid the local school system with that problem (see Figure 6).[19] The model assumes a "package world" in which the local school system is faced with the task of selecting and integrating various curricular packages rather than beginning to design curriculum from scratch. The model suggests that each package is to be evaluated by an instructional theory (what does the package assume about the nature of the learner, how one learns), by practical considerations (how much does it cost, how long are pupils expected to be involved), by the organizational pattern of the school (how many staff members are required, is it designed for small groups or large), and by the mix or diversity that occurs if the package is adopted (how does this unit in history mix with the mathematics pack-

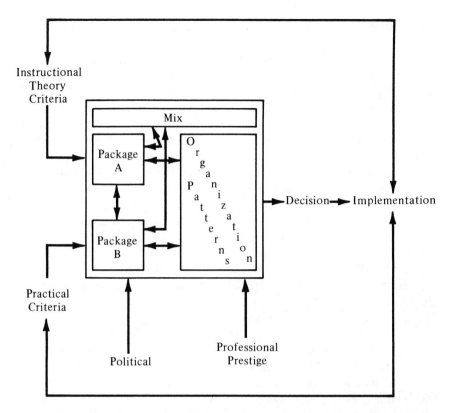

FIGURE 6. A Model for Curriculum Development Decision Making. In *Criteria for Theories of Instruction*. Ira J. Gordon, ed. Washington, D.C.: Association for Supervision and Curriculum Development, 1968, p. 42.

age when both are to be used in a self-contained classroom). Out of this interacting analysis comes the decision to adopt or to reject a curriculum package.

CURRICULUM CONTENT. When university professors and other scientists found that they could influence what was taught in the high schools they moved with much enthusiasm. Emphasis was upon the discreteness of the academic disciplines: not simply science, but physics, chemistry, and biology. The physics curriculum for the high schools was to be designed by physicists, chemistry curriculum by chemists, and so forth. It was suggested that each subject area had its unique structural elements—i.e., concepts, key ideas, principles, and modes of inquiry. If a student learned the structural elements of the subject area he would come to think like a scientist in that area and he would be able to grasp the relationship of a new phenomenon to another phenomenon already experienced.

A set of criteria was established to help the scientists determine the content for the organizing centers of a discipline, an organizing center being defined as the concepts, skills, or values around which specific learning stimuli or educational experiences are to be organized. The content of an organizing center: (a) must be authentic and important to the subject area, (b) must possess linkage value and relate one experience with another, (c) should involve the student so that he is thinking and acting, (d) should present alternatives to the student, and (e) should lead the student to discover for himself.

The involvement of university scholars in fields such as physics, biology, economics, and social studies in the construction of high school curricula was long overdue. The result has been a course of study that possesses unity and structure from the time it is introduced into the school until it is last offered. "Senior physics" (the last physics course that a student takes in a secondary school) is no longer an isolated course but is built on the principles of physics that were introduced to the student in earlier educational experiences.

Two serious gaps are now apparent in this curriculum reform movement. The first gap has to do with the limited subject areas of the high school. College professors first offered help in the physical sciences, then in social studies, economics, and history. Many other subject areas have not had this expert help. One also wonders about the logical conclusion of such efforts. At the college level the academic disciplines are now more discrete. Biochemistry is a branch of chemistry, just as chemistry is a branch of science. Nuclear physics is more discrete than is physics. Will the experts move to have these and other discrete courses introduced at the high school level?

The second serious gap is the fact that the marriage between the subject matter concepts and student considerations did not occur. The initiative for reform came from the top down and from outside of education. Seldom were teachers involved except to judge between two alternatives in the proposed curriculum. A review of the criteria that the scientists evolved for the organizing centers shows an appalling lack of concern for students' past experiences, interests, and self-perceptions.

What has really occurred is a shift in the content of the curriculum. It has lost some child-centered and society-centered concerns and gained more discipline or subject-centered concerns. This gap was particularly true at the beginning of the reform movement but now shows some signs of narrowing as the two forces recognize and talk about the problem. As a consequence of the shift to subject-centered curriculum, there is a great danger that significant mankind problems that grow out of where the student lives, problems that cut across subject lines, may not find their way into the classroom unless the two forces are merged.

THE EMERGENT SCHOOL

The above discussion of implosions and explosions, however brief, hoped only to highlight some of the changes in the educational scene. The list of factors was not exhaustive. Other factors, such as a new guidance philosophy and the technological revolution, are discussed elsewhere in this book.

The educational system has probably changed as much in the decade of the 1960s as it has in any previous half-century. The school entered the sixties as an institution with rather rigid internal and external structures, it emerged as an institution that showed some signs of flexibility in its internal structure. At the outset creativity in the schools was not particularly fostered. Each pupil within a given track—academic, vocational, or general—was exposed to generally the same program. Change from one track was seldom permitted. Student interest was considered primarily from the point of view of groups, not of the individual.

The general public was largely ignored; the schools were thought to be none of their business. After all, the teacher was a trained professional whose judgment should not be questioned. Looking back over this era, Leslie A. Hart suggests that the layman is shocked at school practices as he looks across the chasm between himself and the educator.

On one side of the chasm are those who manage and operate the schools. On the other are those who send their children and pay the taxes—and who are becoming more and more concerned about the competence of educators to provide acceptable education. The gap between the two is dismayingly wide and potentially explosive. Bridging it, it seems to me, must be an urgent objective for all concerned with the future of public education.

In a real sense, those on either side live in different worlds. The working educator as a rule went through school, attended college, and then re-entered the school world as a teacher, specialist, or administrator, with perhaps little more than a glimpse along the way of what all too soon became "the outside world." Moonlighting jobs, summer work, and occasional contacts serve feebly to offset the persistent isolation normally engendered by teaching or other school employment.

To the lay person, looking from his side of the gap, the local school system has long seemed a walled fortress, fiercely resistant to intrusion. Let us admit the fact: those citizens who evidenced curiosity about the how and why of school functioning have likely soon found themselves fended off, none too subtly. The more penetrating their questions and persistent their intent, the more teachers and administrators seem to bridle. They suspect, often correctly, that the information if given may lead to criticism rather than applause; and they may feel also that their "professional" purlieus are being threatened. . . .

—The layman is *shocked* to find that the schools operate in a sea of opinion. Each teacher, each specialist, each administrator constantly makes decisions with little recourse to research, established findings, verifications, or the checking of results in meaningful ways. Myths, folklore, habit, antique practices continue in use because they are seldom checked against readily available knowledge. School people often seem not even to *care* whether what they are doing is the best practice, so long as it suits their convenience and preferences. Pressed to justify their views, they become annoyed and abusive, as though no such obligation exists and the request is a personal attack. To the layman, such behavior seems irresponsible, and so unscientific as to suggest something out of *Alice's Adventures in Wonderland*.

—The layman is *shocked* to discover that teachers are paid almost wholly without regard to assignment or performance. One may get $10,000 for handling a class of 30, while another next door with precisely the same responsibilities (and perhaps more ability) receives $5,800. Two teachers are each paid $7,500, one of whom is considered atrocious, the other the school's best. For almost all teachers, there is nothing approaching an adequate "promotion ladder," no way to get paid more for superior teaching. Locked into a classroom, largely prevented from watching other teachers work, a teacher can readily become less sensitive, more rigid, more outdated and weary each year—yet win a pay increment based on "experience"! The layman gasps in disbelief, and when forced to believe, grows angry.

—The layman is *shocked* to find that the schools expend huge sums, requiring more than half of all local and perhaps state taxes, without the remotest sense of cost accounting. Records show who got the money, but whether a particular expenditure has produced any observable or measurable educational result is usually a total mystery. Money is spent mainly the way it was spent last year. Inertia is the chief guide. Useless, even harmful practices can continue to absorb funds for decades because there is no built-in or provided check or feedback to call a halt—even while the educators cry poverty and ask more taxes each year. Accustomed to having to justify every dollar he spends by proving results, the layman feels his head reeling as he beholds this wanton squandering of public funds.

—The layman is *shocked* to learn that the school operates in a state of near-anarchy, with teachers "owning" their classrooms and doing just about what they please within them—often almost literally thumbing their noses at school, system, or even state policies, and virtually daring their superiors to supervise them. That effective supervision and control has all but vanished is too evident. Principals in turn ignore, defy, or frustrate their central administration. To suppose that such a disjointed, unsteered, diffuse organization can respond to complex and urgent needs of the day seems to the layman purest madness.[20]

Prior to and including the early 1960s it was generally agreed that all activity in the classroom tended to revolve around the activities of the teacher, who was assumed to be "an all-knowing and all-doing" person. The teacher determined what each pupil would do, how long it was to be done, and what the pupil would use in the activity, and he censored any conclusions drawn by the pupil. Such a teacher was said to be authority-centered. E. Paul Torrance, an educational psychologist and one of the leading experts on teaching for creativity, often works with teacher workshops in helping authority-centered teachers to work more creatively with students. He asks that they ask themselves questions like the following:

Would I be willing to let pupils ask questions about whatever puzzles them?

Would I teach something outside my prepared lesson?

Would I permit a child to work alone in the classroom?

Would I permit a child to continue an activity in which he is absorbed, even if he has to miss a planned activity?

Would I allow the child to be successful in some way that is possible for him, even if it is not the way I had planned?

Would I withhold criticism long enough for the child to discover and correct his own errors?

Would I plan a lesson specifically to help one child solve a problem?

Schools have not developed to the point where we can say that they are now pupil-centered. The emergent school, though, is seeking to develop pupil-centered classrooms, to work creatively with students, and to have students assume responsibility as they acquire experiences within a subject area.

By the late 1960s many people had expressed a concern for what would be taught in the school. The question was usually phrased as: What should the high school graduate know about . . . when he graduates? It was assumed that if he should know it, it should be taught. This movement was led by university professors and other scientists. Teachers, by and large, were left out of the process.

Concurrently a new psychological base for instruction emerged: The student was to assume more responsibility for his own learning. Although the scientists ignored the student as new curricula were developed, the school began to find ways of making the interaction of pupil with subject matter a meaningful educational experience. The emergent school also took on a broader area of responsibility within the fabric of society for those pupils staying in school.

NEW CHARACTERIZATIONS OF THE
EDUCATIONAL SYSTEM

The emergent school and the educational system have a number of commitments that are altering their style, if only slightly. The older characterizations of public, free, democratic are as true now as they have ever been. In addition, some new things are happening in the schools of the late 1960s and early 1970s.

1. More flexibility in the internal structure of the school. This flexibility is designed for the student who finds the school relevant and meaningful to him. It permits him some alternatives as he responds within the school environment and it permits him to assume some responsibility for his own learning. We have already mentioned discovery learning. In addition, the school began to institute on a rather large scale such things as flexible scheduling, modular scheduling, team teaching, and independent study. Though these practices are not in a majority of the schools, they are in a significant number and are being added rapidly. Nearly every school, though, has instituted some changes that have resulted in greater flexibility for students.

2. A middle-class institution. At first glance, this may contradict the above point, which suggests that there is now flexibility for those students who find the school a relevant institution. But many students do not find the school relevant. Their only recourse has been to drop out of school or to stay in as a passive participant. Many critics suggest that the school is too rigid to deal with anything other than normal programs, that it is becoming more and more an institution to serve the middle class. For special programs other social institutions need to be created or the task normally assigned to the school should be assigned to other social institutions. An example is the Job Corps. Job Corps participants were at one time in the school system. They did not find it relevant to their needs and dropped out. After discovering that education is necessary to any kind of success in the outside world, they had no place to go to get needed training and educational help. The nation was concerned, as unemployed and underemployed people are wasted human resources. The idea emerged to create the Job Corps to train these people so that they might obtain and hold jobs and to educate them so that they could function in our society. It seemed to some in authority, and especially so to members of Congress, that it was poor policy to assign that task to an institution that had already failed at the job. Consequently, the Job Corps was created apart from the educational system. It was not even assigned to the U.S. Office of Education, but to the Department of Labor.

Another area of rigidity concerns staffing and teacher certification. Schools need a variety of specialized functions performed. Occupational education in particular possesses this need, with nursing programs, shop demonstrations, occupational experience programs, shop skills, and with regular vocational classes. Elementary education in such programs as the nursery school and science also need specialized functions. Persons are available who can perform these skills, but the school system, by and large, has not been able to hire them since they are not "certified." This is particularly true at the elementary and secondary level. (The post–high school area has made some significant inroads.) At the elementary and secondary level some additional personnel has been added under the category of "teacher aides." But these people do not usually possess the specialized knowledge that is often needed, though the teacher aide is a valuable addition to the school system. All in all, the educational system has not been too willing to relax its rigidity to meet current demands.

3. Many persons in the emergent school are committed to letting students seek and discover. This point has been discussed earlier and is mentioned here to remind the reader that the school is becoming committed to the discovery method of teaching at least some subjects.

4. The emergent school is committed to exploring new systems of evaluation. Given team teaching, independent study, and the discovery method of teaching, the old system of evaluation is no longer adequate. The 1967 Yearbook of the Association for Supervision and Curriculum Development (ASCD) says:

There are many ways of looking at learning but the understandings that grow out of them are often hard to translate into classroom procedures. Mechanistic stimulus-response explanations of learning have never appealed to most teachers. Neither have laboratory findings about conditioning, trial and error, reinforcement, extinction, reward, etc., which have seemed to have little to do with the way boys and girls really act in the classroom. Most teachers now know that older notions of training the mind, mental discipline, and transfer of training were based on a kind of mythology. However, while these notions were in command, they generated methods of teaching and ideas about school organization which have been in practice so long that they now seem natural and sensible; thus the procedures linger on, long after their rationale has faded.[21]

The traditional system of evaluation that culminates in a letter grade of A, B, C, D, or F is said to serve administrative, guidance, information, and motivation and discipline functions. Of the four functions, only one really may be identified as helping the student.

The ASCD seriously considered modernizing the evaluation system. It suggested that a first criterion of evaluation must be how well it is converted into genuine feedback to the pupil, leading him steadily toward sharper, more valid perceptions, and therefore toward wiser decisions and actions. The test of an evaluation system is: "Does it deliver the feedback that is needed, when it is needed, to the persons or groups who need it?"[22] According to the ASCD, an evaluation system for modern education must: (a) facilitate self-evaluation, (b) encompass every objective valued by the school, (c) facilitate learning and teaching, (d) produce records appropriate to the purposes for which records are essential, and (e) must provide continuing feedback to the larger questions of curriculum development and educational policy.[23]

One educator comments about evaluating a student's independent study activities:

The effective student in independent study is one who produces results and strives for improvement. The school should report both of these aspects to parents, to college admissions officers, employers, and to interested members of the general public. Too, the student should be in a position to know what he has accomplished in his independent study endeavor. The art student who goes to be interviewed with portfolio in hand suggests a clue as to how to do this. Why should not a poem, a research paper, a painting, a project, a model, a write-up of an original experiment, a musical composition, a short story, a publication, a physically fit body, a piece of sculpture, a specimen of typing, a special device, or other evidence of the quantity and quality of independent study be used as evidence of a productive high school experience?[24]

No magic breakthroughs have occurred yet in getting the majority of school systems to change their evaluation system. Schools are showing evidence that they are trying to break with the tradition of the informal, half-intuitive, complex system of quizzing, testing, and examining and assigning a letter grade.

A Center for the Study of Evaluation has been created at the University of California, Los Angeles. Its three basic areas of study are:

1. Evaluation of instructional programs. Research in this area aims at creation of a means of studying classroom practices, programs and procedures. One goal is to provide methods of gathering information upon which educational decisions can be based.

2. Evaluation of educational systems. Here the focus is on ways of studying total educational organizations—schools or school systems—rather than particular programs.

3. Evaluation theory and methodology. A general model of evaluation is to be constructed. Major emphasis is placed on identifying evaluation problems, simulated evaluation exercises and statistical sampling procedures.[25]

In addition to research activities, the center sponsors symposia on evaluation to assist in the dissemination of research information. The center's publication, *Evaluation Comment,* is widely read in the field of education and aids greatly in the promotion of instructional evaluation. Evaluation is not ignored by other research centers. The Center for Vocational and Technical Education in Columbus, Ohio, conducts many studies related to the evaluation of vocational education.

5. The emergent school is committed to community and industry involvement. During the mid-1960s, it was popular to say "education is too important to be left to the educators." This comment was made by a U.S. Commissioner of Education. What he meant was that the education of our young people is so important, such a variety of experiences are needed, that the walls of the classroom must be extended to involve community resources, industry personnel, tours of industry, and the like. A later commissioner, Harold Howe II, often spoke of the need to involve the community and industry in education. Excerpts from two of his speeches follow:

The partnership must be extended, also, to all those in industry who depend on the human resource development of the educational enterprise and to all those in education who must somehow get a vision of the future for which our youth are being prepared. The key word is cooperation; it is creative cooperation. We look to industry not only to fulfill our demands and prescriptions, but, in the characteristic manner of American industry, to provide innovative and original contributions to the educational process itself. We will have to share problems, tell you of our needs, our pressures, our successes, and our failures. We hope you will do the same. In the past, there has not been enough of this kind of teamwork.[26]

We are getting away from the notion that education is a neatly packaged period of years inserted into a person's life somewhere between the first pair of long pants and his first vote. Education no longer ends with a high school diploma or a college degree. I think within 25 years we will come to regard it as entirely natural for a person to return periodically to a college or a technical institution to renew and refresh his education. . . . When we think of vocational education, there is no reason at all why we should think only of the teenager. In fact, we must not. We must think also of the older, semi-skilled worker who is anxious to elevate his abilities to a new plane of skill and understanding that makes him eligible for more demanding and more fulfilling work. We can depreciate a machine over a period of years and then junk it without serious loss. But we cannot depreciate humans, and we certainly must not junk them.

Industry can help our vocational schools to fashion training courses that confer a mental flexibility as well as manual dexterity. Collaboration between the businessman and the educator can teach us how to train a student, not simply for one job that might be automated out of existence in five years but for a career built on an understanding of the principles underlying a service or production process. Industry and education can investigate together the problem of retraining, of salvaging for a useful, fulfilling, and productive life those older workers whose skills have been made obsolete.[27]

The first quotation is from a speech that Commissioner Howe delivered to a conference on Engineering Systems and Education; the latter is from a speech delivered to the Georgia Vocational Association. He is simply reflecting a trend that is occurring throughout education. Programs in New Jersey, Pennsylvania, California, and Wisconsin have been mentioned in recent journals as examples of educational programs that involve community resources in the schools.

6. The emergent school is an agent for new values. A traditional debate concerns the role of the school in transmitting values from one generation to another. Some persons argue that the school is basically a conservative institution whose role is to mirror the culture, to transmit from one generation to another the time tested and thus "best" values of the culture. Here, the school is seen to be at the trailing edge of a cultural time line. Others argue that the school should perform that role but that in addition, as a partially futuristic institution, it should pick up the emergent values and inculcate new values into the present generation. In this instance the school is at the leading edge of a cultural time line. This whole issue is simply academic, for the school at present is being used to change values.

The schools have been driven by political forces into the position of spearheading societal change as that change is embodied in politically formulated public policy.

As striking an example as any is the way in which the schools have been drafted into the role of principal change agent to affect racial integration.[28]

The authors conclude by stating that "the point intended to be emphasized is that, within the last two decades, the schools have been cast in the role of a principal change agent." The school has always been concerned directly and indirectly with values. Prior involvement was, however, concerned with teaching the tried and true values that stood the test of time and were held by the majority of the population. When the school becomes a change agent, however, its role is reversed and the emerging values examined may clash with the traditional values. This role is inherent with conflict and will keep the school in the limelight for some time to come. Margaret Mead, for example, suggests that all men regardless of past cultural traditions are entering the present at the same point in time.[29] This sets up a condition where youth know more about the society than do the parents. A role reversal is occurring, according to Mead. Young people and their elders must be willing to explore the future on every ground, learning from each other. In such a situation the school has no alternative if it wishes to remain alive but to be an agent for new values.

Clearly, whether we like it or not, some schools are agents for spearheading changes in social values. The extent to which this is happening, however, is a point of considerable debate. All schools are not doing this, and all emerging values are not being examined by the school system.

NOTES

[1]Alvin C. Eurich, *Reforming American Education* (New York: Harper & Row, 1969), p. 199, jacket.

[2]J. Steele Gow, Jr., Berkart Holzner, and William C. Pendleton, "Economic, Social and Political Forces," in *The Changing American School*, ed. John I. Goodlad, 65th Yearbook of the National Society for the Study of Education, Part II (Chicago: University of Chicago Press, 1966), p. 160.

[3]George Arnstein, "Quo Vadis, Vocational Education," *Phi Delta Kappan*, 44, no. 7 (April 1963), 329.

[4]National Education Association, *Education in a Changing Society*, Project on Instruction (Washington, D.C.: The Association, 1963).

[5]Eli Ginzberg, "Social and Economic Trends," in *Vocational Education*, ed. Melvin L. Barlow, 64th Yearbook of the National Society for the Study of Education, Part I (Chicago: University of Chicago Press, 1965), p. 31.

[6]Sigmund Nosow and William H. Form, eds., *Man, Work and Society* (New York: Basic Books, Inc., Publishers, 1962). See pp. 9–55 for a discussion of work and leisure.

[7]Ibid., p. 44.

[8]Eurich, *Reforming American Education* (New York: Harper & Row, 1969), p. 117.

[9]Alvin Toffler, *The Culture Consumers* (New York: St. Martin's Press, Inc., 1964).

[10]Stanford Research Institute, Long Range Planning Report, No. 140, "The Arts and Business," in William J. Baumol and William G. Bowen, *Performing Arts: The Economic Dilemma* (New York: Twentieth Century Fund, 1966), p. 37.

[11]See Robert E. Gard et al., *The Arts in the Small Community—A National Plan*, and Michael Warlum et al., *The Arts and the Small Community* (Madison: University of Wisconsin, Department of Community Arts Development, 1969).

[12]Gow, Holzner, and Pendleton, *The Changing American School*, p. 169.

[13]Percival M. Symonds, *What Education Has to Learn from Psychology* (New York: Teachers College, Columbia University, 1964).

[14]Gordon W. Allport, "Values in Our Youth," *Teachers College Record*, 63 (1961), 217.

[15]J. W. McGuire, "A Multiprocess Model for Paired-Associate Learning," *Journal of Experimental Psychology*, 62 (1961), 335–47.

[16]Robert M. Gagné, *The Conditions of Learning*, 2nd ed. (New York: Holt, Rinehart, & Winston, Inc., 1970), pp. 63–64, 66.

[17]See E. R. Hilgard, ed., *Theories of Learning and Instruction*, 63rd Yearbook of the National Society for the Study of Education, Part I (Chicago: University of Chicago Press, 1964), and Donald Snygg, "A Cognitive Field Theory of Learning," in *Learning and Mental Health in the School*, 1966 Yearbook of the Association for Supervision and Curriculum Development (Washington, D.C.: The Association, 1966), pp. 77–96.

[18]Louis J. Rubin, "Creativity and the Curriculum," in *Teaching for Creative Endeavor*, ed. William B. Michael (Bloomington: University of Indiana Press, 1968), p. 76.

[19]"A Model For Curriculum Development Decision Making," in *Criteria for Theories of Instruction*, ed. Ira J. Gordon (Washington, D.C.: Association for Supervision and Curriculum Development, 1968), p. 42.

20Leslie A. Hart, "The New Breed of School Critic," *Educational Leadership*, 26, no. 7 (1969), 671–73.

21Rodney A. Clark and Walcott H. Beatty, "Learning and Evaluation," in *Evaluation as Feedback and Guide*, ed. Fred T. Wilhelms, 1967 Yearbook, Association for Supervision and Curriculum Development (Washington, D.C.: The Association, 1967), p. 49.

22Fred T. Wilhelms, in ibid., p. 4.

23Ibid., pp. 4–8.

24William M. Griffin, "Schedules, Bells, Groups, and Independent Study," in *Independent Study*, eds. David W. Briggs III, and Edward G. Buffie (Bloomington: University of Indiana Press, 1966), p. 8.

25See *Prospectus*, Center for the Study of Evaluation, University of California Graduate School of Education, Los Angeles, Calif.

26Harold Howe II, "Education and the Changing Technology," in *Picking Up the Options* (Washington, D.C.: Department of Elementary School Principals, 1968), p. 96. Copyright 1968, National Association of Elementary School Principals, National Education Association. All rights reserved. Used with permission.

27Howe, "Recruiting For The New Partnership," in "Education and the Changing Technology: in *Picking Up the Options* (Washington, D.C.: Department of Elementary School Principles, 1968), pp. 21–22. Copyright 1968, National Association of Elementary School Principals, National Education Association. All rights reserved. Used by permission.

28Gow, Holzner, and Pendleton, *The Changing American School*, p. 197.

29Margaret Mead, *Culture and Commitment* (New York: Doubleday & Company, Inc., 1970).

10

THE EMERGENT IN
VOCATIONAL EDUCATION

GROWTH AND DEVELOPMENT CONCERNS

The term "vocational development" describes the processes of development that are involved when individual moves from an awareness of work and work ideas to competence in making a contribution to earning a living. People are not born mature; they grow and develop. One of the areas of an individual's growth is toward an occupational identity. The stages that he grows through in gaining this occupational identity are referred to as life stages; five are normally accepted: growth, exploration, establishment, maintenance, and decline. Within these five life stages there are a number of processes. One with which vocational educators spend a significant portion of time is the process of skill development. There are also other processes. A process coming much earlier in the life of an individual is the awareness that at some point in time he must decide how he is going to earn a living. Another is discovering the available resources as he decides on the best way for him to contribute to the world of work. Still another process—and this one comes in the middle and advanced years of one's career—is that of deciding how to maintain one's style of life and one's level of contribution to the world of work.

VOCATIONAL DEVELOPMENT AS A PROCESS

Vocational development is a *process* of growth and development (cognitive, psychological, affective) that *enables* an *individual to find* a *satisfying work role* and to *become established* in an occupation. Stress is placed on all of the underlined words. A process is something that is dynamic and ever-changing. It implies that there is order, that something must come before something else though several things may be occurring at the same time. "Enable" is to facilitate, to provide the opportunity for something to occur.

The word "individual" provides the central area of focus. An individual is one, is personal, is unique. Each individual has his own unique pattern, rate, and sequence of development, and these rather than the needs of the labor market are the primary determinants of the educational experiences he needs for his vocational development. The educational experiences leading to the selection of a work role and the work role itself must be satisfying to the individual. "Work role" is a very broad term and means much more than an occupation. It includes all of the aspects of life that are determined by one's work. "Establishment in an occupation" refers to the exploratory, trial, and stable phases in getting a job. It is normally thought that a person needs three years in a job before he is established in that occupation.

Vocational development is a sequentially patterned process that is the same for all who develop normally.[1] The rate at which a particular individual passes through the pattern varies. Vocational development also involves a series of decisions made over a period of time, each one built on a previous one. The series of decisions leads to a person's final choice of an occupation. The developmental pattern is largely irreversible. Each experience in the pattern influences later decisions and consequently these experiences cannot be undone. A final occupational choice following the sequential pattern of decisions and experiences ends in a compromise among the individual's interests, capacities, values, and reality considerations.

STAGES IN VOCATIONAL DEVELOPMENT

A young person from an early age until about age ten or eleven is thought to be in a fantasy stage of development, i.e., the young person is

guided by his fantasy. The stage begins with fantasy at its most operational stage. A youngster at age five can, from dinnertime to bedtime,
indicate a preference for and reject being a space pilot, a cowboy, a
policeman, a fireman, and a football player. He is limited only by his
imagination and his fantasy as to the roles he would like to assume.
These considerations are not guided by any consideration of reality. As
the youngster gets older, the range of occupations considered and not
rejected diminishes. This is shown by curve A in Figure 7. As he gets
older he also begins to acquire knowledge about himself, about occupations, and about relating himself to work (curve B in Figure 7). Curve A
is a function of curve B, thus as the individual continues to acquire information, this information is used to narrow the range of occupations
he is considering. This is a very important stage of occupational development.

The concept that vocational development moves through a series of
life stages has been central to much of this work since the days of G.

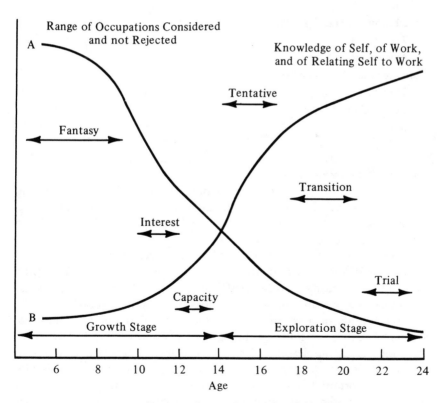

FIGURE 7. Forming an Occupational Choice

Stanley Hall. It has been advanced by a number of researchers, as evidenced in recent years in the works of Buehler, Lazarsfeld, Super, Ginzberg, Dysinger, Pressey and Kuhlen, Cass and Tiedeman, and O'Hara and Tiedeman.[2] Each of the five life stages is thought to have substages and is characterized by certain tasks that the individual encounters in that stage and with which he must successfully cope before he can progress to the next substage.[3] The five life stages and substages along with the general age at which it is encountered are:

Growth Stage (Birth–14)
   Fantasy (4–10)
   Interest (11–12)
   Capacity (13–14)
Exploration Stage (15–24)
   Tentative (15–17)
   Transition (18–21)
   Trial (22–24)
Establishment Stage (25–44)
   Trial (25–30)
   Advancement (31–44)
Maintenance Stage (45–64)
Decline Stage (65 on)
   Deceleration (65–70)
   Retirement (70 on)

Vocational education has traditionally been concerned primarily with a portion of the exploration stage, a narrow portion of this total framework. It is true that vocational education has programs for adults who may be in the establishment and maintenance stages. These programs, however, serve only a small portion of adults who could benefit from such programs.

These stages are in turn composed of five vocational developmental tasks: crystallizing a vocational preference, specifying a vocational preference, implementing a vocational preference, stabilizing a vocational preference, and consolidating status and advancing in a vocation.[4]

Crystallization of a vocational preference is a developmental task encountered during the fourteen- to eighteen-year-old period. During these early and middle adolescent years, the teen-ager is expected to begin to formulate ideas as to appropriate fields and levels of work. He is also expected to formulate concepts about himself and occupations that will enable him to commit himself to a type of education or training that will lead to some partially specified occupation. His preference may be quite vague. The choice of a school curriculum, for example, must be considered exploratory in most cases, as business education may lead to any one of a number of business occupations and may be abandoned at any time for lower level work. Even the preference for a more specific occupational area, as in the case of apprenticeships, must be regarded as nothing more than crystallization, since he can drop out before completion and enter related work.

Specifying a vocational preference is a developmental task of the middle and late adolescent years. It is during this period that the older adolescent is expected to convert a generalized choice into a specific choice and to make a final commitment to it. This is done by embarking upon a specialized educational and training program or by taking a job designed to serve as an entry to a chosen field. The key factors are the singling out of a specific occupation and the attitude of commitment to it. The age at which specification occurs depends in part on the type and length of education pursued by the individual and in part by his age of entry into the labor market. The job-seeking high school graduate is expected to specify what kind of job he desires, the college sophomore is expected to specify a major field of study, and the college senior is expected to have a specific job or area of graduate education in mind as his next goal.

Implementing a vocational preference is a developmental task of late adolescence and early adulthood. During these years from eighteen to twenty-five, the individual makes the transition from general education to specialized education, from school or college to employment; he is expected to convert his specified vocational preference into a reality, to implement his choice. If an individual's implementation is verbal—that is, he voices a liking for a specific job—he is implementing a preference. If it is instrumental—that is, he has at least partially acted upon his preference—he is implementing an occupational choice. In either case, implementation is exemplified by applying for admission to a specific college or taking a job as a mechanic's helper. At its lower levels implementation may take place without having been preceded by specification, just as specification can take place without crystallization. The important point about implementation is that it is primarily instrumental behavior of the individual.

Stabilization in a vocation is a developmental task of late adolescence and particularly of early adulthood. During the years from twenty-one to thirty the individual is expected to settle down, to find himself in a field of work that is compatible with his abilities, skills, interests, and aspirations. There may be a certain amount of changing from one job or employer to another during this period, but the changes should be changes of position, not of occupation.

Consolidation of status and advancement in a vocation is a vocational developmental task that is typically faced in adulthood. It generally begins at about age thirty and continues as the individual advances in his vocation until his middle forties, when the maintenance stage begins. Consolidation and advancement gets the individual firmly established in the occupation in which he has found a satisfactory place; he consolidates the position to insure that he may occupy it with safety and satisfaction as the years go by.

Each developmental task may be broken down into the relevant attitudes and the related behavior. Crystallization, for example, the process of forming a generalized vocational goal during the ages of fourteen to seventeen or eighteen, involves the following eleven items:

1. Awareness of the need to crystallize.
2. Use of resources.
3. Awareness of factors to consider.
4. Awareness of contingencies that may affect goals.
5. Differentiation of interests and values.
6. Awareness of present-future relationships.
7. Formulation of a generalized preference.
8. Consistency of preference.
9. Possession of information concerning the preferred occupation.
10. Planning for the preferred occupation.
11. Wisdom of the vocational preference.[5]

PROGRAMMING FOR STAGES IN THE VOCATIONAL DEVELOPMENT PROCESS

The developmental tasks, as well as the set of attitudes and behaviors listed above, concern the upward slope of career development (exploratory and establishment stages) rather than the plateau of middle adulthood (maintenance) or the decline of later adulthood (decline stage). Career patterns are generally clear at about age thirty-five, when stabilization is likely to be complete and consolidation tends to be well under way.

Additional insight into the problem of building vocational education programs on a growth and development base can be gained by examining page 209. Borow has classified six stages of vocational development. Programming for the early stages of vocational development is discussed around the key concepts of awareness, self-assessment, knowledge about occupational opportunities, differentiation, integration, planning for the tentative occupational choice, and becoming employed.

VOCATIONAL DEVELOPMENT—A LIFELONG PROCESS

STAGES OF VOCATIONAL DEVELOPMENT*	AGE
I. *Identification with a Worker* Father, mother, other significant persons. The concept of working becomes an essential part of the ego-ideal.	5–10
II. *Acquiring the Basic Habits of Industry* Learning to organize one's time and energy to get a piece of work done. School work, chores. Learning to put work ahead of play in appropriate situations.	10–15
III. *Acquiring Identity as a Worker in the Occupational Structure* Choosing and preparing for an occupation. Getting work experience as a basis for occupational choice and for assurance of economic independence.	15–25
IV. *Becoming a Productive Person* Mastering the skills of one's occupation. Moving up the ladder within one's occupation.	25–40
V. *Maintaining a Productive Society* Emphasis shifts toward the societal and away from the individual aspect of the worker's role. The individual sees himself as a responsible citizen in a productive society. He pays attention to the civic responsibility attached to his job. He is at the peak of his occupational career and has time and energy to adorn it with broader types of activity. He pays attention to inducting younger people into Stages III and IV.	40–70
VI. *Contemplating a Productive and Responsible Life* This person is retired from his work or is in the process of withdrawing from the worker's role. He looks back over his work life with satisfaction, sees that he has made his social contribution, and is pleased with it. While he may not have achieved all of his ambitions, he accepts his life and believes in himself as a productive person.	70+

*Henry Borow, ed., *Man in a World of Work* (Boston: Houghton Mifflin Co., 1964), p. 216. Used with permission of Houghton Mifflin Co. and the National Vocational Guidance Association.

AWARENESS. Young children are very aware of the things around them. During their fantasy stage, until about age ten, vocational experiences are very important, though they are not likely to be applied to the youngsters' cognitive, personal style. There is a degree of detachment to all of this pretending, as the youngster knows that he is simply playing a role. As he emerges from the fantasy stage, he is cognitively and personally aware—aware that he must some day decide on an occupation, that he must work, that he must make a personal decision about how he will spend his life, how he will earn a living.

Society has a number of awareness-developing experiences built into its institutions and processes. Awareness may come as a result of parents, peers, school authorities, and others asking the adolescent what he wants to do when he grows up, what curriculum he wants to pursue in high school, what specific course he wants to take. Regardless of when it occurs, awareness is usually an attitude and is usually verbal behavior, as illustrated by the many discussions and questions one has about choosing a career. Awareness may, however, be inferred from such instrumental behavior as an individual reading an occupational pamphlet.

Awareness occurs at all levels of vocational development and is usually the first in a set of behaviors to be dealt with. These have been identified as: awareness of the need to crystallize a general vocational preference, awareness of the need to specify a vocational preference or choice, awareness of the need to implement a preference, awareness of the need to stabilize, and awareness of the need to consolidate and advance.

SELF-ASSESSMENT. We are always assessing ourselves. Self-assessment, however, comes into major focus as and after an awareness of the need to crystallize a vocational preference and is how one gathers information about himself. Information in terms of one's abilities, aptitudes, interests, and aspirations is gathered through self-assessment, which should occur early in any vocational program. It should also be repeated several times in high school, throughout the post–high school educational program, and at points of adjustment after employment. An example of one self-assessing instrument is the *Sextant Profile*.[6]

An ability is something that one can do and is cognitive as well as psychomotor. Self-assessment tries to recognize such abilities as social, scientific, mathematical, physical, creative, and problem-solving. An aptitude is potential for something. Aptitudes such as personal traits, initiative, and courage are important in self-assessment. An interest is something one likes or enjoys. Thus, vocational interests are those occupational activities one likes or enjoys most. One needs to assess occupationally the situations that he has interests in (at a desk, out of doors), his desire for influence over others, his desire for abstractions, and similar criteria. An aspiration is a long-term goal that one would like to attain. One needs to assess the style of life one wants to achieve. This includes such things as the type of house, the neighborhood, friends, and how one wants to spend his leisure time. It is also important to consider the desire for material goods, the degree of security wanted in a job, how much prestige is desired, and to what degree it is necessary to be independent.

There is an intricate and to a large degree inexplicable relationship between abilities, aptitudes, interests, and aspirations. The mere fact that one has potential for something does not necessarily mean that he should or will develop it. Persons may have abilities that they have no interests in developing for occupational purposes. On the other hand, persons may aspire to an occupational area but possess no abilities or aptitudes to back them up. A recent conversation with the owner of a very successful cinema photography company brings home this point. This man had an intense desire to be an artist. He did very poorly in art classes in high school and could not successfully complete art courses after high school, though he did get a college degree in speech and drama. His hobby was photography, where he applied his creative talents with the determination that he would be the best cameraman anywhere. After a three-year assignment overseas for a company, in which he spent all of his spare time photographing the people and their dress, he sold some of his work. With that money he purchased additional equipment and began to produce films on fashions for advertising purposes. Today his company employs thirty-five full-time cinema technicians (cameramen, cutters, splicers). All the time that he was moving his company into its leadership role in the fashion merchandizing industry, he was being motivated by an aspiration to become an artist.

KNOWLEDGE ABOUT OCCUPATIONAL OPPORTUNITIES. If a person is to grow and develop toward an occupational area he must learn about occupational opportunities. One of the more simple areas is knowing how work is classified. It may be classified by type (white collar–blue collar), by level (managerial, professional, technical, skilled, semiskilled, unskilled), by title (president, vice president, principal, teacher, administrator, supervisor), by industry (medical, trades, professional, construction, insurance, equipment), and by function within an industry (production sales, product control, management).

One also needs to learn what is required for a specific occupational entry and advancement. After entry is obtained what is required for advancement? Can one advance in this occupation? What abilities—physical, mental, social, educational—are necessary in this occupational area? A nurse's aide, for example, has very little opportunity for advancement. Although a nurse's aide and a registered nurse may use very similar physical and social abilities, they differ widely in terms of educational abilities both for entry and advancement.

Also important is the availability of opportunities. This is frequently tempered by geographical limitations, for certain jobs and occupations are located in specific regions of a state or country. This factor is not considered by a significant number of students in making plans for post-high school education. One state, for example, was recently experiencing some difficulty in placing graduates of a two-year materials handling program simply because the students expected to return to their home area. When the jobs offered to them were far removed from their homes, and in some cases in another state, the graduates were likely to return to their home town and seek any employment available rather than take the offered job in their area of training.

DIFFERENTIATION. Differentiation may occur simultaneously with learning about occupational opportunities. During the tentative substage of exploration, individuals are very interested in what workers in occupations really do. A milkman, for example, drives a truck, fills out sales slips, is responsible for selling, handles money, explains a product, keeps records of deliveries and sales, reports to a supervisor, and so on. An individual needs to differentiate many jobs into their component areas or kinds of activities.

INTEGRATION. Knowledge about self and about occupations merge as the student puts himself into the occupational arena. "I have persuasive ability. Where may I use it?" is an example of integrating knowledge about self with knowledge about occupations. As the individual moves to the trial (little commitment) substage of the exploratory stage, it is important that he get a job to help him integrate himself with the occupational world. At the end of this stage he should have formulated ideas as to the fields and levels of work that are appropriate for him. Therefore the job is likely to be vague, for it is to help him determine how he feels about being a plumber, a salesman, a typist, a bookkeeper, a medical worker, a construction worker, trades, or a restaurant worker; to help him determine if he could be satisfied working at one level in an industry or if he should seek more education to seek employment at a different level. It is unimportant how many students later enter that occupation if the job is obtained at the senior-in-high-school level.

PLANNING FOR THE TENTATIVE OCCUPATIONAL CHOICE. Specification is involved in planning for the tentative occupational choice. For the individual going to college as well as the one seeking employment right after high school, planning simply involves getting ready to implement. In crystallization he is expected to have a generalized choice, i.e., medical, computer, or data processing field. Now he is expected to develop a specific choice, i.e., X-ray technician, registered nurse, computer programmer, key punch operator.

BECOMING EMPLOYED. Implementation is involved in becoming employed. Generally, this stage occurs when general secondary education terminates and the individual actually begins to work and is fully exposed to the demands of adult society, or seeks admission to a post–high school educational institution. This job is quite specific and the individual has a commitment to it, though he is likely to change jobs or occupations at a later time. Becoming employed involves the individual making contact with employers and securing employment either in the occupation of his choice or in a beginning job that should lead him into a job in his preferred occupation. Keeping the job—satisfying himself and satisfying the employer by his performance—leads to stabilization.

Vocational education has not by and large employed this growth and development base as the primary framework for developing programs. However, increasing numbers of programs are emerging with this framework.

The career education concept actively promoted by the U.S. Office of Education is a case in point. Three models of this concept are being tested. The first, a school-based model, seeks to substitute career education for general education by restructuring the entire local school program around real life (careers). Secondarily, it seeks to integrate academic knowledge and skills with specific job preparation. The Center for Vocational and Technical Education at Ohio State University was awarded an initial grant of $2 million to develop and test this K–14 model. Employer- and home-based models are also being developed and tested by other groups.

It seems imperative that growth and development be used as the building blocks for future vocational education programs. Seen in the growth and development framework, vocational education programs are designed to help young people grow and mature in relation to finding satisfying work roles and becoming established in an occupation in which they can make a contribution. This leads to a different concept of vocational education; the following section develops an emerging definition of vocational education.

VOCATIONAL EDUCATION DEFINED

People are not born aware of their environment. Soon after birth, parents, grandparents, brothers and sisters, and other friends and relatives try to get the youngster to respond to various stimuli, such as smiles, coos, squeaking toys, mobiles on the crib, and creative toys. When normal growth patterns are followed the baby takes on the attributes of responding consistently to the various stimuli. Without them the baby does not respond and is passive in the environment, which has dire consequences for his adult life.

We are speaking here of both cognitive and affective awareness. The concept of self is an old one in religion and philosophy. A part of man's search for awareness has been in answer to the question, "Who am I?" For Descartes, the answer was, "Cogito ergo sum" ("I think, therefore I am"). This statement marked a sharp break with medieval thought. The age of reason, as the era of philosophy ushered in by Descartes was called, held that cognition or reason was superior to emotion or feeling. The self was active, aware; the senses and emotions were passive. Freud broke with the age of reason by centering upon the emotions, by denying free will, and by stressing the influence of the child's earliest years.

Though the age of reason—cognitive self-awareness—has been given little attention since Freud introduced his theories, both positions have validity. The first step in self-awareness is both affective and cognitive. When a youngster puts his thumb or his toes in his mouth, he experiences sensation in both his mouth and his thumb or toes. When he puts a pacifier or a rattle in his mouth, he produces sensation in only one, his mouth. Since these objects do not produce double sensation, he separates self from other. This process provides the first reference point, his first awareness: that of separateness. Without growing through these processes of awareness, a child develops an inadequate concept of self. It is imperative to reinforce the fact that behavior is caused not by cognitive processes, but by way that cognitive information is acquired and internalized by the self. If it is internalized, it guides future behavior because the person "feels" a particular way about something. In short, knowledge is not sufficient for behavioral change; we respond to situations by considering how we feel about what we know. For instance, all of us have heard teen-agers say, "I just wouldn't feel right in that job," when discussing a particular situation. Others respond that it is a good job and they would and could fulfill its work role. Bloom, on the basis of reviews of longitudinal research, indicated that half of what accounts for the variance in adults, in aggressiveness in males and dependence in females, is present by age four.[7]

In general, a child's self-image and awareness are highly developed by the third year and become the organizers of future experiences, as well as the evaluators, selectors, and judges of experiences. As he continues to grow and mature he seeks to enhance and maintain that view of self. Such a view is not harsh and deterministic, though it may appear to be, for the individual possesses a great capacity and possibility for change.

Another type of awareness that a youngster acquires very early in life is an awareness of work: that people work, that he must work, that there are different kinds and types of work, that one can enter work at many different levels, that work determines many aspects of one's life, and that when one chooses a work role, he is implementing a concept of self. Work is not an end in and of itself. Work is the means of earning a living. A person must develop a competency so that he may contribute to earning his living. A part of that competency—but only a part—is competency to perform a skill or a needed service.

Vocational education begins with the first notion that a child has about work. A child in his early education is given some visual stimuli to make him aware of work and some emotional experiences about work. From these a youngster formulates a number of cognitive questions.

The visual stimuli are primarily toys, which are differentiated by work roles. Early in life children are exposed to toy fire engines and police cars. A fireman becomes associated with the fire engine and a policeman with the police car. The child is able to play out each of those roles. Similar toys are dump trucks, tractors, front end loaders, nurses' kits, and astronautical games. Each of these reminds the child that people work at the jobs represented by his toys and that he could contribute to any of these jobs.

A child also has a number of awarenesses of work that center in the affective domain. A traditional emotional experience is associated with the father. The youngster is aware that his father goes to work each day. He may look upon his father's return from work with great excitement so he can tell Dad about the day's events. Students of the present college generation who are turned off by the Establishment relate many emotional experiences concerning their fathers and work. Generally they comment that their fathers came home from work each day in a poor frame of mind, frustrated and perhaps full of disappointment. They further comment that if work does that to people then it must be bad and they want nothing to do with it. It is quite common for both parents of some youngsters to work and with the youngster going to a baby sitter. The child does not like to get up early, be dropped off, spend the day with the sitter, be picked up at night, taken home, and put to bed. Often they rebel, cry, and hang onto Mother's skirt. Mother's only reply is, "But Jimmy, Mother can't stay, she has to work." Work, then, is bad because it takes Mommy away. At age sixteen months my daughter became aware of the fact that work took Daddy away. At about this age, whenever I said I was going to work, she began to respond verbally with "Bye, bye" and overtly with a smile and a vigorous hand wave.

At an early age, youngsters ask some very insightful questions about work. An excellent example concerns my wife and a three-year-old girl for whom she baby-sat. The girl, Jeri, arrived every morning at about 7:30. Her father was an aluminum sider and drove a truck home to and from work. I occasionally spend some time in the morning at home working at my desk before going to the university. One day as I was leaving, Jeri asked where I was going; I responded, "I am going to work." With much puzzlement and deep concern showing in her face, she asked, "Where is your truck?" Since her father went to work in a truck, she assumed that all work roles required the father to have a truck. I then asked her a number of questions such as: "Does your dad drive a truck?" "Do you ever see trucks at any other house on our street?" "How does Ellen's dad get to work?" "How does Monty's dad get to work?" Together we discerned the fact that the fathers of the children in neighboring houses went to work in different types of vehicles. Her father and Ellen's father went to work in trucks. Monty's father went to work in a car as did Amy's and Cathy's fathers. The important point is that at age three Jeri was able to cognitively wrestle with the concept that a work role indicated how one traveled to and from work. Though her initial perception was inadequate she did recognize that, depending on the work the father did, he went to work in a different manner. She learned this too, as quite often in the weeks that followed she commented on the work that each father did and how he went to work differently.

Early formulations of vocational education focused on the development of skills and competencies associated with those skills. Vocational education was for those that had made a choice regarding an occupation. Further, that choice had to require an education of less than college grade. It is now possible, based upon what is known about the importance of life-long vocational education, about how people grow and develop, and about the enhancement of one's self-concept through work roles, to extend the concept of vocational education. In this extension it is important not to lose sight of the core that has been the traditional focus of vocational education. Skills are important in vocational education, and will continue to be important for some time to come, but their acquisition is not all there is to vocational education.

We are now ready to define vocational education as it is the focus of the emerging philosophy: *Vocational education is any education that provides experiences, visual stimuli, affective awareness, cognitive information, or psychomotor skills; and that enhances the vocational development processes of exploring, establishing, and maintaining oneself in the world of work.* Vocational education is important to all individuals, extends from the cradle to the grave, and is concerned with the cognitive, affective, and psychomotor domains of the individual.

Any number of writers have concluded, implied, or inferred that vocational education needs to be extended beyond its psychomotor skill framework. None of them, though, has spelled out a new definition of vocational education. Each has hinted at some of the dimensions of an extended vocational education. Two of these writers were cited in Chapter 5 and are referred to again here.

Some of the conclusions of the Draper report are:

1. An obligation of the public educational system is to prepare all young people for effectiveness in the world of work.

2. Many traditional definitions and requirements need to be modified to allow for expansion and variation in vocational education. It is time to recognize that vocational programs typically offered at the secondary level, in addition to serving only a small fraction of the students and a few types of work, have "been rather narrow, appropriate to the aspirations and abilities of a limited group of students."

3. Vocational competence involves much more than what is generally labeled as occupational, vocational, or technical education. It is appropriate to think of vocational education as beginning when the individual enters school and includes: understanding the processes, agencies, and materials of work; understanding vocational opportunities; exploring vocational experiences; training for a specific occupation; pretechnical education; and a sample employment experience.

4. Vocational education must avoid too-exclusive emphasis on building a specific set of skills. It must teach its subjects in such ways as to develop analytic problem-solving and skills essential in a group situation, as well as the ability to adapt to change.[8]

Frank also suggests that vocational education needs to be modified and extended, to begin at the junior high school level, and be a new path for most students.[9] His report makes five points in regard to extending vocational education.

First, it seeks to have vocational education begin at the junior high school level. Second, it seeks to establish investigation as a method of learning. A project type of goal-oriented process "requiring personal investigative involvement of students" is described as the method. This method can be used by students to seek solutions to other problems. Three sections of the method suggest that students are to learn how to do something, then learn what they are doing, and finally learn the broad principles related to the activity.

Third, the proposal seeks to strengthen both the intellectual elements of vocational education and the manipulative, nonverbal aspects of general or academic education. It is proposed that vocational education students be permitted to make more generalizations and abstractions on the basis of their operational activities. It is also proposed that all students be given the opportunity to study and manipulate materials, processes, and systems; to pull apart and put together all the vital, wordless things so as to discover their characteristics.

Fourth, the proposal seeks to have vocational education become one of the common subject areas along with mathematics, science, and English. Fifth, it suggests a design for implementing the above ideas.[10] It permits no hard lines or tracking of vocational and other students, individualized programs, exploratory and in-depth experiences, and promotes high school education as no longer being terminal in nature.

Of particular significance to the emerging philosophy of vocational education is the "Essex Report," so called because Martin W. Essex was chairman of the 1968 Advisory Council on Vocational Education. The Senate Subcommittee on Education published the Essex Report as did the U.S. Office of Education.[11] There are some differences between the two reports, in that Senate subcommittee's report contains a Part I of fifty-five pages that contains highlights and recommendations from the general report. The Senate subcommittee's report indicates a need for broadening vocational education:

Equally important, we feel, is modification of the school program to provide, as part of the course work of all students, instruction designed to acquaint them with today's world of work. At present we have almost none of this, for the Congress has decreed this off limits to vocational education, and Federal funds may not be used for this purpose.[12]

The report also suggests that

there is particular backwardness, with notable exceptions, in undertaking an orientation to the world of work in the junior high school or earlier to better prepare students for future vocational choices. There has also been a general failure to recognize that vocational education may have as much or more to offer as a technique for motivating students to learn by doing as it does as a method of skill training.[13]

The reports mentioned here are only three of many that suggest that my proposed definition of vocational education draws much support from the literature. Again it is necessary to emphasize two points. First, the emerging philosophy does not deemphasize skills; on the contrary, skills remain an important and integral part of vocational education. Nor does skill acquisition automatically shift to post–high school education. It must be recognized, however, that many of the highly specialized skill preparation programs are more appropriate at the post–high school level and are being expanded in that direction. Getting a job and earning money in the work role of one's potential occupation are very important dimensions of self-concept development of many youngsters, and thus will remain significant content for programs at the secondary school level.

Second, when it is suggested that the new concepts of vocational education require that it be extended to the lower grade levels, it encompasses an area that is not totally foreign to vocational educators. Vocational educators have traditionally referred to these activities as being "prevocational." In this context, they are not "pre-"; they are vocational experiences.

LEARN WHAT AN OCCUPATIONAL AREA IS ALL ABOUT

VOCATIONAL EDUCATION WILL CONCERN ITSELF WITH PROVIDING EXPERIENCES THAT PERMIT STUDENTS TO FIRST LEARN WHAT WORK IS ALL ABOUT BEFORE THEY LEARN ALL ABOUT A JOB. The distinction between the approaches is one of profound importance. An observation is in order before we proceed with an analysis of the two approaches. I have worked with students and this concept at both the graduate and undergraduate levels. Undergraduates immediately see the distinction between the two approaches and identify a number of differences, then discuss what those differences mean in terms of curricular organization and teaching strategies. In general, graduate students do not immediately see the distinction, and are hesitant to discuss changed curricular organization and teaching strategies once the distinctions are identified. Perhaps this says something about the socialization that occurs in our profession, about the commitment that occurs in the social process, especially in that phase where one is establishing himself in an occupation. In essence, the commitment that the worker develops to an occupation may tend to put blinders on him that limit his thinking.

Vocational education has tended to have the student learn all about an occupation. This approach stresses the human performance requirements of the occupation without relating these to the industry. An auto mechanics curriculum, for example, is designed so that the psychomotor skills of that job constitute one's training program. The student spends all of his time acquiring the skills associated with tuning an engine, with adjusting the carburetor, grinding valves, boring cylinders, replacing seals and inserts, and the like. These skills are not related to the individual who is performing the skill or to the social function that the industry performs.

When such teaching occurs, and it permeates much of the instruction in vocational education, it is *nonhumane* as it assumes that man is an extension of the machine on which he is working. Man is to assist the machine in doing the task rather than the machine assist the worker. Technology has forced a uniformity upon many factory operations. Many products are assembled out of prepunched parts. The worker is to assemble the parts in a uniform manner, and all workers perform the same repetitive task as their part of the uniform operation. In this situation, distinctions between the craftsman, the product, and the machine are obscured. At one stage in our technological development it was possible to say that products were indeed *manu*-factured, but at present products are *machine*-factured. When products were manu-factured, the individual worker was the hub around which products and materials evolved; he was the element of control. In that situation the worker acquired his skills and became acquainted with the contribution that he made to the industry and the contribution that the industry made to society. In the present situation the machine is the hub of the work environment and our approach to teaching reinforces that very point.

Without really analyzing what was happening in industry, we have gradually altered our vocational curriculum to coincide with the changes in industry. Shifting from handmade to machine-made products was an evolutionary process. The job analysis technique, for example, was very good at picking up, at each stage in the evolution, what the worker was doing, but the technique provided no way of relating the job to the past or the future. Curriculum was to be based on what type of work the worker was currently doing. This helps to explain why our curriculum in occupational education, to a large extent, is designed to prepare the worker to be an extension of the machine.

Further, the approach of teaching all about a job is nondemocratic: It defies the democratic principle of the creativeness of man and forces all into a mold of likeness. The curriculum does not permit the worker to ask how he might do the job better, how he can make a more significant contribution to his industry. The worker is expected to be an extension of the machine, to perform a specific skill in a repetitive manner. An airline industry made this point very dramatically in an advertising campaign in 1969. TWA suggested that, in order to serve its customers, its employees needed to break out of their mold and really serve the people. It offered "A Million Dollar Bonus" to those employees who did a better job and made a significant contribution to the industry.

Perhaps the best illustration of this concept is being pointed out to us by biomechanists, scientists who are anatomists and engineers. A biomechanist seeks to improve the fit between man and machine. *Time* recently carried a story about Erwin R. Tichauer, one such biomechanist, of New York University.[14] Tichauer's knowledge of human anatomy permits him to understand the human body thoroughly as it performs various activities. He is helping industry understand and accept the indisputable truth that man cannot be redesigned but that tools and machines can. An electrical plant was having trouble with production. After examining the assembly line, Tichauer designed a new pair of pliers with a thirty-degree bend in the handle. The new pliers considered the anatomy of the human wrist, which tires quickly when contorted. Efficiency of the production line improved immediately and remarkably.

At another plant, Tichauer eliminated a work situation that resulted in severe chest pains of the workers. They were required to sit too low in relation to their work level and to keep their arms up and off the table. Tichauer raised the workers' chairs and modified the seating angle. Other examples of Tichauer's work include redesigning the handle of the snow shovel, designing a new stepladder, and hinging the oven door laterally.

It seems imperative, therefore, that students in vocational education programs learn what an occupation is all about. An occupation is all about life, is all about man trying to improve the whole spectrum of human activity, is applying a skill in a creative manner, is living in a society. Learning with such an orientation includes a number of elements.

First, learning what an occupation is all about includes learning a skill in relation to the contribution that the performer of that skill makes to a particular industry. Each worker is not an isolate; he makes a contribution to his industry.

Second, each industry makes a social contribution.

Third, the performance of an occupation is all about earning a living.

Fourth, an occupation is all about living in society. The occupation that one follows determines the style of life that one will have: who one's friends are, one's associates, the type of car one drives, the type of home one lives in, where one's home will be located.

Learning what an occupation is all about helps the student understand what he has to do to qualify for work in an occupation. It also avoids stereotyping an individual so that he can move horizontally and vertically in his occupational area. A welder who knows only his welding skills can move horizontally from one welding job in a company to another, and from one company to another to perform the same tasks. If he understands that, in welding, the machine is used to fasten or to fuse material, and that he can use that machine to perform that function in a variety of ways, he is likely to find that he can move vertically in an organization. He can move from being an operator of a machine to areas of supervision.

The learning approach that we mention here is to be used before getting into the specifics of entry employment. That is, a vocational student needs to learn much about the occupational role before he obtains in-depth skill development. A creative approach to the industry is important. The student needs to discover what a worker does, how he does it, the educational level that is associated with the job, what his function in the industry is, how this relates to the total industry, how he can maintain his self-identity as he performs that job, and the style of life that is associated with the job.

Vocational education has not, by and large, studied jobs creatively but as they exist. Job analysis has been the classical method employed. Vocational education curriculum was then designed on the basis of what the worker did so that he could go to industry prepared to perform the job as it was currently designed and was performed in the past.

Conversely, when a man knows what an occupation is all about, he can exert a building influence on the occupation that he enters; he can improve on the way that the occupation is performed. In addition it decreases learner-worker frustration. A young lady recently related her experience in a twenty-hour course on electric tape typewriters. The course was designed to teach a crew of girls how to operate such a machine. The instructor began and continued to say to the class, "First you do. . . . then you. . . . then you. . . ." By the end of eight to ten hours of this, the young lady, as well as the class, was frustrated. She commented that she thought the operation too complex for her to learn. Then she decided to change her outlook toward the machine. She decided that she should control the machine rather than let it control her. She began to ask herself, as the instructor said to perform some acts, "now, what is it that she wants me to get the machine to do." With that orientation she soon had the operation of the machine down pat and at the end of the twenty hours was one of the few girls in the class who indicated that she did not need additional hours of training. With the approach of "What do I want the machine to do for me," she was creating an architectural influence on her work environment.

A UNIFYING EFFECT

The individual parts of an industry, such as retail stores, processing plants, and wholesale distributors, are interrelated in many ways. This interrelationship is expressed, in part, through the functions and at different levels performed throughout the industry. Workers in many parts of the total industry contribute to the performance of a wide variety of functions. Fairly obvious are contributions to sales and public relations by employees at levels from the delivery truck driver to the manager, or contributions to processing made by the research function.

We must recognize our long-standing educational tradition of attempting to teach disciplines in the same context with which the scientist has dissected them for research and analysis. The student has been responsible for unifying bits and pieces of information into some kind of a whole as it related to the performance of a job in an industry. He was not prepared to do this when he was taught only the bits and pieces of his job and possessed few tools that allowed him to unify isolated bits and pieces. It is imperative that vocational educators accept the responsibility of unifying the bits and pieces of information into a whole related generally to life and specifically to a particular job.

We have already discussed the searches for occupational competency that have occurred in the context of vocational education. Techniques of job analysis and clustering have dominated the field. Neither approach permits the bits and pieces of a job to be unified into a meaningful whole. One approach to occupational competency that does permit a unifying concept has been highly developed under the tutelage of Professor Raymond M. Clark at Michigan State University. Called the function approach, it was described in Chapter 8.

Underlying the function approach to identifying curricular inputs and planning vocational-technical education programs is a philosophy of vocational education. The focus is on preparation for a particular "world of work" based on the identification of (a) the specific requirements for performance by individuals in terms of activities contributing to a particular function in relationship to the unity of the over-all industry and (b) the general requirements for living related to the specific relationships of the industry to the unity of society. That is, we are concerned with mobility of individuals, their vocational satisfactions, with specific non-work-related contributions to society, and with education to prepare for further study. Successful employment is interpreted to mean not only highly satisfactory performance in the industry but also excellent performance as a citizen in the society.[15]

The function approach then becomes one method of unifying the unique information from one or more traditional disciplines into a whole that becomes the curriculum for educational programs. Programs that rely on the structure of a traditional discipline for content become increasingly out of step with the characteristics of the world of work that are shaped by our technology. The unifying effect of the function approach offers hope in combining content from the academic disciplines in the physical and the social sciences in a manner that is meaningful to students. Such a unifying effect offers educators a method of developing a structural framework that may prove helpful in their quest to exert an influence on the development of society and the technology that serves that society.

A CONTEMPORARY MODEL FOR VOCATIONAL EDUCATION

PRINCIPLES

"A conventional model" of vocational education was presented in Chapter 6. With the new definition discussed now, it is obvious that the traditional model must give way to a new one. The basic ingredients of a contemporary model for vocational education are shown in Figure 8. The model is designed for flexibility to allow students to move from one

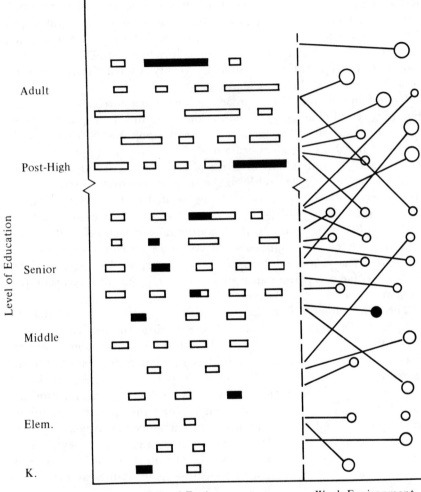

Experiences, Visual Stimuli, Affective Awareness, Cognitive Information, and Psychomotor Skills About Occupations and Jobs.

O   Occupations and Jobs.

FIGURE 8.   Contemporary Model for Vocational Education

area of the educational environment to another without having to back up and take courses that were missed. Vocational education would begin in the lower grades and continue throughout the educational system. The work environment is important at all levels, including the lower levels. This is to prevent an aseptic consideration of the work environment as is now the case in so many of the vocational attempts at the lower levels. The following operational principles guide the model.

1. Occupational education should begin in the elementary schools with a realistic picture of the world of work. Its fundamental purposes should be to familiarize the student with his world, to help him discover himself, to discover the intellectual tools and rational habits of thought that give meaning to a satisfying occupational role in society.

2. The primary objective of vocational education should be the development of the individual. One of the functions of an economic system is to structure incentives in such a way that individuals will freely choose to accomplish the tasks that need to be done. Preparation for employment should be flexible and capable of adapting the system to the individual's need rather than the reverse. The system for occupational preparation should supply a framework for exploring, establishing, or maintaining a position in the world of work at any terminal point chosen by the student, yet no doors should be closed to future progress and development.

3. Some type of formal occupational preparation must be a part of every educational experience. Though it may be appropriate to delay final occupational choice until all the alternatives are known, no one ought to leave the educational system without a framework for exploring, establishing, or maintaining himself in the world of work.

4. Occupational education should be based on a spiral curriculum that treats concepts at higher and higher levels of complexity as the student moves through the program. Occupational experiences, visual stimuli, affective awareness, cognitive information, and psychomotor skills form the content of the curriculum. In short, the vocational curriculum is expanded from manipulative content to manipulative and intellectual content.

5. It is no longer possible to compartmentalize students for the purpose of assigning them to general, academic, and vocational components of education. Nor can education itself, for that matter, be compartmentalized. We can talk about experiences that contribute to the individual's vocational education, but students are not to be rigidly assigned to it as a track. Education is a crucial element in all students' preparation for successful working careers. The educational skills of spoken and written communication, computation, problem-solving, social awareness, and self-awareness are vital to all students regardless of their

planned occupation. On the other hand, occupational skills are equally essential to the field of education. Culture and vocation are inseparable and unseverable aspects of humanity.

The shaded areas of the model are quite important. One cluster of careers from the work environment is shaded. The shaded blocks in the school environment represent how education might deal with the career cluster. I would suggest that a career cluster may be diffused throughout all educational levels. Key concepts of the career cluster may be introduced at the elementary education levels, with a full course combining many key concepts being offered at the senior high level. An associate degree program offering specialization in an occupational area may be available at the post–high school level. Each time the school environment instructs about a career cluster it does so by offering experiences, visual stimuli, affective awareness, cognitive information, and/or psychomotor skills about occupations and jobs.

A CRITIQUE OF THE NEW MODEL

In Chapter 6 we discussed the traditional model of vocational education, stating that it had a marketable skill orientation, a work environment orientation, a narrow social base, specific career expectations, and was oriented to having the worker produce a product. Vocational education was to provide each student with a marketable job skill that was taught as an isolated activity and that was acquired by the students with varied precision. The real world of the occupation was to be duplicated for the vocational program, the real world being one in which the worker had a wide span of work and semiautonomous control of his work environment.

The new model describes vocational education as performing a far different set of purposes than it did according to the traditional model.

LIFE SKILL ORIENTATION. As a society we are developing a new kind of life, one characterized by affluence, by increased leisure time, by technological evolutions, by technological convenience, and, of late, by a despairing concern for our evaporating individuality. Since the procession of man's innovations as well as the evolutionary aspect of our society are not likely to come to an end in the foreseeable future, we have little choice but to base education of the young on the expectation of uncertainty. It is important to recognize the fact that as the functions of man shift with each cultural evolution, his need for skill mastery does not decrease.

By life skills, then, we mean the total array of skills that are needed by an individual to discern meaning out of life, to assess his own abilities, interests, capacities, and to assert a building influence on his society. The 1969 Yearbook of the Association for Supervision and Curriculum Development (titled, appropriately, *Life Skills in School and Society*) suggests that life skills are of two kinds, primary and secondary:

Solving an equation, repairing a faucet, performing a piano sonata, and driving a golf ball can all be conceived as *secondary* skills. Underlying the secondary skills and defining the whole realm of human potential are the *primary* skills by which people adapt to and master their life situations. Primary skills are grounded in indispensable rather than accessory knowledge. For example, one can survive quite adequately without mastering golf, but unless one can fulfill the role expectations of his social group, life will not be truly gratifying. Primary skills give individuals a means for perceiving and responding to life's significant events. What we choose to define as primary skills will vary according to place and time. Whereas command of language is an essential primary skill in all societies, the capacity to hunt food is crucial in some but not in others.

In our culture, skills which allow one to earn a living are still important for most males and for some females, but they will become less important for succeeding generations if our economic system continues at its present trend. On the other hand, skills which enable one to achieve inner peace and *joie de vivre* will always be indispensable. Primary skills, in brief, are those skills which are necessary for the individual's physical and emotional well-being. If these primary skills can be developed systematically with greater efficacy than if they have been attained incidentally, education may be able to discharge its obligation to prepare the young for an unpredictable and troublesome new world.[16]

This distinction between primary and secondary life skills seems logical and educationally sound. We would propose, however, that if our society continues to develop a new kind of life-style, much of what we define as vocational education will be a primary life skill. Man will always need to know about shaping and directing his technology, using it creatively to master his life situations. Thus vocational education, as viewed here, will become increasingly important as our culture evolves.

WORK ENVIRONMENT. Work environment is important to education at all levels. At present some exposure to vocations does occur at the lower grade levels but much of this is antiseptic in nature. Only a few occupations—fireman, policeman, postman, and perhaps the banker and the grocer—are introduced to the children and they seldom get to learn about the duties of these jobs.

There are a variety of work environments. The poultry processing plant (see page 153) is an example of a work environment in which the man is truly an extension of a machine, is not permitted to be creative, and in general does nothing to enhance his self-concept. A recent research effort, after analyzing the nonsupervisory jobs in eleven major industries, reports that 34 percent of these jobs are "dead-end jobs," "those which allow a minimum opportunity for the exercise of independent judgment and which do not provide a reasonable expectation for advancement."[17] These facts are even more shocking when the number of jobs is considered. Over 7,000,000 jobs were analyzed, of which 2,390,000 were classified as being dead-end. In the auto industry, which employs in excess of 800,000 workers, more than 70 percent of the workers have their moves detailed down to the second, operate in set work stations, and perform repetitive tasks.[18] One's self-concept in such a job setting is not likely to be enhanced. On the other hand, if permitted, many jobs in a grocery store do permit one to be creative and the work environment can be so structured as to permit much enhancement of one's self-concept.

At the other end of the continuum are occupations and jobs in the professional and service areas that permit maximum amounts of creativity and self-concept enhancement. The college professor, dental technician, registered nurse, and computer programmer all have jobs with a very creative work environment. A college professor, for example, can work varied hours, can engage himself in a number of ways (teaching, writing, research, extension, advising students, consulting with industry), and within each of these areas can be as creative as his personality and psychological orientation will permit.

SOCIAL BASE. The social base for vocational education is the same as the social base for all of education. Education can no longer be compartmentalized and students assigned to tracks within the educational system. Vocational education is not a separate discipline within education but is a basic objective of all education. It is not possible to select any one student and say that he needs communication, social, economic, decision making and other skills less than another student. It is true that there are differences in occupations and there are differences in the style of life of individuals associated with varied occupations, but when viewed from the point of view of the individual, social foundations are as important to one as to another. Each person, in order to lead a meaningful life and to contribute to an occupation and to society, must participate in society, must vote intelligently, must abide by laws, must solve economic and budget problems for his family, and so on. To provide a kind of education that prepares one to do this better than another is not only poor education or poor vocational education but is nondemocratic as well.

EXIT POINT. There are purposely no exit points on the proposed model for vocational education. It is recognized that people do leave the formal educational system at various times. A research project at the University of California at Berkeley attempted to discover the relationship between students leaving the educational system and the educational scale.[19] It was discovered that out of a thousand students, 703 exit the system at Level I, with a minimum of vocational education; 163 exit at Level II, having completed junior college occupational programs, or having gained competency at upper division university work; and 134 exit at Level III, with four or more years of college. Draper adjusted these figures and suggested the following:

Level III—College graduates and above	20 percent
Level II—Junior college and special school graduates	25 percent
Level I—High school dropouts, high school graduates, junior college dropouts	40 percent
—Those not entering the labor market or not wanting vocational education	15 percent
	100 percent

Vocational education's task is to enhance the vocational development process of exploring, establishing, or maintaining oneself in the world of work. This is just as important an objective for the individual who exits at Level III as it is for the one who exits at Level I. Consider, for example, the tragedy and wasted human resources if a person completes a four-year college program or a two-year junior college program and enters a job in which he has had no exploratory experiences; upon getting the initial job he finds that it is not what he wanted and is not at all like what he had "imagined" it to be.

In essence, it is not possible to postpone education on the basis that another agency will provide a needed experience if it is omitted. "Education is not preparation for life, it is life," to paraphrase John Dewey; life is finding out about life, or exploring the world of work. This vocational development process is important for all students.

NOTES

[1]Eli Ginzberg et al., *Occupational Choice: An Approach to a General Theory* (New York: Columbia University Press, 1951).

[2]Charlotte Buehler, *Der menschliche Lebenslauf als Psychologisches Problem* (Leipzig: Hirzel, 1933); P. Lazarsfeld, *Jegend and Beruf* (Jena: C. Fisher, 1931); Donald E. Super, *The Dynamics of Vocational Adjustment* (New York: Harper & Bros., 1942); Super, *The Psychology of Careers* (New York: Harper & Row, Publishers, 1957); Ginzberg et al., *Occupational Choice*; W. S. Dysinger, "Maturation and Vocational Guidance," *29 Occupations* (1950), pp. 198–201; S. L. Pressey and R. G. Kuhlen, *Psychological Development Through the Life Span* (New York: Harper & Row, Publishers, 1957); J. C. Cass and David V. Tiedeman, "Vocational Development, the Election of a Secondary School Curriculum, and Public Policy," *Harvard Studies in Career Development*, No. 13 (Cambridge: Graduate School of Education, Harvard University, 1959); Robert P. O'Hara and David V. Tiedeman, "The Vocational Self-Concept in Adolescence," *Journal of Counseling Psychology*, 6 (1959), 292–301.

[3]Ginzberg et al., *Occupational Choice*; Super et al., *Vocational Development: A Framework for Research*, Career Pattern Study Monograph No. 1 (New York: Teachers

College, Columbia University, 1957), p. 132; Super, "Vocational Development in Adolescence and Early Adulthood: Tasks and Behaviors," in *Career Development: Self-Concept Theory* (New York: College Entrance Examination Board, Research Monograph No. 4, 1963), p. 81.

4Ibid., pp. 81–84.

5Ibid., p. 84.

6Sextant Systems, Inc., Milwaukee, Wis. 53210, publishes vocational guidance materials of many types.

7B. Bloom, *Stability and Change in Human Characteristics* (New York: John Wiley & Sons, 1964).

8Dale C. Draper, *Education For Work* (Washington, D.C.: National Committee on Secondary Education, 1967), pp. 109–11. Reprinted by permission of the National Association of Secondary School Principals. Copyright: 1970 by the National Association of Secondary School Principals.

9Nathaniel H. Frank, *Final Report of the Summer Study on Occupational, Vocational and Technical Education* (Cambridge: Science Teaching Center, Massachusetts Institute of Technology, 1965).

10Ibid., pp. 54–60.

11*Vocational Education, The Bridge Between Man and His Work* (Washington, D.C.: Government Printing Office, 1968).

12*Notes and Working Papers Concerning the Administration of Programs Authorized Under Vocational Education Act of 1963 Public Law 88–210, as Amended*, prepared for the Subcommittee on Education of the Committee on Labor and Public Welfare (Washington, D.C.: Government Printing Office, 1968), p. 38.

13Ibid., p. 40.

14*Time*, 93, no. 18 (May 2, 1969), 46–51.

15Raymond M. Clark and O. Donald Meaders, *Function Approach to Identifying Curricular Content Appropriate to Vocational-Technical Education Programs* (East Lansing: Michigan State University, College of Education, 1968), pp. 4–6.

16Louis J. Rubin, "The Object of Schooling: An Evolutionary View," in *Life Skills in School and Society*, ed. Louis J. Rubin (Washington, D.C.: Association for Supervision and Curriculum Development, 1969), pp. 19–20.

17William Grinker, Donald D. Cooke, and Arthur W. Kirsch, *Climbing the Job Ladder* (New York: E. F. Shelley and Co., 1970), p. 13.

18Ibid., p. 41.

19Reported by Draper, *Education For Work*, pp. 16–19.

11

OCCUPATIONAL EDUCATION FOR ALL

Public education as it is supported in America is established as the means for maintaining, perpetuating, and improving the society it serves. Increased reliance is placed upon education to examine, solve, and prevent problems that deter social progress and improvement. There are a number of major social issues confronting today's society: urbanization, population growth, civil rights, student unrest, ethnic problems, poverty, slums, housing, and crime. Each of these conditions must be improved if social progress is to be maintained and all aspects of public education are asked to assist in this improving process. Vocational education was created to help improve a social condition, and today it is still being asked to improve a social condition. The 1968 General Report of the Advisory Council on Vocational Education states:

Vocational education was created in response to a social need for an educated labor force, and was designed as a function and responsibility of public education. Vocational education in its total environment is, and must continue to be, sensitive to the dynamism of contemporary society. As society changes, vocational education adjusts accordingly. But throughout these adjustments its concern is directed toward people, in an educational setting, who provide the goods and services required by society.[1]

Is vocational education sensitive to the dynamism of contemporary society? Many of its critics say, emphatically, no. There is little doubt, however, that vocational education has enjoyed a number of very outstanding successes, and many vocational educators want to hold on to these past successes. Changes within contemporary society do demand changes in vocational education. Vocational education, like any other social institution, can undergo change from within, guided by its own practitioners, with less stress and with much greater freedom than it can if it is put in the position of reacting to pressures from the outside. Rather than asking if vocational education is sensitive, a more appropriate question might be: How can vocational education be more sensitive than it is at present to the dynamism of contemporary society? An answer to that question was presented in Chapters 4, 5 and 6. It was suggested that vocational education needs to develop a higher level of consistency between verbal and instrumental behavior—between actions and beliefs—in planning and conducting its programs.

Also discussed was a list of the basic principles that have emerged within vocational education and on which actions of vocational educators are based. It was suggested that these basic principles, by and large, are not adequate for contemporary society. One way in which vocational education can narrow the gap between actions and beliefs, and thus be more sensitive to the needs of contemporary society, is to develop a new set of basic assumptions about vocational education. I have designed such a set of assumptions, which it seems appropriate to present and discuss at this point.

A MODERN PHILOSOPHY

A modern philosophy of vocational education concerns developing a view of man and a view of society. A view of man, a philosophical perspective, examines what man is, what is his greatest potential, and what he is capable of achieving. A sociological perspective relates man to the conditions that permit him to develop his potential. Though this book does not deal extensively with the psychological conditions of vocational education, a psychological perspective is also offered, as a vocational educator needs to have a view about the nature of being.

A VIEW OF MAN: A PHILOSOPHICAL PERSPECTIVE

If vocational education is to increase its sensitivity toward social problems it must enlarge its philosophical perspective of man. It is necessary to assume that *man as an individual is unique and important.* Man is unique from all other species of animals. Though similarities of life experiences tend to produce similar personality characteristics in different persons, each individual grows at his own rate, has his own thought patterns, responds to stimuli differently, and may reach a different conclusion than another from the same set of facts. Each man is also important. We cannot turn our backs on any one person or any one group of persons because they do not fit in, because he or they are different, or because he or they have been on welfare for two generations.

MAN CAN ADAPT TO A CHANGING ENVIRONMENT. Both man and the environment are active, with each exerting an influence on the other. As our environment becomes altered, crowded, and impersonal, man can adapt himself to it. Man is flexible rather than rigid and is a rational problem-solver, enabling him to direct forces in society. *Man desires maximum control over his environment.* His desire is to control, shape, and direct the environment to his needs, desires, and wants.

MAN IS A SOCIAL BEING. Man does not grow and develop in an isolated environment, but as he interacts with people and objects in his environment. Lacking interaction, man becomes very disoriented. Social interaction enters all phases of one's life: social, professional or work, leisure, and family.

MAN PROJECTS HIS THOUGHTS TOWARD WHAT HE IS CAPABLE OF BECOMING. Seldom is man satisfied with what he has. Man is constantly thinking about (sometimes acting toward) what he can become that is different and better than what he is. Man projects himself into many imaginary roles just to try them out. Man also aspires to very realistic changes in his life.

THE NATURE OF SOCIETY: A SOCIOLOGICAL PERSPECTIVE

A SOCIETY IS A SYSTEM OF AGREED-UPON RELATIONSHIPS AMONG INDIVIDUALS AND GROUPS. On most occasions, individuals with similar geographic, professional, or social boundaries interact with other individuals, forming to some degree a group. As an individual member of society dies, he takes to his grave the complex aggregate of behavior patterns and beliefs that we speak of as "the American way of life." This way of life is not in the possession of a baby at birth; he must be socialized, so to speak, into it. If society did not provide some method of social and psychological procreation, we might conceivably survive as a physical group, but we would certainly perish as an integrated society, with beliefs, values, and ways of life. Any interactions between members of the group and other individuals to provide for social and psychological procreation are governed by an agreed-upon set of relationships. Such agreements are formal and informal, simple and complex, direct and indirect, and are woven together to form a system. Societies exist in the formal sense but they also exist as subsystems within any group. Thus this assumption also carries to units within a society. It is true for an automobile assembly plant, for a university faculty, for a medical clinic, for a paving contractor, and for a group of men on a garbage truck. Unless an agreed-upon set of relationships exists, none of the functions to be performed by the above groups is likely to be achieved in a consistent manner.

A number of conditions make this assumption particularly significant for vocational education. Through conglomerates and mergers, industries are becoming more and more complex, with management in many instances being placed far beyond the proximity of the work. Another consideration is the changing value pattern of Americans, particularly those of the younger generation. Many such individuals are not likely to participate in activities in which their opinions and views are not considered. A third factor concerns the word "bureaucracy." Many institutions are rigid and permit little interaction between the worker and the philosophy behind his job. Bureaucracy involves increasing specialization of work and at the same time coordination of the specialized activities into a functioning whole. Among other processes, bureaucratization involves the centralization of authority and the standardization of work routines.

This gives rise to another assumption. *There must be a reciprocity between the needs of man and the needs of society.* If the first assumption was recognized in all cases there would be little need to consider the second. Each and every individual wants to feel that he is making a contribution. Workers like to know that they can be heard within the system and they like to be involved in decisions concerning changes in their particular job. Decisions made some distance from the work and imposed upon the work environment are likely to suffer considerable distortion. More and more the worker cares less and less about the company. It becomes evident that the goals of the worker are different from the larger set of goals held by the company.

A problem on which I spent considerable energy in 1968 involves a large industrial firm. Essentially a problem existed between the industrial engineering (IE) and production staffs. The union contract specified the standard of work routines. These could be changed by the IE staff under specific conditions. More often than not the production worker was informed on Thursday that beginning Friday his standard was changed. The production worker would do everything in his power to see that his standard was not changed. Production workers were always suspicious of an IE on the floor, as they never knew what he was up to. A procedure was developed whereby the IE told production workers what he was doing, solicited their advice, and involved them in setting new standards. An in-service training program was held in which the goals of each individual were related to the goals of his department, which were then related to the goals of the company. As a result of this, more harmonious relationships have emerged between production and IE staffs, morale is alleged to be higher, and job standards are more readily accepted by the workers. In essence, the workers' needs are now in closer interchange with management's (society's) needs than before.

Today's society is a mass, protean society rather than being nascent. Formerly society was described as primordial, traditional, and hierarchical. Our present society is one in which

the integration occurs, not through kinship, but through the exercise and acceptance of authority in the major sub-systems of the society, in the policy, the economy, and the status and cultural orders, i.e., in educational and religious institutions and their associated norms and beliefs. Integration occurs in two directions—vertically and horizontally. A society is vertically integrated in a hierarchy of power and authority and a status order; it is horizontally integrated by the unity of elites of the various sectors of life or sub-systems of the society.[2]

Modern society is a large-scale society. It involves populations running into the hundreds of millions and it covers large territories. Government is more continuously and effectively in contact with much of the population through the variety and comprehensiveness of its legislation, through the continuity and intensity of administration, through nearly universal public education. The economy is integrated so that scarcely any part of the economic order of the society lives in isolation from its rules or competitors.

Culture, once confined to a narrow circle at the center, is now spread over a far greater radius through such means as radio, television, books, records, periodicals, and a higher level of educational attainment. Modern society is consensual in terms of bringing nearly all persons living within a bounded territory into the fabric of governmental action, economic participation, and civic disposition.

When we say that this new order of mass society is a consensual society, this does not mean, however, that it is completely consensual, a fabric of seamless harmony. The competition and conflict of corporate bodies resting on diverse class, ethnic, professional, and regional identifications and attachments are vigorous and outspoken in this new order of society.[3]

What is specific in modern society is the establishment of consensually legitimate institutions within which much of this conflict takes place and which imposes limits on this conflict.

Modern society also has a less authoritative relationship between adults and children. The parent is less "charismatic." This dispersion of charisma also carries over to working classes, women, and ethnic groups, and has manifested itself through a greater stress on individual dignity and individual rights in all strata, in both sexes, and in ethnic groups. This internalization of individualism does not, however, extend equally to all such groups or to all spheres of life.

A concern has grown for the well-being of others, for government to establish a "floor" below which no member of the society can fall, giving rise to modern society being labeled a welfare society. Social security, Medicare, Medicaid, welfare, Aid for Dependent Children, and old-age pensions are examples of governmental actions that seek to establish an economic base for all citizens. Modern society is also an industrial society, creating an elaborate network of transportation and communications that make it possible for the various parts of society to have a frequency of contact with each other not possible before.[4]

Within this set of characteristics of modern society, sociologists are able to discern at least two major subthemes that run counter to the dominant themes.

SOCIAL LEADERSHIP BY INDIVIDUALS IS ATTENUATED. At one point social leadership was provided by the elite in society. To this elite fell the task of running the social institutions. A protean society does not permit this to happen, for the quality of individuals is not at issue. What is at issue is the relationship between classes within a society. The gap between the social elite and the common man has narrowed, giving the common man direct contact with areas of cultural incubation and development. All institutions of society have been affected by this process. Among the consequences is that those participating in the social leadership functions of a protean society have lower standards of knowledge and conduct than did the social elite who ran the nascent society.

ALIENATED PERSONHOOD. In a mass society large groups of persons lose faith in traditional values and find the older patterns of family activity broken. And in a bureaucratic organization man may not find meaning to his work and life. The need that man has to belong is unfulfilled; insecurity and alienation follows. Being counterthemes these trends do not necessarily permeate the society uniformly and are not dominant at this point in time.

THE ECONOMIC SYSTEM OF A DEMOCRATIC SOCIETY MUST SERVE THE GOALS OF THE SOCIETY AND EVERY INDIVIDUAL IN THE SOCIETY. Documentation exists to show that the economic system of our society favors some persons more than it favors others and that this favoritism leads to deficiency, hardship, and injustice.[5] It was pointed out in the press in the fall of 1969, as Congress examined a number of measures on tax reform, that the tax system was so inequitable that those who made the most money escaped nearly all taxes through special loopholes.

For families at low income levels, income is less than consumption by wide margins.[6] In fact, for families at the lowest income levels, expenditures for current consumption exceeded income by 71 percent. The difference between what is spent and what is taxable income implies the wide use of credit, the receipt of public or private assistance, and gifts. Families of low income, considering all sources of revenue, salary, and assistance, spend 10 percent more of their total budget on food than do the average nonfarm families. (The percents are respectively, 24 and 34.) Nutritional information is lacking in such families, causing their diet to be nutritionally inadequate though they are spending approximately a third of their income on food.

About a third of the families with incomes below the poverty line in 1960 lived in housing that was dilapidated or lacked plumbing. Such persons buy lower quality and possibly smaller appliances than do similar-sized families earning from $6,000 to $7,500. For example, the low income families paid an average of $176, $140, and $68 respectively for refrigerators, washing machines, and vacuum cleaners. Families in the $6,000 to $7,500 class paid an average price of $266, $197, and $85 for the same items. Data are also available that show that young men receive greater benefits from the economic system than do older men, men more than women, educated more than the less well educated, white more than the nonwhite, and urban more than rural.

Two additional assumptions are important when considering a sociological perspective for vocational education. These are: (1) *Society is collectively responsible to provide every individual the opportunity to develop himself to the maximum extent of his ability, and* (2) *Society's educational institutions need to exert an architectural influence on society.*

THE NATURE OF BEING: A PSYCHOLOGICAL PERSPECTIVE

To complete the philosophical and sociological perspectives, a psychological perspective is needed. The following is a set of psychological assumptions that I developed:

1. Human development is a dynamic process.

2. Human development is patterned, sequential, and largely irreversible.
3. Man is motivated by needs.
4. Change in individual man occurs only through learning.
5. Humans learn through experiences affecting their
   a. affective (feeling) domain.
   b. cognitive (thinking) domain.
   c. psychomotor (acting) domain.
6. Man is continuously in a state of becoming.
7. Man's development in a vocational sense begins at a very early age and frequently extends throughout his lifetime.
8. Man's successful vocational development is dependent upon experiences that assist him in understanding the opportunities from the world of work in terms of his needs and desires.

THE PURPOSE OF VOCATIONAL PROGRAMS

PURPOSE: A CRUCIAL ISSUE

These assumptions lead to a rethinking of the purposes of vocational education at its various levels. Many books concerned with the history of American education suggest that America and its educational community have not really come to grips with the fundamental question of purpose. The report of the Committee of Ten and those of other groups have been cited, but these suggestions have never really been agreed upon by the American people. Thus any discussion of purpose generally stays very general. Hicks and Blackington, for example, comment: *"Nevertheless, the point of reference in this chapter has been that of educational purpose. It would be extremely difficult to maintain that anything remotely resembling agreement exists concerning the purpose of the public school."*[7]

Lieberman, on the other hand, contradicts the notion that the American people disagree about the purpose of the school system. He indicates that Americans desire the school to accomplish the development of critical thinking, effective communication, creative skills, and social, civic, and occupational competence.[8] The disagreement, according to Lieberman, is one of means of achieving the agreed-upon purposes. The type of disagreement that exists concerning purpose in American education is not a moot question. In fact, it is the most crucial question facing vocational education today.

Philosophically, vocational education does not agree with all of education that vocational education is a legitimate part of the school system, much less as to its purposes. That is, a significant number of nonvocational educators have always argued that vocational education should not be a part of the school system. Within vocational education it is often difficult to move beyond nominal agreement to programmatic agreement. Some vocational educators would argue that vocational programs are for specific job preparation only. Some would argue that agricultural education should not be offered in high school; others would argue that trade and industrial programs should not be offered then either. Lacking nominal agreement with other educators and lacking programmatic agreement within, vocational educators are not likely at this time to develop a clear set of purposes that all can agree upon.

GENERAL PURPOSES

The purposes of vocational education must be consistent with the purposes of occupational development. Occupational development has been defined as a process of growth and development that enables an individual to find a satisfying work role and to become established in an occupation. The generalized purpose of vocational education, then, is to assist an individual to grow and develop, to become separate from other things and other persons, to discover a satisfying role in an occupational area. A secondary purpose is to help the labor market maintain a balance between jobs and unemployment, between employment opportunities and trained manpower.

Another way of saying this is that in a democratic society it is assumed that free choice of an occupation is preferred to coercion. Efficient functioning of the economy and the attainment of personal and social adjustments by workers are not opposing ideas in a democratic society. If a person has experiences that permit him to really know his own strengths and weaknesses, know the world of work, and know how to relate himself to the world of work, he will seek out a satisfying work role. The incentives provided by the free enterprise economy will insure that various job shortages are filled. The reverse is not true. If experiences and educational programs are provided only in the jobs that the economic system finds in short supply, there is no guarantee that individuals will find satisfying work roles. Free choice of occupations in a democratic society assumes that (1) there are alternative courses of action, and (2) one is free to choose among these alternatives. Free choice does have limitations, which include rate of turnover, expanding or contracting economy, level of education planned for, age, and incentives provided by the economic system. Learning about these limitations is important as one looks for a satisfying work role.

In this context it is important to mention a changing role of industry in the preparation of workers. Generalizations in vocational education are difficult to support. Nevertheless, industry must be allowed to play a more important role in preparing workers than it has been permitted to in the past. It is interesting to take the question "What do you as an industry person expect of beginning workers in your industry?" and ask it at various levels in industries. If the question is asked at the lower levels of the industry—the worker, immediate supervisor, or foreman— the reply is likely to indicate that they expect the worker to do and know everything prior to coming on to the job. He is expected to know how to operate a specific type of machine, to perform a specific skill, or to know the characteristics of the latest materials used in the industry. In addition he is expected to have acquired all the desirable work habits, to be polite, to get along with fellow workers, to respect his superiors, and so on. If the question is asked of higher-level persons in the same industries a different answer is obtained. Executive vice presidents, managers, and directors indicate that they desire a worker who knows the industry, knows how one function of an industry is related to another, knows how one function is performed at the various levels in the industry, has desirable work habits, and has the ability to get along with fellow workers. Higher-level industry people indicate that industry will provide training on the specific machines and techniques used if the new worker understands the basic purposes and function of a machine. They indicate that they would prefer that he not have extensive training on one specific machine prior to coming to their industry, for such a machine, if found in the school, is likely to be an older model and it may not be the kind of machine that they employ. Understanding relationships, the new worker is likely to consider other aspects of the company in considering alternatives in his own work area.

The purpose of vocational education must permit a concentration on specific job preparation only after the individual has made a tentative choice of an occupation. Some persons would argue that vocational education prior to high school graduation is not appropriate and therefore should be the exclusive function of community, junior, or vocational-technical colleges. If you accept the above assumptions, the question is not that simple. Many traditional vocational programs have, in fact, been offered to high school–age youth with the general assumption that they had made an occupational choice, and these programs consisted of specific job preparation. This is only one phase of a sound vocational education program, however. It can occur for some youngsters prior to high school graduation, but is likely to be appropriate for most young people afterward. On-the-job experiences are very important for high school youth who want to know what it is like to work at a particular job. Thus, so-called exploratory experiences are an important part of vocational education.[9]

The purposes of vocational education must be consistent with a human development base and serve to further the vocational development of its clientele, as discussed in Chapter 10.

THE PURPOSE OF VOCATIONAL EDUCATION IN THE ELEMENTARY SCHOOL

Young people of elementary school age are in what has been described as the fantasy stage of development. Growth and maturity is unique to each young person. At the same time, people share certain kinds of experiences as they mature physically, socially, and occupationally. From the way each person uniquely knows these shared experiences he learns to value certain kinds of relations with his world. The young person primarily seeks acceptance. He wants to know that his thoughts and his actions are acceptable to the people that are important to him.

In the early fantasy stage, a young person is usually in a direct, one-to-one relationship with himself and things. He moves from that to an examination of relationships between the things themselves. He needs to know, "How is this related to this?" Then he must continue to explore, "How is this related to that, and how does the resulting relationship affect me?" From what the young person knows, he reaches toward expanding relations, concepts, and integrations while he continues to establish new firsthand relations, so that there is an ever-expanding base of knowledge. It is important that vocational education be introduced to the young person while he is exploring all these relationships.

A generalized set of objectives for vocational education at the elementary school level would include having each youngster acquire cognitive information and affective awareness that

1. there are a variety of ways that one makes a living and the way one makes a living is called his occupation.

2. within each occupation there are numerous jobs.

3. within each job, a worker performs a variety of tasks.

4. man has dignity and what he does occupationally contributes to that dignity.

5. there is an interrelationship between jobs and occupations.

These and similar objectives could be implemented with only two areas of improvement: new teacher orientation and new curriculum materials. It is not necessary to add new specialized teachers at the elementary school level. An example of the new curriculum materials is a volume of books being published entitled *Come to Work with Us*.[10] The first six books give the children a guided tour of a television station, a hospital, an airport, a construction project, an aerospace complex, and a toy factory. The young person sees the surroundings and equipment of an occupational area. He sees children his own age in a wide range of realistic work situations and learns what each job involves through a rhyme accompanying each photograph. Accompanying the picture of a dietitian, for example, is the following rhyme:

> I'm in charge of patients' food
> and plan what they will eat.
> I check on how it's cooked and served,
> make every meal complete.[10]

Such a set of books in the hands of a skillful elementary teacher could do much to increase the cognitive information and affective awareness of the young person about himself and vocational education.

THE PURPOSE OF VOCATIONAL EDUCATION IN THE MIDDLE SCHOOL

In the junior high school, industrial arts for boys is primarily concerned with development of leisure-time pursuits, with activities limited largely to those pursued by the individual. The view of industry given the student is that of 200 years ago when goods were produced by individual craftsmen on a custom-order basis. Home economics at the junior high level does a better job, although it introduces girls primarily to the middle-class home where the wife has both time to sew and money for expensive appliances. Little or nothing is taught about the problems of the working wife or about occupations other than home-making.[11]

The above paragraph is quoted from the highlights and recommendations of the Essex Report published by a Senate Subcommittee on education. It summarizes from the point of view of vocational educators what vocational education is currently like at the middle school level. One point should be made in its defense. To many vocational educators, vocational education cannot make a contribution to students in the middle school and thus has no place in its curriculum. To classify what goes on there as the "development of leisure-time pursuits" is right and proper, according to their view.

The young person attending the middle school is likely to be in the latter phase of the fantasy stage of development and is emerging into the exploratory stage. Particularly crucial to a person of this age is learning how people and objects affect him. Borow has classified this as the Acquiring the Basic Habits of Industry Stage, Ages 10–15.[12] During this stage the young person learns to organize his time and energy to get a piece of work done, to put work ahead of play in appropriate situations.

In essence, the young person is learning self-expression, which implies a flexibility, independence, and self-discipline in relation to his mental growth.

A generalized objective for vocational education at the middle school is to have each individual obtain a broad, fundamental understanding of the world of work as well as a personal sense of his ability to control and manipulate this world. The youngster is to express himself in and become sensitive to the problems in the world of work. This can be done at this level by having the students work with materials, which are the vehicles for the induction of changes in learners, changes that are behavioral as well as cognitive.

Excellent examples of curricula based on this concept were developed in 1965 by the Summer Study on Occupational, Vocational and Technical Education held at Massachusetts Institute of Technology.[13] Contained in the final report is a "Proposal for a Laboratory Oriented Vocational Course in Materials Science at the Seventh Grade Level" and a "Sample Program in Mechanical Sciences." The new kind of vocational education that is suggested here requires the development of interdisciplinary units that are rooted in a child's knowledge, enlist his reasoning power, deepen his understanding, and open new vistas for exploration. The final report also contains four interdisciplinary units to teach the young person much about the world of work: Systems and Processes, Boats, Electricity, and Currency and Finance. The previously mentioned sample program in Mechanical Sciences is reprinted here.[14]

The primary academic goal is to provide a unified course from which the student will obtain a broad, fundamental understanding of a part of the world in which he lives, as well as a personal sense of his ability to control and manipulate this "world." Links are expected to develop logically outwards to discipline such as mathematics, history, etc.

A very necessary and immediate aim of the course is to instill a sense of realism, excitement, personal participation, and personal accomplishment. Hence, for many, and presumably most, this requires a laboratory-oriented, vocational course. The teaching of salable skills is a matter for later years, and certainly courses for this purpose are expected to build logically on the proposed course.

For many reasons, discussed at length elsewhere, we have made the initial assumption that some vocational education is desirable for all students at about the seventh grade level, as well as, presumably, above and below this level. The goal of these vocational courses is to provide broader fundamental understanding than is now generally being taught.

The exact field of study (i.e. "Materials Science," "Design," etc.) is clearly less important than broader academic and social goals. However, a percept of this study is that some well defined field should be studied in depth, and that only in this way can the primary academic goal be met. Materials Science offers the following potential advantages: it brings realistic experiences to all students; it can be presented as a laboratory-oriented course; it is a suitable vehicle for meeting the primary academic goal.

A requisite for the proposed course structure is a course based on natural interests in materials, systems or processes. The course must employ open-ended experimentation instead of the standard canned experiments and should develop competence and interest in basic concepts and materials. Another vital purpose of the course is to help students discover a need for mathematics, quantitative measurement, etc. This need is to be discovered through real experience. Finally, the course structure and philosophy should ensure continual updating.

We recommended that the course be built around a series of laboratory experiments, such as that in Table I below. The laboratory work should be divided

OUTLINE OF SIMPLE LABORATORY EXPERIMENTS FOR
VOCATIONAL COURSE IN MATERIALS PROCESSING*

A. Creativity with Materials—Shape Manipulation
   Metal Casting
   Electroforming
   Pottery-making-powder Metallurgy
   Crystal Growing
   Metal Forging—Plastic Forming
   Glass Blowing
B. Measurement of Properties of Materials
   1. Physical Properties
      Thermal conductivity
      Electrical conductivity
      Thermal expansion
      Density
      Magnetic properties
      Hardness
      Melting point
      Color, transparency, opaqueness
      Corrosion
   2. Mechanical Properties
      Tensile properties (including those associated with elevated temperature)
C. Manipulation of Properties
   Alloying
   Cold-working
   Cross-linking of Polymers
   Heat Treatment
   Composite Fabrication
   Corrosion Control

*Topics listed are for example only.

into three phases. Initially, creative shape manipulation would be emphasized. Later on, laboratory experiments would focus on the properties of materials, and finally manipulation of those properties.

The underlying thread of the course is to be materials; specifically, basic, lasting concepts of materials. Such lecture material and outside reading as are to be assigned would deal with these concepts logically and in conjunction with the course structure and introduce principles only as a natural part of the laboratory-oriented course.

SAMPLE EXPERIMENTS:

A. Experiment in "Creativity with Materials—Shape Manipulation"

Problem: As homework, take home a piece of foam plastic (styrofoam) and carve, or otherwise shape, whatever you wish (a piece of sculpture, an ash tray, a cooking utensil). Bring it in to class next week and cast it, using the sand molding process.

Suggestions: For shaping the styrofoam, a pocket knife, file, sandpaper, etc., are ideal tools. Also, if you paint parts black and leave others white, and then expose the styrofoam to a bright light or heat lamp, you will find a depression in your model forms wherever you painted black.

For casting, aluminum is ideal, and prepared sand is available. Necessary materials and furnaces are available. Some sketches in the laboratory show suitable methods of forming the molds. You may wish to plan your own molding procedure after consulting these sketches.

Suitable recipes for melting aluminum are placed near the small bench furnace. Be sure to wear gloves, face mask, and asbestos apron when melting and ask your instructor for assistance in pouring.

NOTE: No attempt is made in this or other experiments to use language suitable for student use. The aim is only to describe, for purposes of this conference, the type of laboratory envisioned.

In addition, no attempt is made here to include material suitable for presentation as lecture material, homework, or outside reading. It is assumed that this "academic" material is to be developed to follow and logically to support the experiments performed and, most important, to provide the continuous thread to the course. This thread is to be a fundamental understanding of materials and methods of manipulation of these materials. Through this thread, ties are to develop outwards to mathematics, physics, history, economics, etc.

B. Experiment in "Measurement of Properties of Materials"

Problem: Cookingware is generally, although not always, made from metals. This is because certain properties of metals make them particularly useful for this application. These properties of metals include ductility, high temperature strength, cheapness in initial cost of materials and in fabrication, and ability to transmit heat. Consider the materials to which you have been exposed from the standpoint first of only their ability to transmit heat. What material do you recommend for use in making a frying pan?

PURPOSE OF VOCATIONAL EDUCATION
AT THE SENIOR HIGH LEVEL

During the high school years, nearly all young persons have left the fantasy stage of development and are in the tentative substage of the exploration stage of vocational development and are concerned with the vocational developmental task of crystallization. Crystallization of a vocational preference is a developmental task typically encountered during the fourteen- to eighteen-year-old period. During this developmental task the teen-ager is expected to begin to formulate ideas as to fields and levels of work that are appropriate for him. He is also expected to formulate concepts about self and occupation that will enable him to commit himself to a type of education or training that will lead him to some partially specified occupations.

From this type of vocational development base, three generalized objectives for vocational education in the high school emerge:

1. Assist the individual in assessing himself.
2. Assist the individual in formulating a tentative occupational choice.
3. Provide occupational experience that enables the individual to explore an area of tentative choice.

Thus vocational education at the high school level in the decades ahead is to be much more exploratory than it has been admitted to be in the past. The critical shift is viewing skill development at the high school level from a different perspective. Skill development was thought to be very specific. One means of evaluating vocational education in the past was what percent of the graduates of a particular high school vocational program were employed in that occupational area. If the percentage was high—55 to 75 percent—the high school program was evaluated as being quite good. In the generalized objective, skill development is very important but for different reasons. It is important to recall the stage of vocational development in which the high school youngster finds himself. He is in the exploratory stage and therefore it is educationally sound to give him experiences that permit exploration of an occupational area. Having a job at the senior year level, in which he acquires in-depth skills in an occupational area, is one way of attaining exploration. We are more interested in knowing if the acquisition of skills, the exploration, associated with a job helped the individual mature vocationally than we are in knowing if he follows the occupation after he leaves high school.

An outline of a curriculum supported by these generalized objectives might resemble the following:

• Assessment of individual self in terms of abilities (social, scientific, mathematical, physical, creative, problem-solving, etc.), aptitudes (personal traits), interests (outdoor, indoor, painting, sketching), and aspirations (style of life). This may be accomplished at an early grade level (ninth or tenth) through a testing and assessment program, field trips, movies, slides.

• Introductory courses. An introductory course can be given to acquaint the student with the general subject matter of an area, the classification of work levels in an occupational area, and how an individual can express himself in an area of work.

• Content courses. A content course moves beyond the general material and deals with specific subject matter. The individual assesses himself in terms of abilities, aptitudes, interests, and aspirations, and if he feels he can make a contribution to that arena of work.

• Occupational experience. Occupational experience is a means of helping a student make a tentative occupational choice. It would normally be offered at the senior year of high school but it needs to be supported by other types of occupational experience. Simulated work experience, projects, and even field trips, where ninth-graders simply observe and analyze what workers do, are all types of occupational experience and support the vocational development of students.

• Specific content courses. These are a continuation of the content courses mentioned above and are likely to be offered in conjunction with or after the type of occupational experience in which the student is actually holding a job.

VOCATIONAL EDUCATION FOR ADULTS

This topic is very complex and merits a separate book. The adult has an occupational age range from eighteen to sixty-five. These ages may be grouped in stages of occupational development, as was done earlier in Chapter 10.

A capsule of the primary substages are as follows:

SUBSTAGE	TYPICAL AGE RANGE	PRIMARY FOCUS OF THE INDIVIDUAL
Transition	18–21	Convert a generalized choice into a specific choice and make a final commitment to it by embarking upon a specialized education and training program or by taking a job designed to serve as entry to a chosen field.
Trial (little commitment)	18–25	Implement the choice. The young person is in transition from general to specialized education or from school to employment. He is expected to convert a pref-

SUBSTAGE	TYPICAL AGE RANGE	PRIMARY FOCUS OF THE INDIVIDUAL
		erence into reality. During this time shifts in occupational areas may occur.
Trial (commitment)	21–30	Stick with one occupational area. Job changes rather than occupational changes are likely to occur.
Advancement	30–45	Get firmly established in the occupation so that the job provides security and comfort.
Maintenance	45– retirement	Concern not to lose status, money, style of life, etc.

Vocational education needs to be concerned with the individual as he progresses through all of these stages. As he leaves high school, a young person is likely to have a tentative occupational choice. In adult life he is expected to convert that general preference into a specific choice and to make a final commitment to it. He does this by enrolling in an educational or training program such as a four-year college program, a program at a vocational-technical school, or a training program provided by a business firm. He may also implement his preference by taking a job designed to serve as entry to a chosen field. A young girl, for example, may want to be the manager of the china department of a large store. After graduating from high school where she had distributive education, she takes the job of clerk in a china department. She has little commitment to the job in the sense that she has little invested in it and is willing to continually assess herself in relation to it. From a different perspective, emotionally, the commitment may be thought to be great in that few people take such a job with the expectation they will not like it.

The young lady is still assessing her potential and is trying to find a way in which she can contribute to the job. After a year, she concludes that this is not the type of work for her as her interests are really more inclusive. She is interested in china, yes, but is also interested in how it is arranged, how it is displayed in the home, the complementary furniture, and even the room in which it is used. She decides that she would like the work of interior decorating and such a job would likely enhance all of her interests in china. She seeks and obtains a job with an interior decorator. After having this job for about six months, she finds it is to her liking and enrolls in the local vocational-technical school for night courses so that she can advance and learn more about the occupation. She develops a commitment to this occupational area and advances within it, all the while seeking more knowledge and experience within it.

There are many types of vocational education for adults, which may be grouped into the following four broad categories:

• Formal education programs. Such programs are offered through vocational-technical schools and private business and other colleges to prepare a worker for occupational areas such as electronics, data processing, and nursing.

• Industrial training programs. Industrial training programs are usually sponsored within a given industry to train new workers to fit into a specific job or position. Such programs may last from a few hours to nearly a year in length.

• Inservice. The primary purpose of inservice programs are to upgrade the worker. Professional groups such as teachers and doctors use this type of adult education constantly. Industries also upgrade their workers through inservice programs, but they may not be as frequent as the professional groups.

• Hobbies. Adult education usually offers a significant number of programs that are designed as hobby or personal interests programs. These are regarded as avocational as they do not directly assist a person to grow and mature vocationally.

This introduction is meant to convey three general impressions about vocational education for adults:

1. Adult education is a large, complex area of study.

2. The adult continues to grow and mature occupationally.

3. The human development base is an appropriate base for programming adults who are maturing occupationally.

SUMMARY

Vocational education has its parallel with each stage in the development of man. It was added to the curriculum of the public educational system, however, less than a hundred years ago to meet a particular social condition. It was seen as a means of helping man develop and advance in an occupational area. As technological advances were made in our society, advances or rather changes were made in vocational education and in its purpose. It changed from being primarily concerned with the developing man to giving man the technology that he needed to fill an existing, unfilled job that society needed.

Vocational education has always known strife and stress. However, the current stress is probably stronger than vocational education has faced in any other stage of its development. There are pressures from within vocational education to stay as it is and pressures to change. From without come similar pressures of both types.

It seems defensible to say that vocational education is not as responsive to contemporary society as it could be. There is a need for more congruency between what vocational educators believe and what they do. To begin to develop this congruency is to rethink what vocational educators believe about man and society rather than to begin with program changes. Then it is possible to rethink the general purposes of vocational education, which in turn should reveal new actions to be carried out in conjunction with specific vocational education programs.

NOTES

[1]*Vocational Education—The Bridge Between Man and His Work*, General Report of the Advisory Council on Vocational Education (Washington, D.C.: Government Printing Office, 1968), p. 156.

[2]Edward Shils, "The Theory of Mass Society," in *America as a Mass Society*, ed. Philip Olson (New York: The Free Press, 1963), pp. 22–23.

[3]Ibid., p. 36.

[4]Walter L. Thomas, "Values and Youth," *Home Economics Journal*, 61, no. 10 (1969), 748–54.

[5]See E. B. Sheldon and W. E. Moore, eds., *Indicators of Social Change* (New York: Russell Sage Foundation, 1968), Chaps. 4, 9.

[6]Helen H. Lamale, "Levels of Living Among the Poor," No. 238–12 (Washington, D.C.: Bureau of Labor Statistics, 1965), p. 6.

[7]W. Vernon Hicks and Frank H. Blackington III, *Introduction to Education* (Columbus, Ohio: Charles E. Merrill Books, Inc., 1965), p. 93.

[8]Myron Lieberman, *The Future of Public Education* (Chicago: University of Chicago Press, 1960), p. 17.

[9]See a later section of this chapter called "Purpose of Vocational Education at the Senior High School Level."

[10]*Come to Work with Us* (Milwaukee: Sextant Systems, 1970).

[11]U.S. Senate, Subcommittee on Education of the Committee on Labor and Public Welfare, *Notes and Working Papers Concerning the Administration of Programs Authorized Under Vocational Education Act of 1963*. (Washington, D.C.: Government Printing Office, 1968), p. 39.

[12]Henry Borow, ed., *Man in a World of Work* (Boston: Houghton Mifflin Co., 1964), p. 216.

[13]Nathaniel H. Frank, *Final Report of the Summer Study on Occupational, Vocational, and Technical Education* (Cambridge: Science Teaching Center, Massachusetts Institute of Technology, 1965), pp. 61–93.

[14]Ibid., pp. 68–69.

INDEX

Academic track, 120, 128, 193, 225. *See also* differentiated goals; Vocational track
Accident theory, 105–7
　related to vocational education, 105, 112
Adult education
　agriculture, 135
　business, 137
　developmental framework, 247–49
　distributive, 138
　emergent view of, 247–50
　health, 140
　stages of vocational development, 247–48
　technical, 142
　trade and industrial occupations, 142
Advisory Committee on Education, 1938, 36–37
Advisory committees, 46, 99

Advisory Council on Vocational Education, 1968, 18–20, 38–43, 81, 213–14, 218
　part of 1968 Vocational Education Act, 38
　recommendations
　　for The Commissioner, 43
　　for legislation, 41–43
　　toward a unified system of vocational education, 38–41
Agrarian society
　change, 28
　frontier needs, 65
　limited vocational education, 65
　maturation into an industrial society, 28
　self-sustaining family units, 28
Agricultural education
　adult farmer classes, 135
　agribusiness, 135, 136

Agricultural education (*cont.*)
  curriculum, 161–65, 170–71
  defined by Smith-Hughes Act of 1917,
    135
  defined by Vocational Education Act of
    1963, 135
  enrollment, 134
  in-school students, 134
  objectives, 135
  out-of-school students, 134
  in rural areas, 135
  young farmer classes, 135
Agricultural mechanics, 164
ALLEN, CHARLES R., 95, 101, 118, 121, 165,
    166, 167
ALLPORT, GORDON W., 186
American Association of Junior Colleges,
    182, 189
American culture. *See* Culture, American
American Industry Project, 172
American Institute of Research, 102
American Vocational Association, 72, 86,
    182
ANDERSON, VERNON E., 156
Apprenticeship
  business, 137
  in Colonial America, 48
  colonies, 59
  compulsory, 59
  control by labor, 45
  declined with mass production, 48
  early form, 30
  in Great Britain, 58
  labor support of, 45–46
  no longer adequate, 106
  and occupational crystallization, 207
  purpose of, 46
  trade and industrial, 143
  voluntary, 59
Appropriations, 80
Area Redevelopment Act of 1961, 17
ARNOLD, JOSEPH P., 168
ARNSTEIN, GEORGE E., 101, 182
Arts, national endowment for, 185
Association for Supervision and Curricu-
    lum Development, 188, 189, 190,
    197, 226–27
Assumptions
  defined, 89
  democratic, 90–93
  occupational competency, 150–51
  reliability, 89
  validity, 90
  world of work, 93–104
Assumptions of Vocational Education, 89–
    104. *See also* Philosophy; World of
    work assumptions

BAKER, RICHARD, 168
BARLOW, MELVIN L., 78, 84, 93, 94, 113,
    114, 142–43, 184
BATESON, WILLARD M., 170
BEAUMONT, JOHN A., 138, 139
Biomechanists, 220–21
BLACKINGTON, FRANK H., III. *See* Hicks,
    W. Vernon
BORROW, HENRY, 208–9, 242
BOWMAN, CLYDE A., 123
BOYNTON, PAUL W., 126, 127
BRIGGS, VERNON M., 46
BROOKOVER, WILBUR B., 14, 127, 155
BROWN, ANNE F., 16
BRUBACHER, JOHN S., 96
BRUNER, JEROME S., 171–72
BSCS, 180, 181
BUCKINGHAM, WALTER, 50
Bureaucracy, 234
Business and office education, 136–38
  implementing occupational choice in,
    207

CAMPBELL, DOAK S., 155
Career choice
  accident theory, 106
  awareness process, 209–16
  stages, 204–8
Career education, 213
Career expectations
  narrowing process, 127–28
  tentative commitment, 127
CASWELL, HOLLIS L., 155
Categorical funding
  discontinued, 134
  1968 amendments discontinued, 81
  Smith-Hughes Act in 1917, 81
Chamber of Commerce, U.S., 46–47
  support for Smith-Hughes Act of 1917,
    46
Character traits, 126–27, 154
Child labor, 45, 145
Church and state, 58, 60–61
CLARK, RAYMOND M., 170, 171, 223
Commission on National Aid to Voca-
    tional Education, 1914, 35–36
Commissioner of Education, U.S., 134
Community
  curriculum, 98–100, 157
  manpower needs, 98–100
  new role of, 100
  occupational clusters related to, 169
  questions regarding, 157
Community colleges
  enrollment, 189
  growth of, 189, 190
  influenced by war, 33

Community colleges (*cont.*)
  teacher certification, 197
Community survey, 99
CONANT, JAMES B., 113
Concept, 171–73
Constitution, 64
Contemporary program, 133–49. *See also*
    Agricultural education; Business
    and office education; Distributive
    education; Health educations;
    Home economics education; Tech-
    nical education; Trade and indus-
    trial education
  administration, 134
  cross section of occupational world, 133
Cooperative education, 143–46
CRONBACH, LEE J., 122–23
CROWTHER, BEATRICE, 140
Culture, 8, 9
Culture, American, 10
Curriculum
  adjustment in vocational education, 15
  agricultural education, 161–65, 170–71
  altered by change, 220
  American Industry Project, 172
  analysis techniques, 160
  business and office education, 137–38
  community, 98–100, 157
  concept approach, 171–73
  content changes in, 191–92
  content selection, 158–60
    analytical procedure, 159, 165, 168
    consensual procedure, 159–60, 168, 170
    experimental procedure, 158–59
    judgmental procedure, 158, 170, 172
  content shift, 192
  and crystallization process, 206
  defined, 155
  factors that have influenced, 156–57
  flexibility, 163
  health occupations, 140
  history, 155
  history in agriculture, 161
  industrial functions, 170–71, 223
  integrated approach, 161–65
  involvement of university scholars, 192
  methods of instituting change, 190
  for middle school, 242–45
  model for decision making, 190
  more sophisticated, 160
  occupational analysis, 165–68
  occupational clusters, 168–70
  reform, gaps in, 192
  reform in public schools, 180
  spiral, 225
  technical, 142, 165–68
  trade and industrial, 165–73

DECA. *See* Distributive Education Clubs
    of America
DEYOE, GEORGE P., 163
Decision making
  for curriculum, 190–92
  in education, 12
Deluder Satan Act, 59
Democratic assumptions, 90–93
Development of technology
  applying power to machines, 47–48
  automation applied to assembly lines,
    50–51
  mass production and assembly lines,
    48–50
  miniaturization, 51
Differentiated goals. *See also* Dualism
  English heritage, 59
  implemented, 118, 120, 123, 128, 193
  intent of early legislation, 103
  new view of, 225
Discovery learning, 196
Discovery method, 188
Distributive education, 75, 138–39, 146–47
Distributive Education Clubs of America
    (DECA), 84, 146–47
Division of labor, 9
Douglas Commission, 35, 46
  conclusions, 44
  educated labor force, 45
DOUGLAS, PAUL H., 30
DRAPER, DALE C., 114, 216–17, 228–29
Dualism. *See also* Academic track; Differ-
    entiated goals; Vocational track
  intent of early legislation, 108
  vocational and general education, 96–97

EATON, THEODORE H., 161
Economic Opportunity Act of 1964, 17
Economic system, and vocational educa-
    tion, 17, 18, 29, 67, 85, 93–95, 97,
    100–101
Economic theory, and vocational educa-
    tion, 95–96
Education
  in Colonial America, 58–60
  and culture, 7
  decision making, 12
  differentiated, 59
  for elites, 59
  man and work, 103
  the nature of, 7
  normative, 7
  for poor, 59
  purpose, 238
  social change, 7
  solve social problems, 231
  universal concern, 59

Education and work, in conflict, 30
Educational policies commission, 91
Educational system
  and labor market, 133
  prepare for work, 217
Embargo Act, 67
Employer, 49
Employer associations, 42, 46–47
Employment policy
  manpower policy, 16
  prevails in the 1970s, 17
  Smith-Hughes Act of 1917, 19
English Grammar School, 62
English Poor Law of 1601, 58, 59
Enrollment
  agriculture, 134–35
  business and office, 136
  distributive, 138
  education, 5
  health, 140
  home economics, 140–41
  technical, 142
  trade and industrial, 142
  vocational education, 5
Entry employment, 97–98, 124
  in emergent vocational education, 229
  in trade and industrial occupations, 142
Equal opportunity, 95
Essex, Martin, 38
Essex Report. See Advisory Council on
  Vocational Education, 1968
Eurich, Alvin C., 179, 184–85
Evaluation system, test of, 198
Evans, Rupert N., 160
Expenditures, 80
  categorical funding, 134
  during World War II, 33
  vocational education, 4

Fair Labor Standards Act, 45
FBLA. See Future Business Leaders of
  America
Federal Board for Vocational Education,
  32
Federal participation, influence on voca-
  tional education, 113
Fen, Sing-Nan, 96
FFA. See Future Farmers of America
FHA. See Future Homemakers of Amer-
  ica
Fischer, Louis, 7, 12, 13, 83, 92, 99–100
Frank, Nathaniel H., 17, 115, 214, 243–
  45
Franklin, Benjamin, 62
Free Enterprise Economic System, 29
Friese, John F., 167

FSA. See Future Secretaries Association
Future Business Leaders of America
  (FBLA), 84, 147
Future Farmers of America, 84, 135, 146
Future Homemakers of America (FHA),
  84, 147
Future Secretaries Association (FSA), 147

Gagné, Robert M., 122–23, 187
Gebhart, Richard H., 172
Geiger, George R., 96
George-Barden Act (1947–1968), 76, 107
George-Deen Act (1937–1947), 76, 107
George-Elizey Act (1934–1937), 76
George-Reed Act (1930–1934), 75
GI Bill, 76
Ginzberg, Eli, 184, 204, 206
Gleason, William E., 170
Griffin, William M., 198
Grinker, William, 227–28

Haines, Peter G., 146
Hamlin, Herbert M., 161, 162, 164
Hammonds, Carsie, 114
Hart, Leslie A., 193–94
Hawkins, Layton S., 32, 67, 73
Health occupations, 139–40
Herzberg, Frederick, 23
Hicks, W. Vernon, 7, 69, 238
History. See Vocational education, devel-
  opment
Home economics education, 140–41
Hosler, Russell J., 136–37
Howe, Harold II, 199–200
Howell, Kathleen M., 141
Hughes, Dudley, 73–74
Human Resources Development Policy,
  16, 151

Illiteracy, mathematical and scientific, 181
Independent study, evaluation, 198
Individual
  importance of, 22, 233
  welfare of, 113
Individual differences, 122
Individual needs, curriculum for, 162–63
Individuals, 182
Industrial functions, 170–71
Industrial Revolution. See Development
  of technology
Industry
  changing role in training, 239–40
  cooperation with vocational schools, 199
  vocational programs in, 6
Innes, Jon T., 18
Institution, 10, 11

Institutional change, 189
Institutionalizing, 10
Instruction, new psychological base, 195

JEFFERSON, THOMAS, 63, 91
Job analysis. See Occupational analysis
Job corps, 82–83, 196
   related to manpower policy, 19
Junior college. See Community colleges;
   Technical schools

KAUFMAN, JACOB J., 16
Knowledge explosion, 183

Labor, 16
Labor, Department of, 82, 196
Labor force, 53, 54
Labor groups, 44–46
Labor market, opportunity forecasting, 15
Labor organizations, 43–46
Labor productivity, 94
Labor supply, 101
LAMALE, HELEN H., 237
LAMAR, CARL F., 114
Land Grant College Movement, 68
LATHRUP, FRANK W., 70
Latin Grammar School, The, 59, 61
Learning
   cognitive organization, 188
   contemporary theory, 188
   new insights, 186
   new psychological base, 195
   stimulus-response, 186
   types of, 187
LEE, SYLVIA L., 141
Legislative acts. See specific legislation by
   title
Legislative impact, 83
LEIGHBODY, GERALD B., 52
Leisure, 183, 184
LIEBERMAN, MYRON, 238
Life skills, 226–27
Low income families, 237

McCARTHY, JOHN A., 35
MALEY, DONALD, 168
Man
   changing view of, 27
   concerned with sets of events, 180
   economic view, 29
   fashions change, 181
   new view of, 180
   societal context, 181
Management, beyond work environment,
   234
MANGUM, GARTH L., 17

Manpower allocation policy, 16, 101
Manpower Development and Training
   Act, 17, 19, 82
Manpower needs, 116
   of community, 98–100
   long range, 15
Manpower policy, 16, 19, 151. See also
   Employment policy; Manpower
   allocation policy
Manpower programs, matching philos-
   ophy, 151
Manpower projections, 16
Marketable skills, 121
MARSHALL, F. RAY, 46
MASON, RALPH E., 144, 146
Mass society, 235–36
Massachusetts General Court, 59, 60
MEAD, MARGARET, 200
MEADE, EDWARD J., 21
MEADERS, O. DONALD, 223
MICHAEL, DONALD N., 152
MOBLEY, MAYOR D., 78, 84
Modern society, 235, 236
MOORE, W. E., 237
Morrill Act of 1862, 69

National Association of Manufacturers,
   The, 46
National Association of Secondary School
   Principals, 114, 182
National Business Education Association,
   136, 147
National Child Labor Committee, 45
National Education Association, 183
National Retail Merchants Association, 46
National Society for the Promotion of
   Industrial Education, 35, 72
   influences definition, 107–8
National Society for the Study of Educa-
   tion, 180, 185, 188, 200
National Study Panels, 34–42. See also
   Panel of Consultants on Vocational
   Education; Advisory Council on
   Vocational Education, 1968
Nationalism, 64
Nature of educational decisions, 12
Non-Intercourse Act, 67
NORGREN, PAUL H., 46
Northwest Ordinance of 1787, 66
NOSOW, SIGMUND, 14, 51, 124, 127, 155, 184

Occupational abilities, 210, 211
Occupational analysis, 101, 159, 165–68,
   220
Occupational aptitude, 210, 211
Occupational aspirations, 210, 211

Occupational changes, 156
Occupational choice, 11
Occupational choice process, 204–8
    awareness, 209–10, 214–16
    becoming employed, 212–13
    differentiation, 212
    integration, 212
    knowledge about occupations, 211–12
    planning for tentative choice, 212
    self-assessment, 210–11
Occupational clusters, 96, 168–70
Occupational competency
    developing, 150–76
    flexibility, 152
    job relationships, 153–54
    a needed skill, 154–55
    nonpermanency of skill, 152
    social compatibility, 154
Occupational development, 239
Occupational experience programs, 143–46
Occupational goals, 164
Occupational identity, individual's growth
    toward, 203
Occupational interest, 210, 211
Occupational objectives, 168
Occupational opportunity, geographical
    limitations, 211
Occupational roles, 14, 15
Occupational selection, 9
Occupational skill, 155
Occupational structure, 53–55
Occupations
    cultural setting, 9
    cultural specialties, 8–9
    in early America, 61
    as institution, 10
    self-concept, 17
    source of personal identity, 16
    survival skills, 20
Office education. See Business and office
    education
Office Education Association, 148

PAGE, CARROLL S., 70–73
Page Bill, The, 71–73
Panel of Consultants on Vocational Edu-
    cation, 18, 37, 93–94, 182
Philadelphia society, 70–71
Philosophy
    assumptions, 89
    behavior of vocational education, 90
    consistency, 90
    democratic assumptions, 90–93
    instrumental behavior, 90
    matching man to job, 106, 150
    reliability, 89
    validity, 90

verbal behavior, 90
world of work assumptions, 93–104
    equal competition, 95–99
    outdated, 103
    vocational education and manpower
        needs of the community, 98–100
    vocational education can develop a
        marketable man, 95–97
    vocational education evaluated on the
        basis of economic efficiency, 100–101
    vocational education for initial em-
        ployment, 97–98
    vocational education geared to job
        market, 93–95
    vocational education insures labor
        supply, 101
    vocational education is economic
        education, 93–95
    vocational education to serve the
        economic system, 97
Philosophy, emergent
    Advisory Council of Vocational Educa-
        tion, 218
    architectural influence, 222
    contemporary model, 223–28
    creative approach to industry, 221
    defines vocational education, 213–19
    expands vocational education, 217–19
    extends to lower grades, 218
    importance of skills, 218
    learn what an occupational area is all
        about, 219–22
    life long process, 216
    nature of being, 237–38
    nature of society, 233–37
    purpose of vocational education, 238–50
    rationale, 213–19
    understanding before entry employ-
        ment, 221
    a unifying effect, 222–23
    a view of man, 233
PHIPPS, LLOYD J., 160
Pluralism, 30
Poverty, 237
Principles, as assumptions, 89–104, 223–26
Proprietary schools, 6, 64
Prosperity, 181
PROSSER, CHARLES A., 32, 67, 72, 73, 95,
    118, 121
Psychology, 121, 186–88, 195
Public education, 3
Public school. See also Education; Schools
    current problems, 179
    differentiated goals, 119–20
    emergence, 62
    experimenting, 179
    objectives, 91

Public school *(cont.)*
  principal change agent, 7
  rationale for, 91
  reform, 179
  reform movement, 180–92
PUMPER, FRED J., 100
Purpose, 238–50

RAY, ELIZABETH M., 16, 20
Reform forces
  concern for all students, 182
  curriculum content shift, 191
  discovery method, 188–89
  illiteracy, mathematical and scientific,
    181
  institutional change, 189
  knowledge explosion, 183
  learning, new insights, 186–88
  leisure, 183–84
  man concerned with sets of events,
    180–81
  methods of curriculum change, 190
  prosperity, 181
  urbanization, 185–86
  values, 183
RICARDO, DAVID, 94
ROBERTS, ROY W., 44, 59, 93, 101, 102, 148
RUBIN, LOUIS J., 188, 189, 226–27

SANDERS, GEORGE, 139
SANFORD, CHARLES W., 162
SCHILL, WILLIAM J., 168
School system, authority, 3
Schools, emergent
  agent for new values, 200
  change in the 60s, 193
  citizen concern, 193–94
  committed to discovery, 197
  community involvement, 199
  evaluation, 197
  flexibility in the internal structure, 196
  industry involvement, 199
  middle-class institution, 196
  new psychological base, 186–88, 195
  principal change agent, 200
  pupil-centered, 195
Schools, traditional, 195
SELDEN, WILLIAM, 142–43
Self-concept, 17
SELVIDGE, ROBERT W., 166, 167
Sextant profile, 210
Sextant systems, 242
SEXTON, PATRICIA, C., 93
SHELDON, E. B., 237
SHORES, J. HARLAN, 9, 158–59
Shorthand, 122
SMITH, ADAM, 94

SMITH, B. OTHANEL, 9, 158–59
SMITH, HOKE, 71–74
SMITH, PATRICIA, 141
Smith-Hughes Act of 1917, 70, 72, 73
  accident theory, 105
  amendments, 75
  compromise reached, 72
  defines vocational education, 106–7
  manpower allocation for war, 101
  manpower allocation policy, 16
  passage of, 35
  toward war effort, 101
  World War I, 31
SMSG, 180, 181
Social base, 25
Social change, and education, 200
Society
  and culture, 9–10
  current perspective, 233–37
  and institutions, 10
  protean, 235
Span of work, 124
STANLEY, WILLIAM O., 9, 158–59
State Advisory Council, 81
State plan, 74, 134, 136, 144
State supervisors, 134
State vocational board, 74
STERN, JACOB, 170, 171
STEWART, W. F., 22
STIMSON, RUFUS W., 70
STRUCK, THEODORE, 72, 93, 113
Student, unify subject matter, 222–23
SUPER, DONALD E., 206, 208
SYMONDS, PERCIVAL M., 186

Teacher aides, 197
Teacher certification, 197
Teacher coordinator, 139, 144
Teaching, context of the scientist, 222–23
Technical education
  adult programs, 142
  advisory committee, 99
  curriculum, 142, 165–68
  enrollment, 142
  in health occupations, 139–40
  occupational clusters, 168
  postsecondary, 142
Technical schools, 189, 190, 197
Technical skill, 127, 154
Technical trends, 52
Technological change, 156–57
Technological gaps, closing of, 66
Technology, 27, 51, 157. *See also* Develop-
    ment of technology
THOMAS, DONALD R. *See* Fischer, Lewis
THOMAS, WALTER L., 236
THOMPSON, JOHN F., 172

TICHAUER, ERWIN R., 220–21
TOFFLER, ALVIN, 185
Toys, visual stimuli, 215
Track, academic. *See* Academic track
Track, vocational. *See* Vocational track
Trade and industrial education, 142, 143, 165–73
Training, public mistrust of industry, 106
TRUE, A. C., 72, 73

Unemployed, 92
Unemployed out-of-school youth survey, 92
Unemployment, 54, 94
Uniformity, 107–8
Urbanization, 28, 185

Value conflict, in education, 7
Values, 200
   changing patterns, 234
   in decision making, 13
   explicit, 13
   new, 183
VENABLE, TOM C., 90
VENN, GRANT, 31, 103, 107–9, 152
VETTER, LOUISE, 141
VICA. *See* Vocational Industrial Clubs of America
Vocational development
   awareness, 209–10, 214–16
   becoming employed, 212
   defined, 204
   differentiation, 212
   integration, 212
   knowledge about occupational opportunities, 211
   life stages, 203
   lifelong process, 209
   processes, 203–4
   programming for stages, 208
   self-assessment, 210
   stages, 204–12, 241, 242, 246
   stages for adults, 247–49
   stages for elementary school, 241
   stages for high school, 246–47
   stages for middle school, 243–44
   tasks, 206–8
   tentative occupational choice, 212
Vocational education
   allocation of occupational roles, 14
   applying technology, 28
   appropriations, 80
   assumptions, 89–104
   assures an adequate labor supply, 16
   basic objective of all education, 228
   community, 99, 100

concept of the learner, 21
contemporary manpower needs, 16–17
conventional model, 118–29
   exit point, 126
   marketable skills, 121
   related to general education, 118–20
   social base, 125
   work environment orientation, 123
defined, 105–17. *See also* Vocational education, emergent
definition, 107–9, 116
demand for after Civil War, 70
development, 68, 69–70
differentiated goals, 123
in early America, 60
early formulations of, 216
is economic education, 93–95
economic effects, 18
economic efficiency, 100–101
economic policy, 17
economic rationale, 85
economic theory, 95
economic well being, 85
educational agencies, 11
elementary school, 116
enrollment, 4, 5
enters public school, 106
entry employment, 97–98
expands, 182
expenditures, 4
expenditures during World War II, 33
extends to lower grades, 225
framework for early growth, 64
and general education, 69
growth and development base, 202–13
growth in social conditions, 28
inconsistent with democratic principles, 94–95
individual's welfare, 113
in industry, 6
influence of federal participation, 113
and institutions, 10
instrument of national manpower policy, 19–20
job market orientation, 93–95
labor productivity increased, 94
labor supply, 101
legislation for war effort, 33
link between education and labor, 14
manpower policy, 17, 19–20
as national economic policy, 67
needs today, 85
nonpublic, 6
not exploratory, 127
number involved in, 4

Vocational education (*cont.*)
  output of goods and services, 18
  for the poor, 64
  primitive society, 31
  principles, 89–104
  product of the democratic culture, 8
  proprietary schools, 6
  scope, 6
  secondary school goals, 23
  sensitive to contemporary society, 232
  serve the economic system, 18, 97
  social base, 213
  social contribution, 23
  social foundations, authority base, 4
  social setting, 14
  specialized knowledge and skills, 10
  subculture, 11
  teachers, number of, 4
  traditional role, 24
  understanding technology, 28
  unemployment lowered, 94
  uniformity, 107–8
  upgrade economic position, 29
  variety, 6
  vast, 4
  what a job is all about, 24, 25
Vocational education, emergent
  architectural influence, 222
  contemporary model, 226–29
  defined, 213–19
  in early child, 215
  expanding, 217
  expands occupational concept, 225
  extends to lower grades, 218
  growth and development concerns,
    202–13
  life skills, 226–27
  lifelong process, 216
  model for, 223–24
  occupational concept, expands, 218
  philosophical view of man, 232–33
  primary objective, 225
  principles, 223–26
  purpose, 238–50
    for adults, 247, 249
    elementary school, 241–42
    general, 239–41
    middle school, 242–45
    senior high, 246–47
  rationale, 213
  social base, 234
  spiral curriculum, 225
  toys, visual stimuli of work, 215
  work environment, 225
Vocational Education Act of 1963, 17,
  77–81

amended in 1968, 79–80
manpower policy, 19
passage, 77
provisions, 78, 109–10, 110–11
Vocational educators, 14
Vocational Industrial Clubs of America,
  148
Vocational track, 120, 123, 128, 193, 225.
  See also Academic track; Differentiated goals
Vocational training, 31, 112

WALSH, JOHN P., 142–43
War of 1812, 67
WARMBROD, J. ROBERT, 18, 94
Wars, 31–34, 83
WEST, MARGARET D., 140
West, settlement of
  Agrarian Society, 65
  technological gaps, 65–68
WHITMARSH, RUTH J., 168
WILBER, DWIGHT L., 140
WILLIAMS, WILLIAM A., 167
WOLFBEIN, SEYMOUR L., 45, 54, 152
Women
  in labor force, 54, 141
  and occupational structure, 54
WOODHALL, MAUREEN, 94
Work
  affective, 215
  begins in early child, 215
  classified by function within an in-
    dustry, 211
  classified by industry, 211
  classified by level, 211
  classified by type, 211
  emotional experiences, 215
  functions of, 184
  man and education, 103
  toys, visual stimuli of, 215
Work ethic, 183
Work experience programs, 145. *See also*
  Occupational experience programs
Work roles, classified, 11
Worker
  adjusting to technology, 157
  changed conditions, 49
  character traits, 126, 154
  components of skill, 154
  as consumer, 49
  control of work, 125
  controlled work environment, 125
  dead end jobs, 227–28
  dependent, 154
  education for, 30
  extension of machine, 219, 220

Worker (*cont.*)
    job changes him, 151
    job relationships, 153
    and leisure, 183–84
    losing identity with company, 234
    machine-facturing, 220
    manufacturing, 220
    mass society, 235–36
    motivation, 23
    need for identity, 23
    needs more technology, 190
    nonpermanency of skill, 152
    not getting promoted, 126, 154
    occupational flexibility, 152
    producing a consumer product, 126
    as property owner, 29, 30
    quality of life, 29
    reasons for discharge, 126, 154
    resource for institution, 29
    skill, 154
    social skills, 126, 154
    span of work, 123
    subsystems, 234
    system of payment, 29
    technical skill, 126, 154
    tool of production, 94
    women, 141
World of work assumptions, 93–104
WRIGHT, JOHN C., 32, 67, 73

Youth, out of school, 92
Youth organizations, primary purpose,
    146. *See also* Distributive Educa-
    tion Clubs of America; Future
    Business Leaders of America; Fu-
    ture Farmers of America; Future
    Homemakers of America; Future
    secretaries Association; Office Edu-
    cation Association; Vocational In-
    dustrial Clubs of America